Bloom's Modern Critical Interpretations

Bloom's Modern Critical Interpretations

Bloom's Modern Critical Interpretations

Richard Wright's
BLACK BOY

Edited and with an introduction by
Harold Bloom
Sterling Professor of the Humanities
Yale University

CHELSEA HOUSE
P U B L I S H E R S
An imprint of Infobase Publishing

Bloom's Modern Critical Interpretations: Black Boy

©2006 Infobase Publishing

Introduction © 2006 by Harold Bloom

Chelsea House
An imprint of Infobase Publishing
132 West 31st Street
New York NY 10001

Library of Congress Cataloging-in-Publication Data
Richard Wright's Black Boy / Harold Bloom, editor.
    p. cm. — (Bloom's modern critical interpretations)
 Includes bibliographical references and index.
 ISBN 0-7910-8585-6 (hardcover)
 1. Wright, Richard, 1908-1960. Black boy. I. Title: Black boy. II.
Bloom, Harold. III. Series.
 PS3545.R815R53 2006
 813'.52—dc22   2006001772

Chelsea House books are available at special discounts when purchased in bulk quantitie for businesses, associations, institutions, or sales promotions. Please call our Special Sale Department in New York at (212) 967-8800 or (800) 322-8755.

You can find Chelsea House on the World Wide Web at http://www.chelseahouse.com

Contributing Editor: Amy Sickels
Cover design by Keith Trego
Cover photo © Josh Mitchell

Printed in the United States of America
Bang EJB 10 9 8 7 6 5 4 3 2 1

This book is printed on acid-free paper.

All links and web addresses were checked and verified to be correct at the time of publication. Because of the dynamic nature of the web, some addresses and links may ha changed since publication and may no longer be valid.

Contents

Editor's Note

My Introduction contrasts *Black Boy* with *Native Son*, and states a personal aesthetic preference for the autobiography over the novel. What endures in *Black Boy* is both a memorial to American racism and a strong version of the birth of a writer.

Ralph Ellison, the author of the great novel *Invisible Man*, impressively finds the formal origin of *Black Boy* in the blues, and thus establishes a highly useful context for reading Richard Wright's autobiography.

The voyage into knowledge is set forth as the pattern of *Black Boy* by Dan McCall, after which Claudia C. Tate traces the growth in Wright of Unamuno's tragic sense of life.

Charles T. Davis praises *Black Boy* for what he judges to be its sustained eloquence, while Horace A. Porter invokes the analogue of James Joyce's *Portrait of the Artist as a Young Man*.

Wright's extraordinary labor of self-molding is detailed by Yoshinobu Hakutani, after which Keneth Kinnamon traces an intertextual relationship between *Black Boy* and Maya Angelou's *I Know Why the Caged Bird Sings*.

Donald B. Gibson describes Wright's traumatic break with his father, while Elizabeth J. Ciner expands this to a double-break, with the grandmother's God as well as with the biological father.

The tradition of African-American autobiography is taken as *Black Boy*'s context by William L. Andrews, after which Warren J. Carson emphasizes Wright's visions were of Southern American realities during his childhood.

In this volume's final essay, Petar Ramadanovic invokes comedy, in modes defined by Jacques Lacan and by Paul de Man, as the genre of *Black Boy*.

HAROLD BLOOM

Introduction

I

What remains of Richard Wright's work if we apply to it only aesthetic standards of judgment? This is to assume that strictly aesthetic standards exist, and that we know what they are. Wright, in *Native Son*, essentially the son of Theodore Dreiser, could not rise always even to Dreiser's customarily bad level of writing. Here is Bigger Thomas, condemned to execution, at the start of his death vigil:

> In self-defense he shut out the night and day from his mind, for if he had thought of the sun's rising and setting, of the moon or the stars, of clouds or rain, he would have died a thousand deaths before they took him to the chair. To accustom his mind to death as much as possible, he made all the world beyond his cell a vast gray land where neither night nor day was, peopled by strange men and women whom he could not understand, but with those lives he longed to mingle once before he went.
>
> He did not eat now; he simply forced food down his throat without tasting it, to keep the gnawing pain of hunger away, to keep from feeling dizzy. And he did not sleep; at intervals he closed his eyes for a while, no matter what the hour, then opened

them at some later time to resume his brooding. He wanted to be free of everything that stood between him and his end, him and the full and terrible realization that life was over without meaning, without anything being settled, without conflicting impulses being resolved.

If we isolate these paragraphs, then we do not know the color or background of the man awaiting execution. The intense sociological pathos of Wright's narrative vanishes, and we are left in the first paragraph with an inadequate rhetoric: "shut out the night and day," "died a thousand deaths," "a vast gray land," "strange men and women," "with those lives he longed to mingle." Yet the second paragraph is even more unsatisfactory, as the exact word is nowhere: "gnawing pain of hunger," "resume his brooding," "full and terrible realization," "conflicting impulses being resolved." Wright's narrative requires from him at this point some mode of language that would individuate Bigger's dread, that would catch and fix the ordeal of a particular black man condemned by a white society. Unfortunately, Wright's diction does not allow us even to distinguish Bigger's horror from any other person's apprehension of judicial murder. Nor does Bigger's own perspective enter into Wright's rhetorical stance. The problem is not so much Wright's heritage from Dreiser's reductive naturalism as it is, plainly stated, a bad authorial ear.

It is rather too late to make so apparently irrelevant an observation, since Wright has become a canonical author, for wholesome societal purposes, with which I am happy to concur. Rereading *Native Son* or *Black Boy* cannot be other than an overdetermined activity, since Wright is a universally acknowledged starting point for black literature in contemporary America. Canonical critics of Wright speak of him as a pioneer, a man of rare courage, as a teacher and forerunner. None of this can or should be denied. I myself would praise him for will, force, and drive, human attributes that he carried just over the border of aesthetic achievement, without alas getting very far once he had crossed over. His importance transcends the concerns of a strictly literary criticism, and reminds the critic of the claims of history, society, political economy, and the longer records of oppression and injustice that history continues to scant.

II

Bigger Thomas can be said to have become a myth without first having been a convincing representation of human character and personality. Wright listed five "Biggers" he had encountered in actuality, five violent youths called "bad Niggers" by the whites. The most impressive, Bigger No. 5, was a knife-wielding, prideful figure "who always rode the Jim Crow streetcars without paying and sat wherever he pleased." For this group of precursors of his own protagonist in *Native Son*, Wright gave us a moving valediction:

> The Bigger Thomases were the only Negroes I know of who consistently violated the Jim Crow laws of the South and got away with it, at least for a sweet brief spell. Eventually, the whites who restricted their lives made them pay a terrible price. They were shot, hanged, maimed, lynched, and generally hounded until they were either dead or their spirits broken.

Wright concluded this same "Introduction" to *Native Son* with his own vision of the United States as of March 7, 1940:

> I feel that I'm lucky to be alive to write novels today, when the whole world is caught in the pangs of war and change. Early American writers, Henry James and Nathaniel Hawthorne, complained bitterly about the bleakness and flatness of the American scene. But I think that if they were alive, they'd feel at home in modern America. True, we have no great church in America; our national traditions are still of such a sort that we are not wont to brag of them; and we have no army that's above the level of mercenary fighters; we have no group acceptable to the whole of our country upholding certain humane values; we have no rich symbols, no colorful rituals. We have only a money-grubbing, industrial civilization. But we do have in the Negro the embodiment of a past tragic enough to appease the spiritual hunger of even a James; and we have in the oppression of the Negro a shadow athwart our national life dense and heavy enough to satisfy even the gloomy broodings of a Hawthorne. And if Poe were alive, he would not have to invent horror; horror would invent him.

The citation of James, Hawthorne, and Poe is gratuitous, and the perspective upon the United States in the months preceding the fall of France lacks authority and precision, even in its diction. But the dense and heavy shadow athwart our national life indubitably was there, always had been there, and for many is there still. That shadow is Richard Wright's mythology, and his embryonic strength. He was not found by Henry James, or by Hawthorne, or by Poe, and scarcely would have benefited by such a finding. A legitimate son of Theodore Dreiser, he nevertheless failed to write in *Native Son* a *Sister Carrie* or a new version of *An American Tragedy*. The reality of being a gifted young black in the United States of the thirties and forties proved too oppressive for the limited purposes of a narrative fiction. Rereading *Native Son* is an experience of renewing the dialectical awareness of history and society, but is not in itself an aesthetic experience.

And yet, I do not think that *Native Son*, and its reception, present us with a merely aesthetic dilemma. In the "afterword" to the current paperback reprint of *Native Son*, one of Wright's followers, John Reilly, defends Bigger Thomas by asserting that: "The description of Mary's murder makes clear that the white world is the cause of the violent desires and reactions" that lead Bigger to smother poor Mary. I would think that what the description makes clear enough is that Bigger is indeed somewhat overdetermined, but to ascribe the violence of his desires and reactions to any context whatsoever is to reduce him to the status of a replicant or of a psychopathic child. The critical defenders of *Native Son* must choose. Either Bigger Thomas is a responsible consciousness, and so profoundly culpable, or else only the white world is responsible and culpable, which means however that Bigger ceases to be of fictive interest and becomes an ideogram, rather than a persuasive representation of a possible human being. Wright, coming tragically early in what was only later to become his own tradition, was not able to choose, and so left us with something between an ideological image, and the mimesis of an actuality.

III

I remember reading *Black Boy: A Record of Childhood and Youth* when Wright's autobiographical book first appeared, in 1945. A boy of fifteen, I was frightened and impressed by the book. Reading it again many years later, the old reactions do not return. Instead, I am compelled to ask the Nietzschean question: who is the interpreter, and what power does he seek to gain over the text, whether it be his own text or the text of his life? Wright, an anguished and angry interpreter, wrote a far more political work in *Black Boy* than in *Native Son*. What passes for a Marxist analysis of the relation between society and Bigger Thomas seems to me always a kind of authorial afterthought in *Native Son*. In *Black Boy*, this pseudo-Marxism usurps the narrator's function, and the will-to-power over interpretation becomes the incessant undersong of the entire book. Contrast the opening and closing paragraphs of *Black Boy*:

One winter morning in the long-ago, four-year-old days of my life I found myself standing before a fireplace, warming my hands over a mound of glowing coals, listening to the wind whistle past the house outside. All morning my mother had been scolding me, telling me to keep still, warning me that I must make no noise. And I was angry, fretful, and impatient. In the next room Granny lay ill and under the day and night care of a doctor and I knew that I would be punished if I did not obey. I crossed restlessly to the window and pushed back the long fluffy white curtains—which I had been forbidden to touch—and looked yearningly out into the empty street. I was dreaming of running and playing and shouting, but the vivid image of Granny's old, white, wrinkled, grim face, framed by a halo of tumbling black hair, lying upon a huge feather pillow, made me afraid.

With ever watchful eyes and bearing scars, visible and invisible, I headed North, full of a hazy notion that life could be lived with dignity, that the personalities of others should not be violated, that men should be able to confront other men without fear or shame, and that if men were lucky in their living on earth they might win some redeeming meaning for their having struggled and suffered here beneath the stars.

The young man going North, scarred and watchful, in search of redemption by meaning, has remarkably little connection with the four-year-old boy, impatient for the dream of running, playing, and shouting. Wright's purpose is to explain his fall from impulse into care, and his inevitable explanation will be social and historical. Yet much that he loses is to his version of the family romance, as he himself describes it, and some of what vanishes from him can be ascribed, retrospectively, to a purely personal failure; in him the child was not the father of the man.

What survives best in *Black Boy*, for me, is Wright's gentle account of his human rebirth, as a writer. At eighteen, reading Mencken, he learns audacity, the agonistic use of language, and an aggressive passion for study comes upon him. After reading the *Main Street* of Sinclair Lewis, he is found by the inevitable precursor in Theodore Dreiser:

"That's deep stuff you're reading, boy."
"I'm just killing time, sir."
"You'll addle your brains if you don't watch out."
I read Dreiser's *Jennie Gerhardt* and *Sister Carrie* and they

revived in me a vivid sense of my mother's suffering; I was overwhelmed. I grew silent, wondering about the life around me. It would have been impossible for me to have told anyone what I derived from these novels, for it was nothing less than a sense of life itself. All my life had shaped me for the realism, the naturalism of the modern novel, and I could not read enough of them.

Steeped in new moods and ideas, I bought a ream of paper and tried to write; but nothing would come, or what did come was flat beyond telling. I discovered that more than desire and feeling were necessary to write and I dropped the idea. Yet I still wondered how it was possible to know people sufficiently to write about them? Could I ever learn about life and people? To me, with my vast ignorance, my Jim Crow station in life, it seemed a task impossible of achievement. I now knew what being a Negro meant. I could endure the hunger. I had learned to live with hate. But to feel that there were feelings denied me, that the very breath of life itself was beyond my reach, that more than anything else hurt, wounded me. I had a new hunger.

Dreiser's taut visions of suffering women renew in Wright his own memories of his mother's travails, and make him one of those authors for whom the purpose of the poem (to cite Wallace Stevens) is the mother's face. There is an Oedipal violence in Wright that sorts strangely with his attempt to persuade us, and himself, that all violence is socially overdetermined. *Black Boy*, even now, performs an ethical function for us by serving as a social testament, as Wright intended it to do. We can hope that, some day, the book will be available to us as a purely individual testament, and then, may read very differently.

RALPH ELLISON

Richard Wright's Blues

If anybody ask you
    who sing this song,
Say it was ole [Black] Boy
    done been here and gone.

(*signature formula used by blues
singers at conclusion of song*)

As a writer, Richard Wright has outlined for himself a dual role: To discover and depict the meaning of Negro experience and to reveal to both Negroes and whites those problems of a psychological and emotional nature which arise between them when they strive for mutual understanding.

Now, in *Black Boy*, he has used his own life to probe what qualities of will, imagination, and intellect are required of a southern Negro in order to possess the meaning of his life in the United States. Wright is an important writer, perhaps the most articulate Negro American, and what he has to say is highly perceptive. Imagine Bigger Thomas projecting his own life in lucid prose, guided, say, by the insights of Marx and Freud, and you have an idea of this autobiography. Published at a time when any sharply critical approach to Negro life has been dropped as a wartime expendable, it should do much to redefine the problem of the Negro and American democracy. Its power

From *The Antioch Review* Vol. 5, No. 2. © 1945 by the Antioch Review, Inc. (renewed 1972).

can be observed in the shrill manner with which some professional "friends of the Negro people" have attempted to strangle the work in a noose of newsprint.

What in the tradition of literary autobiography is it like, this work described as a "great American autobiography"? As a nonwhite intellectual's statement of his relationship to western culture, *Black Boy* recalls the conflicting pattern of identification and rejection found in Nehru's *Toward Freedom*. In its use of fictional techniques, its concern with criminality (sin) and the artistic sensibility, and in its author's judgment and rejection of the narrow world of his origin, it recalls Joyce's rejection of Dublin in *A Portrait of the Artist*.... And as a psychological document of life under oppressive conditions, it recalls *The House of the Dead*, Dostoyevsky's profound study of the humanity of Russian criminals. Such works were perhaps Wright's literary guides, aiding him to endow his life's incidents with communicable significance, providing him with ways of seeing, feeling, and describing his environment. These influences, however, were encountered only after these first years of Wright's life were past and were not part of the immediate folk culture into which he was born. In that culture the specific folk-art form that helped shape the writer's attitude toward his life and that embodied the impulse that contributes much to the quality and tone of his autobiography was the Negro blues. This would bear a word of explanation:

The blues is an impulse to keep the painful details and episodes of a brutal experience alive in one's aching consciousness, to finger its jagged grain, and to transcend it, not by the consolation of philosophy, but by squeezing from it a near-tragic, near-comic lyricism. As a form, the blues is an autobiographical chronicle of personal catastrophe expressed lyrically. And certainly Wright's early childhood was crammed with catastrophic incidents. In a few short years his father deserted his mother, he knew intense hunger, he became a drunkard begging drinks from black stevedores in Memphis saloons; he had to flee Arkansas where an uncle was lynched; he was forced to live with a fanatically religious grandmother in an atmosphere of constant bickering; he was lodged in an orphan asylum; he observed the suffering of his mother who became a permanent invalid, while fighting off the blows of the poverty-stricken relatives with whom he had to live; he was cheated, beaten, and kicked off jobs by white employees who disliked his eagerness to learn a trade; and to these objective circumstances must be added the subjective fact that Wright, with his sensitivity, extreme shyness, and intelligence was a problem child who rejected his family and was by them rejected.

Thus along with the themes, equivalent descriptions of milieu, and the perspectives to be found in Joyce, Nehru, Dostoyevsky, George Moore, and

Rousseau, *Black Boy* is filled with blues-tempered echoes of railroad trains, the names of southern towns and cities, estrangements, fights and flights, deaths and disappointments, charged with physical and spiritual hungers and pain. And like a blues sung by such an artist as Bessie Smith, its lyrical prose evokes the paradoxical, almost surreal image of a black boy singing lustily as he probes his own grievous wound.

In *Black Boy*, two worlds have fused, two cultures merged, two impulses of western man become coalesced. By discussing some of its cultural sources I hope to answer those critics who would make of the book a miracle and of its author a mystery. And while making no attempt to probe the mystery of the artist (who Hemingway says is "forged in injustice as a sword is forged") I do hold that basically the prerequisites to the writing of *Black Boy* were, on the one hand, the microscopic degree of cultural freedom that Wright found in the South's stony injustice and, on the other, the existence of a personality agitated to a state of almost manic restlessness. There were, of course, other factors, chiefly ideological; but these came later.

Wright speaks of his journey north as "taking a part of the South to transplant in alien soil, to see if it could grow differently, if it could drink of new and cool rains, bend in strange winds, respond to the warmth of other suns, and perhaps, to bloom...." And just as Wright, the man, represents the blooming of the delinquent child of the autobiography, just so does *Black Boy* represent the flowering—cross-fertilized by pollen blown by the winds of strange cultures—of the humble blues lyric. There is, as in all acts of creation, a world of mystery in this, but there is also enough that is comprehensible for Americans to create the social atmosphere in which other black boys might freely bloom.

For certainly, in the historical sense, Wright is no exception. Born on a Mississippi plantation, he was subjected to all those blasting pressures which, in a scant eighty years, have sent the Negro people hurtling, without clearly defined trajectory, from slavery to emancipation, from log cabin to city tenement, from the white folks' fields and kitchens to factory assembly lines; and which, between two wars, have shattered the wholeness of its folk consciousness into a thousand writhing pieces.

Black Boy describes this process in the personal terms of one Negro childhood. Nevertheless, several critics have complained that it does not "explain" Richard Wright. Which, aside from the notion of art involved, serves to remind us that the prevailing mood of American criticism has so thoroughly excluded the Negro that it fails to recognize some of the most basic tenets of western democratic thought when encountering them in a black skin. They forget that human life possesses an innate dignity and mankind an innate sense of nobility; that all men possess the tendency to dream and the compulsion to make their dreams reality; that the need to be ever dissatisfied and the urge ever to seek satisfaction is implicit in the human organism; and that all men are the victims and the beneficiaries of the goading, tormenting, commanding, and informing activity of that process known as the Mind—the Mind, as Valéry describes it, "armed with its inexhaustible questions."

Perhaps all this (in which lies the very essence of the human, and which Wright takes for granted) has been forgotten because the critics recognize neither Negro humanity nor the full extent to which the southern community renders the fulfillment of human destiny impossible. And while it is true that *Black Boy* presents an almost unrelieved picture of a personality corrupted by brutal environment, it also presents those fresh human responses brought to its world by the sensitive child:

> There was the *wonder* I felt when I first saw a brace of mountainlike, spotted, black-and-white horses clopping down a dusty road ... the *delight* I caught in seeing long straight rows of red and green vegetables stretching away in the sun ... the faint, cool kiss of sensuality when dew came on to my cheeks ... the vague *sense of the infinite* as I looked down upon the yellow, dreaming waters of the Mississippi ... the echoes of nostalgia I heard in the crying strings of wild geese ... the love I had for the mute regality of tall, moss-clad oaks ... the hint of *cosmic cruelty* that I *felt* when I saw the curved timbers of a wooden shack that had been warped in the summer sun ... and there was the *quiet terror* that suffused my senses when vast hazes of gold washed earthward from star-heavy skies on silent nights... [italics mine].

And a bit later, his reactions to religion:

> Many of the religious symbols appealed to my sensibilities and I responded to the dramatic vision of life held by the church, feeling that to live day by day with death as one's sole thought was to be so compassionately sensitive toward all life as to view all men as slowly dying, and the trembling sense of fate that welled up, sweet and melancholy, from the hymns blended with the sense of fate that I had already caught from life.

There was also the influence of his mother—so closely linked to his hysteria and sense of suffering—who (though he only implies it here) taught him, in the words of the dedication prefacing *Native Son*, "to revere the fanciful and the imaginative." There were also those white men—the one who allowed Wright to use his library privileges and the other who advised him to leave the South, and still others whose offers of friendship he was too frightened to accept.

Wright assumed that the nucleus of plastic sensibility is a human heritage—the right and the opportunity to dilate, deepen, and enrich sensibility—democracy. Thus the drama of *Black Boy* lies in its depiction of what occurs when Negro sensibility attempts to fulfill itself in the undemocratic South. Here it is not the individual that is the immediate focus, as in Joyce's Stephen Hero, but that upon which his sensibility was nourished.

Those critics who complain that Wright has omitted the development of his own sensibility hold that the work thus fails as art. Others, because it presents too little of what they consider attractive in Negro life, charge that it distorts reality. Both groups miss a very obvious point: that whatever else the environment contained, it had as little chance of prevailing against the overwhelming weight of the child's unpleasant experiences as Beethoven's Quartets would have of destroying the stench of a Nazi prison.

We come, then, to the question of art. The function, the psychology, of artistic selectivity is to eliminate from art form all those elements of experience that contain no compelling significance. Life is as the sea, art a ship in which man conquers life's crushing formlessness, reducing it to a course, a series of swells, tides, and wind currents inscribed on a chart. Though drawn from the world, "the organized significance of art," writes Malraux, "is stronger than all the multiplicity of the world; ... that significance alone enables man to conquer chaos and to master destiny."

Wright saw his destiny—that combination of forces before which man feels powerless—in terms of a quick and casual violence inflicted upon him by both family and community. His response was likewise violent, and it has been his need to give that violence significance that has shaped his writings.

II

What were the ways by which other Negroes confronted their destiny?

In the South of Wright's childhood there were three general ways: They could accept the role created for them by the whites and perpetually resolve the resulting conflicts through the hope and emotional catharsis of Negro religion; they could repress their dislike of Jim Crow social relations while striving for a middle way of respectability, becoming—consciously or unconsciously—the accomplices of the whites in oppressing their brothers; or they could reject the situation, adopt a criminal attitude, and carry on an unceasing psychological scrimmage with the whites, which often flared forth into physical violence.

Wright's attitude was nearest the last. Yet, in it there was an all-important qualitative difference: it represented a groping for individual values, in a black community whose values were what the young Negro critic, Edward Bland, has defined as "pre-individual." And herein lay the setting for the extreme conflict set off, both within his family and in the community, by Wright's assertion of individuality. The clash was sharpest on the psychological level, for, to quote Bland:

> In the pre-individualistic thinking of the Negro the stress is on the group. Instead of seeing in terms of the individual, the Negro sees in terms of "races," masses of peoples separated from other masses according to color. Hence, an act rarely bears intent against him as a Negro individual. He is singled out not as a person but as a specimen of an ostracized group. He knows that he never exists in his own right but only to the extent that others hope to make the race suffer vicariously through him.

This pre-individual state is induced artificially—like the regression to primitive states noted among cultured inmates of Nazi prisons. The primary technique in its enforcement is to impress the Negro child with the omniscience and omnipotence of the whites to the point that whites appear as ahuman as Jehovah, and as relentless as a Mississippi flood. Socially it is effected through an elaborate scheme of taboos supported by a ruthless physical violence, which strikes not only the offender, but the entire black community. To wander from the paths of behavior laid down for the group is to become the agent of communal disaster.

In such a society the development of individuality depends upon a series of accidents that often arise, as in Wright's case, from conditions within the Negro family. In Wright's life there was the accident that as a small child he could not distinguish between his fair-skinned grandmother and the white women of the town, thus developing skepticism as to their special status. To this was linked the accident of his having no close contacts with whites until after the child's normal formative period.

But these objective accidents not only link forward to those qualities of rebellion, criminality, and intellectual questioning expressed in Wright's work today. They also link backward into the shadow of infancy where environment and consciousness are so darkly intertwined as to require the skill of a psychoanalyst to define their point of juncture. Nevertheless, at the age of four, Wright set the house afire and was beaten near to death by his frightened mother. This beating, followed soon by his father's desertion of the family, seems to be the initial psychological motivation of his quest for a new identification. While delirious from this beating Wright was haunted "by huge wobbly white bags like the full udders of a cow, suspended from the ceiling above me [and] I was gripped by the fear that they were going to fall and drench me with some horrible liquid...."

It was as though the mother's milk had turned acid, and with it the whole pattern of life that had produced the ignorance, cruelty, and fear that had fused with mother-love and exploded in the beating. It is significant that the bags were of the hostile color white, and the female symbol that of the cow, the most stupid (and, to the small child, the most frightening) of domestic animals. Here in dream symbolism is expressed an attitude worthy of an Orestes. And the significance of the crisis is increased by virtue of the historical fact that the lower-class Negro family is matriarchal; the child turns not to the father to compensate if he feels mother-rejection, but to the grandmother, or to an aunt—and Wright rejected both of these. Such rejection leaves the child open to psychological insecurity, distrust, and all of those hostile environmental forces from which the family functions to protect it.

One of the southern Negro family's methods of protecting the child is the severe beating—a homeopathic dose of the violence generated by black and white relationships. Such beatings as Wright's were administered for the child's own good; a good which the child resisted, thus giving family relationships an undercurrent of fear and hostility, which differs qualitatively from that found in patriarchal middle-class families, because here the severe beating is administered by the mother, leaving the child no parental sanctuary. He must ever embrace violence along with maternal tenderness, or else reject, in his helpless way, the mother.

The division between the Negro parents of Wright's mother's generation, whose sensibilities were often bound by their proximity to the slave experience, and their children, who historically and through the rapidity of American change, stand emotionally and psychologically much farther away, is quite deep. Indeed, sometimes as deep as the cultural distance between Yeats's *Autobiographies* and a Bessie Smith blues. This is the historical background to those incidents of family strife in *Black Boy* that have caused reviewers to question Wright's judgment of Negro emotional relationships. We have here a problem in the sociology of sensibility that is obscured by certain psychological attitudes brought to Negro life by whites.

III

The first problem is the attitude that compels whites to impute to Negroes sentiments, attitudes, and insights which, as a group living under certain definite social conditions, Negroes could not humanly possess. It is the identical mechanism that William Empson identifies in literature as "pastoral." It implies that since Negroes possess the richly human virtues credited to them, then their social position is advantageous and should not be bettered; and, continuing syllogistically, the white individual need feel no guilt over his participation in Negro oppression.

The second attitude is that which leads whites to misjudge Negro passion, looking upon it as they do, out of the turgidity of their own frustrated yearning for emotional warmth, their capacity for sensation having been constricted by the impersonal mechanized relationships typical of bourgeois society. The Negro is idealized into a symbol of sensation, of unhampered social and sexual relationships. And when *Black Boy* questions their illusion they are thwarted much in the manner of the occidental who, after observing the erotic character of a primitive dance, "shacks up" with a native woman—only to discover that far from possessing the hair-trigger sexual responses of a Stork Club "babe," she is relatively phlegmatic.

The point is not that American Negroes are primitives, but that, as a group, their social situation does not provide for the type of emotional relationships attributed to them. For how could the South, recognized as a major part of the backward third of the nation, see flower in the black, most brutalized section of its population, those forms of human relationships achievable only in the most highly developed areas of civilization?

Champions of this "Aren't-Negroes-Wonderful?" school of thinking often bring Paul Robeson and Marian Anderson forward as examples of highly developed sensibility, but actually they are only its promise. Both received their development from an extensive personal contact with European culture, free from the influences that shape southern Negro personality. In the United States, Wright, who is the only Negro literary artist of equal caliber, had to wait years and escape to another environment before discovering the moral and ideological equivalents of his childhood attitudes.

Man cannot express that which does not exist—either in the form of dreams, ideas, or realities—in his environment. Neither his thoughts nor his feelings, his sensibility nor his intellect are fixed, innate qualities. They are processes that arise out of the interpenetration of human instinct with environment, through the process called experience; each changing and being changed by the other. Negroes cannot possess many of the sentiments attributed to them because the same changes in environment which, through experience, enlarge man's intellect (and thus his capacity for still greater change) also modify his feelings; which in turn increase his sensibility, i.e., his sensitivity to refinements of impression and subtleties of emotion. The extent of these changes depends upon the quality of political and cultural freedom in the environment.

Intelligence tests have measured the quick rise in intellect that takes place in southern Negroes after moving north, but little attention has been paid to the mutations effected in their sensibilities. However, the two go hand in hand. Intellectual complexity is accompanied by emotional complexity; refinement of thought, by refinement of feeling. The movement north affects more than the Negro's wage scale, it affects his entire psychosomatic structure.

The rapidity of Negro intellectual growth in the North is due partially to objective factors present in the environment, to influences of the industrial city, and to a greater political freedom. But there are also changes within the "inner world." In the North energies are released and given intellectual channelization—energies that in most Negroes in the South have been forced to take either a physical form or, as with potentially intellectual types like Wright, to be expressed as nervous tension, anxiety, and hysteria. Which is nothing mysterious. The human organism responds to environmental stimuli by converting them into either physical and/or intellectual energy. And what is called hysteria is suppressed intellectual energy expressed physically.

The "physical" character of their expression makes for much of the difficulty in understanding American Negroes. Negro music and dances are frenziedly erotic; Negro religious ceremonies violently ecstatic; Negro speech strongly rhythmical and weighted with image and gesture. But there is more in this sensuousness than the unrestraint and insensitivity found in primitive cultures; nor is it simply the relatively spontaneous and undifferentiated responses of a people living in close contact with the soil. For despite Jim Crow, Negro life does not exist in a vacuum, but in the seething vortex of those tensions generated by the most highly industrialized of western nations. The welfare of the most humble black Mississippi sharecropper is affected less by the flow of the seasons and the rhythm of natural events than by the fluctuations of the stock market; even though, as Wright states of his father, the sharecropper's memories, actions, and emotions are shaped by his immediate contact with nature and the crude social relations of the South.

All of this makes the American Negro far different from the "simple" specimen for which he is taken. And the "physical" quality offered as evidence of his primitive simplicity is actually the form of his complexity.

The American Negro is a western type whose social condition creates a state that is almost the reverse of the cataleptic trance: Instead of his consciousness being lucid to the reality around it while the body is rigid, here it is the body that is alert, reacting to pressures which the constricting forces of Jim Crow block off from the transforming, concept-creating activity of the brain. The "eroticism" of Negro expression springs from much the same conflict as that displayed in the violent gesturing of a man who attempts to express a complicated concept with a limited vocabulary; thwarted ideational energy is converted into unsatisfactory pantomime, and his words are burdened with meanings they cannot convey. Here lies the source of the basic ambiguity of *Native Son*, where in order to translate Bigger's complicated feelings into universal ideas, Wright had to force into Bigger's consciousness concepts and ideas that his intellect could not formulate. Between Wright's skill and knowledge and the potentials of Bigger's mute feelings lay a thousand years of conscious culture.

In the South the sensibilities of both blacks and whites are inhibited by the rigidly defined environment. For the Negro there is relative safety as long as the impulse toward individuality is suppressed. (Lynchings have occurred because Negroes painted their homes.) And it is the task of the Negro family to help the child adjust to the southern milieu; through it the currents, tensions, and impulses generated within the human organism by the flux and flow of events are given their distribution. This also gives the group its distinctive character. Which, because of Negroes' suppressed minority position, is very much in the nature of an elaborate but limited defense mechanism. Its function is dual: to protect the Negro from whirling away from the undifferentiated mass of his people into the unknown, symbolized in its most abstract form by insanity, and most concretely by lynching; and to protect him from those unknown forces *within himself* which might urge him to reach out for that social and human equality that the white South says he cannot have. Rather than throw himself against the charged wires of his prison, he annihilates the impulses within him.

The pre-individualistic black community discourages individuality out of self-defense. Having learned through experience that the whole group is punished for the actions of the single member, it has worked out efficient techniques of behavior control. For in many southern communities everyone knows everyone else and is vulnerable to his opinions. In some communities everyone is "related" regardless of blood-ties. The regard shown by the group for its members, its general communal character, and its cohesion are often mentioned. For by comparison with the coldly impersonal relationships of the urban industrial community, its relationships are personal and warm.

Black Boy, however, illustrates that this personal quality, shaped by outer violence and inner fear, is ambivalent. Personal warmth is accompanied by an equally personal coldness, kindliness by cruelty, regard by malice. And these opposites are as quickly set off against the member who gestures toward individuality as a lynch mob forms at the cry of rape. Negro leaders have often been exasperated by this phenomenon, and Booker T. Washington (who demanded far less of Negro humanity than Richard Wright) described the Negro community as a basket of crabs, wherein should one attempt to climb out, the others immediately pull him back.

The member who breaks away is apt to be more impressed by its negative than by its positive character. He becomes a stranger even to his relatives and he interprets gestures of protection as blows of oppression— from which there is no hiding place, because every area of Negro life is affected. Even parental love is given a qualitative balance akin to "sadism." And the extent of beatings and psychological maimings meted out by southern Negro parents rivals those described by the nineteenth-century Russian writers as characteristic of peasant life under the Czars. The horrible thing is that the cruelty is also an expression of concern, of love.

In discussing the inadequacies for democratic living typical of the education provided Negroes by the South, a Negro educator has coined the term *mis-education*. Within the ambit of the black family this takes the form of training the child away from curiosity and adventure, against reaching out for those activities lying beyond the borders of the black community. And when the child resists, the parent discourages him, first with the formula "That there's for white folks. Colored can't have it," and finally with a beating.

It is not, then, the family and communal violence described by *Black Boy* that is unusual, but that Wright recognized and made no peace with its essential cruelty—even when, like a babe freshly emerged from the womb, he could not discern where his own personality ended and it began. Ordinarily, both parent and child are protected against this cruelty—seeing it as love and finding subjective sanction for it in the spiritual authority of the Fifth Commandment, and on the secular level in the legal and extralegal structure of the Jim Crow system. The child who did not rebel, or who was unsuccessful in his rebellion, learned a masochistic submissiveness and a denial of the impulse toward western culture when it stirred within him.

IV

Why then have southern whites, who claim to "know" the Negro, missed all this? Simply because they too are armored against the horror and the cruelty.

Either they deny the Negro's humanity and feel no cause to measure his actions against civilized norms, or they protect themselves from their guilt in the Negro's condition and from their fear that their cooks might poison them, or that their nursemaids might strangle their infant charges, or that their field hands might do them violence, by attributing to them a superhuman capacity for love, kindliness, and forgiveness. Nor does this in any way contradict their stereotyped conviction that all Negroes (meaning those with whom they have no contact) are given to the most animal behavior.

It is only when the individual, whether white or black, rejects the pattern that he awakens to the nightmare of his life. Perhaps much of the South's regressive character springs from the fact that many, jarred by some casual crisis into wakefulness, flee hysterically into the sleep of violence or the coma of apathy again. For the penalty of wakefulness is to encounter even more violence and horror than the sensibilities can sustain unless translated into some form of social action. Perhaps the impassioned character so noticeable among those white southern liberals active in the Negro's cause is due to their sense of accumulated horror; their passion—like the violence in Faulkner's novels—is evidence of a profound spiritual vomiting.

This compulsion is even more active in Wright and the increasing number of Negroes who have said an irrevocable "no" to the southern pattern. Wright learned that it is not enough merely to reject the white South, but that he had also to reject that part of the South which lay within. As a rebel he formulated that rejection negatively, because it was the negative face of the Negro community upon which he looked most often as a child. It is this he is contemplating when he writes:

> Whenever I thought of the essential bleakness of black life in America, I knew that Negroes had never been allowed to catch the full spirit of Western civilization, that they lived somehow in it but not of it. And when I brooded upon the cultural barrenness of black life, I wondered if clean, positive tenderness, love, honor, loyalty, and the capacity to remember were native to man. I asked myself if these human qualities were not fostered, won, struggled and suffered for, preserved in ritual from one generation to another.

But far from implying that Negroes have no capacity for culture, as one critic interprets it, this is the strongest affirmation that they have. Wright is pointing out what should be obvious (especially to his Marxist critics): that Negro sensibility is socially and historically conditioned; that western culture must be won, confronted like the animal in a Spanish bullfight, dominated by the red shawl of codified experience, and brought heaving to its knees.

Wright knows perfectly well that Negro life is a by-product of western civilization, and that in it, if only one possesses the humanity and humility to see, are to be discovered all those impulses, tendencies, life, and cultural forms, to be found elsewhere in western society.

The problem arises because the special condition of Negroes in the United States, including the defensive character of Negro life itself (the "will toward organization" noted in the western capitalist appears in the Negro as a will to camouflage, to dissimulate) so distorts these forms as to render their recognition as difficult as finding a wounded quail against the brown and yellow leaves of a Mississippi thicket—even the spilled blood blends with the background. Having himself been in the position of the quail—to expand the metaphor—Wright's wounds have told him both the question and the answer that every successful hunter must discover for himself: "Where would I hide if I were a wounded quail?" But perhaps that requires more sympathy with one's quarry than most hunters possess. Certainly it requires such a sensitivity to the shifting guises of humanity under pressure as to allow them to identify themselves with the human content, whatever its outer form; and even with those southern Negroes to whom Paul Robeson's name is only a rolling sound in the fear-charged air.

Let us close with one final word about the blues: Their attraction lies in this, that they at once express both the agony of life and the possibility of conquering it through sheer toughness of spirit. They fall short of tragedy only in that they provide no solution, offer no scapegoat but the self. Nowhere in America today is there social or political action based upon the solid realities of Negro life depicted in *Black Boy*; perhaps that is why, with its refusal to offer solutions, it is like the blues. Yet, in it thousands of Negroes will for the first time see their destiny in public print. Freed here of fear and the threat of violence, their lives have at last been organized, scaled down to possessable proportions. And in this lies Wright's most important achievement: he has converted the American Negro impulse toward self-annihilation and "going-underground" into a will to confront the world, to evaluate his experience honestly, and throw his findings unashamedly into the guilty conscience of America.

DAN McCALL

An American Life

When Richard Wright realized the final meaning of Bigger Thomas he saw there was no place to go. He was facing a wall. So, as he had done so often in his life when he faced a wall, he went straight ahead. To *Black Boy*. The book had begun as "The Ethics of Living, Jim Crow," the essay Wright prepared for the anthology of the Federal Writers' Project; now he was ready to keep all the promises in the "Ethics" and explore larger questions. There were other, exciting projects in the five-year interval between *Native Son* and *Black Boy*—his text for the photo-collection of *12 Million Black Voices*, stories to write, reviews to get in, speeches to deliver—but his autobiography was slowly taking shape in his mind. *Native Son* is a story of the North, of the city, where enraged violence expresses itself in overt assault. Bigger is just coming into his manhood, into the full terms of the curse which corrodes his brain and leads him to kill. *Black Boy* is a Southern story, a story of the country; a boy who must painfully, gradually learn the curse, who totters beneath the blows he receives. The books go together, novel and autobiography, fiction and fact, the twin peaks of Richard Wright's career. Both take us into the mind of a single black boy in America, one destroyed by crippling hate and the other making an uncanny survival.

Wright's effort in *Black Boy* would not be to exorcise another version of "the bad nigger" that was living in his skull; here he would inspect all his own

---

From *The Example of Richard Wright*. © 1969 by Dan McCall.

old scars, make them open wounds again, assess the pain and try to heal. Proust could symbolize his ideal ecstasy in the moment when *Maman* kissed him good night each evening, sealing the warm world of total pleasure; in this black boy's remembrance of things past the mother beats her son into unconsciousness. Daily terror leads to feverish dreams of Granny's sick flaming hair and "huge wobbly white bags, like the full udders of cows, suspended from the ceiling above me" and goggled-eyed kittens hanging by the neck, spitting in air, ready to claw his eyes. In *Black Boy* Wright would re-enter the haunted house of his youth, and summon the gross spirits to intelligence.

Black Boy clarifies the nature of Wright's importance. In any strictly literary sense, he broke no new ground, established no new devices or techniques or methods. He did not make us see our experience in new ways; he made us see new experience. He had a perception about America, a perception of a part of America that was unknown territory. His importance is not really literary but what we should call cultural. We come to him not for new ways of saying things but for the new things he has to say. When he does get "literary" on us, when he draws himself up into "writing," he is merely fancy, and he fails. He would say of his effort in *Black Boy*, "If I could fasten the mind of the reader upon words so firmly that he would forget words and be conscious only of his response, I felt that I would be in sight of knowing how to write narrative. I strove to master words, to make them disappear...." His ability to do that is a major achievement of *Black Boy*, a book virtually uncontaminated by his old rhetoric. In *Native Son* there was too much forensic slag, too many set pieces, a prose racing in all directions, and an explanatory moral. Five years later, Wright has freed himself of his revolutionary slogans and all that went with them; he has grown into his craft and his sense of his life's meaning.

The book is extremely difficult to describe. The power of the prose is explainable largely by its effect. Wright wanted the words, as he said, to disappear. He had to set the facts down in front of us, carefully in clear light, and then we would see. When we do see, what more is there to say? Surely no one needs to "interpret" what we perceive when young Richard, famished for books, gets the permission of a white Irish Catholic, a "Pope lover ... hated by the white Southerners" to forge his name on a note to the white librarian in Memphis (where black people were forbidden to patronize the shelves): "*Dear Madam: Will you please let this nigger boy have some books by H. L. Mencken?*" One of Wright's wisest choices was not to "interpret" that encounter—what should he say that we cannot see?—and one of his finest achievements was to make a note that embodied the situation.

Although Lillian Smith's review of *Black Boy* in PM was generally quite favorable, she complained:

> His childhood is still, in large part, a closed door to him. He has not yet found the key that will unlock old memories and bring back deeply buried childhood feeling. He tells little incidents, little, heart-breaking, pitiful, and sometimes amusing anecdotes. But they are told with a strange lack-of-feeling tone, with little of that quality of imagination that interprets even as it narrates....

Exactly the opposite is true: that "strange lack-of-feeling tone" (whatever it means) may be Miss Smith's way of objecting to the starkness, the unrelieved pain. All life is perceived here in such brutal and corrosive terms that to interpret the details or events would be to draw us away from Wright's accuracy, to swamp his sharp, swift craft with baggy yards of sail. Wright's refusal to provide what Lillian Smith asks for is his dignity as a writer and contributes to the difficult integrity of his book. The story is too important for us to weep over, and the implications of that story cannot be adequately understood if we have been lulled into tears.

Black Boy is, as the subtitle says, "A Record of Childhood and Youth." Here we will not find the unbearable fantasies of the culture, which Wright had previously embodied in Bigger Thomas. In *Native Son* we were shown almost nothing of Bigger's background; while his early life may have been no great mystery to us, it did not exist in any detail. The facts about him, before that dreadful winter day, were sketched in only as answers to Jan's questions in Ernie's Kitchen Shack. Bigger says he was born in Mississippi, quit school at the eighth grade, had been in Chicago five years, and his father had been killed long ago in a riot in the South. In *Black Boy* we can see Richard Wright's similarity to Bigger: born in Mississippi, a formal schooling that ended at the eighth grade, bereft of his father at an early age, and going north to Chicago at the end of his adolescence.

But Richard Wright did not become Bigger Thomas; he created him. If *Black Boy* can be made to fill in all Bigger's blanks, it also raises another significant question: how did it happen that Richard escaped? Malcolm X wrote near the end of his autobiography:

> I feel, and I hope, that if I honestly and fully tell my life's account, read objectively it might prove to be a testimony of some social value.
>
> I think that an objective reader may see how in the society to

which I was exposed as a black youth here in America, for me to
wind up in a prison was really just about inevitable.

Wright, too, is presenting "honestly and fully" his "life's account" and he is
obviously intending it "to be a testimony of some social value." In Bigger's
story Wright had shown that when the "black youth" ended up in an electric
chair it was "really just about inevitable." In *Black Boy* he was showing how
all the horror could make a Bigger, how the whole black society was ripped
up and torn apart by that horror, but he was also showing how he himself
escaped it.

Most of it was sheer luck. That saves the book from any hint of mere
strutting; we see over and over again that when Richard pulled out of a
beating, or escaped a fire, or didn't get a bullet in his brain—all those
survivals had little to do with his own power or his own brains. When he wins
a fight, he wins it out of utter desperation, backed against a wall fighting for
his life; his tormentors lay off because they don't want to get hurt (one of
those wild blows might, after all, land), but they're not afraid of getting
beaten. If Richard had only wised up, he would have been saved innumerable
beatings at home, countless disgraces by the white men. His survival is no
puffing pride at his own cunning or strength; too often we see him duped and
flat on his back.

But his survival is not only luck, and what else it was involves
considerable moral force. *Black Boy* was Wright's second enormous best
seller, and when he wrote to Gertrude Stein on May 27, 1945, he could bring
the news that again a book of his had been out only a few months and the
sales were in the hundreds of thousands. To explain his success he confesses,
"Frankly, I don't know why people read my work; it upsets them terribly...."
But we should get upset in the right way, and Wright knew it more clearly
than his flip "frankly I don't know why people read my work" might imply.
It was absolutely remarkable that the pickaninny he describes could grow up
to be a writer; on all sides people were constantly turning him from that goal,
shaming him out of it, laughing him out of it, beating him out of it. From the
beginning his "Granny" had "always burned the books I had brought into the
house, branding them as worldly." When at the end he looked back, he saw
that his dream of being a writer was one "which the entire educational system
of the South had been rigged to stifle." That he should be able to live to tell
the tale was a freak of determination.

It is also central to our sense of what the "record" means. When
Lionel Trilling reviewed *Black Boy* in the *Nation* (April 7, 1945), he said that
here was "a remarkably fine book," but its fineness could not be understood
merely by those who saw it as another report of misery and oppression. We

had several of those books, and too many readers had enjoyed them cheaply:

> To sit in one's armchair and be harrowed can all too easily pass for a moral or political action. We vicariously suffer in slippers and become virtuous; it is pleasant to exercise moral indignation at small cost; or to fill up emotional vacancy with good strong feeling at a safe distance; or to feel consciously superior to the brutal oppressor; or to be morally entertained by poverty....

Trilling felt that Wright did not allow us those luxuries. In *Black Boy* Wright "does not wholly identify himself with his painful experience, does not, therefore, make himself a mere object of the reader's consciousness, does not make himself that different kind of human being, a 'sufferer.' He is not an object; he is a subject...."

At the Memphis bank young Richard got to know a "round, yellow, fat elevator operator" named Shorty. He was "the most amazing specimen of the southern Negro I had ever met" not only because of his grotesque appearance ("the complexion of a Chinese, a short forehead, and three chins"), but also because this "hardheaded, sensible reader of magazines and books ... proud of his race and indignant about its wrongs" would "play the role of a clown of the most debased and degraded type" whenever white folks were around. One day Shorty needed a quarter for lunch; he told Richard he would get it from the first white man who came by. When one walked in, Shorty went into his act, begging, then refusing to run the elevator, "drooling, drawling, grimacing, clowning." And finally he gets the white man to ask what he'd do for a quarter. Shorty—giggling all the while—bent down, "poked out his broad, fleshy ass" and offered it to be kicked. For two bits.

> The white man laughed softly, jingled some coins in his pocket, took out one and thumped it to the floor. Shorty stooped to pick it up and the white man bared his teeth and swung his foot into Shorty's rump with all the strength of his body, Shorty let out a howling laugh that echoed up and down the elevator shaft.

After Shorty's laugh—"This monkey's got the peanuts"—young Richard goes up to him with "only disgust and loathing" and asks, "How in God's name can you do that?"

"Listen, nigger," he said to me, "my ass is tough and quarters is scarce."

Richard Wright despised that man. In *Black Boy* young Richard always clings to his dignity, even in moments of great suffering, even when that precarious dignity of his gets another white boot in the ass. Shorty is partially redeemed by his humor, by his gross indifference to the sanctity of his rear end. He is redeemed, too, by the fact that he has made his ass tough enough to trust it, and he does inhabit a world where quarters are extremely scarce. But Richard Wright had none of Shorty's capacity for buffoonery and he set a higher price on his person. Over two decades later, Eldridge Cleaver would take a similar stand, quoting a central article of faith from Norman Mailer: "Being a man is the continuing battle of one's life, and one loses a bit of manhood with every stale compromise to the authority of any power in which one does not believe." And that is the continuing cry in all the battles of Black Boy's life: No compromise.

In Arthur Miller's *The Crucible*, a frosty Salem elder is accused of witchery. The old man will not give in. To get the admission out of him the judges pile stone after stone upon his chest. As he dies, he utters only two words, "More weight."

"More weight" is adequate to the horror and to the moral splendor of *Black Boy*. Young Richard is an object of a mass aberration, a witch-hunt in which he is a little black devil. The community keeps piling the crushing circumstances upon him. As he grows he grows to an awareness of just how heavy are the things pressing down on him, begins to see just how hard the white world has to crush. He refuses to give in. No matter how much "more weight" the culture heaps upon him, he will not die into the lowly "nigger" that they want him to be. And when he finally escapes that system, there is a subsequent determination in the writing not to tidy the ordeal with facile pathos. Given all his luck, all his dignity, and all his will, it was unlikely that the boy would survive. But if he did, he could tell us just how much energy had been expended on both sides of the rocks, the world that pressed them down and the small voice that called up from below. Some reviewers objected that Wright's book only showed that the system could not have been as bad as he said—his survival proved, that is, his survival. What it does prove is that all the rocks had not yet killed all the black boys. One that got away was able to tell us why they had not—and how close they had come. He told us in such a way that if we chose to shed our tears we would have to see that they only watered the rocks.

II

The book opens with the house burning down. Richard was bored, it was winter night, and all the attention went elsewhere; he could not play outside and he could not make noise inside because "in the next room Granny lay ill." The scene sets the pitch for the book as a whole: throughout, someone is in deep trouble, wasting away, sick, in the immediate vicinity of a new and even ghastlier trouble. Out of boredom and sickness, a fire. Everywhere in the book Wright is showing us how the ennui, the varieties of illness, and the explosions are hopelessly linked together in an unending and unbreakable circle of oppression.

Richard's "first triumph over my father" is the desperate victory of a false literalness. The kitten outside disturbs the father's sleep and so he yells, "Get rid of it, kill it." Richard, thirsting for excitement and desperate to prove his own power in the world, strings the kitten up. The way to vent all one's bottled-up hate (and not get whipped for it) is to take exasperations as imperatives. But if the father will not whip, the mother will.

His first school is an outdoor privy. He learns to identify his neighbors by their backsides, to gauge their determination by the "projectile force of their excretions." Knowledge begins at the back end of an open-end commode; the course is the law of bodily functions. And this school will be in every school he attends, schools of endurance and dirt. Unable to escape a paralysis at the blackboard, he comes away with all the schoolyard graffiti, spreading it in soap on the neighborhood windows. And when Fundamentalist Granny scrubs his backside in the bath,

> My mind was in a sort of daze, midway between daydreaming and thinking. Then, before I knew it, words—words whose meaning I did not fully know—had slipped out of my mouth.
> "When you get through, kiss back there."

As usual, he has learned too much of the wrong thing. Granny says he has done "something he ought to be killed for." After his beating he is told that he has been whipped for learning "foul practices" and "when I asked what 'foul practices' were, my mother beat me afresh." His schooling takes place in the toilet; he is beaten on the way in and on the way out.

He has nothing to hold him together, to keep him whole. *Black Boy* is a portrait of unending hunger. When his father won't provide food, Richard hates him with a "biological bitterness." Each night he sees "hunger standing at my bedside, staring at me." Later, at the foster home, when he has to mow the lawn by pulling up the grass in his hands, "I was too weak from hunger ... I would grow dizzy and my mind would become blank and I would find myself, after an interval of unconsciousness, upon my hands and knees, my head whirling, my eyes staring in bleak astonishment at the green grass...." Wherever we enter the narrative, we can read hardly a page before we see again the intolerable effects of not having enough to eat. At Uncle Hoskins's house, he is told that he should "get used to food," but every time he leaves the table he has to steal a little bread for his pockets. "In washing my clothes

my mother found the gummy wads and scolded me to break me of the habit;
I stopped hiding the bread in my pockets and hid it about the house, in
corners, behind dressers." And he was right to store it away for very soon
Uncle Hoskins gets killed by whites. He "had simply been plucked from our
midst"—and the ordeal of hunger is on again. At Granny's house they rarely
have any meat. "For breakfast I ate mush and gravy made from flour and lard
and for hours afterwards I would belch it up into my mouth." He concludes
that his diet "would have stunted an average-sized dog." His pride will not
allow him to get the little food that is available from others; in the
playground with the other kids, "whenever they asked me if I wanted food, I
would say no, even though I was starving." And one of the quietest moments
in the book is the end of chapter two where his single Christmas gift is an
orange. He eats it all day long, and at night, just before going to bed, "I tore
the peeling into bits and munched them slowly."

Hunger is the most important thing in his life; over the years we
continue to see how "hunger would make me weak, would make me sway
while walking." But the hunger in his belly is only the most numbing
physical pang of a general hunger. Midway through the book, "I vowed that
someday I would end this hunger of mine, this apartness, this eternal
difference." Hunger is wanting to have, to eat, to be filled.

Except for one brief paragraph about the boy's infatuation with the
Reverend's wife in the choir, there is no sexual love in *Black Boy*—not even
puppy love. When he tries to find out about sex he peeks into a whore house,
falls from the window, and the madam comes out to scold. "Evidently I had
done something terrible"—as usual. Years later as a bellboy he looks at a naked
white prostitute strutting in front of him, and a white man says, "Keep your
eyes where they belong if you want to be healthy!" When in Memphis a simple
little black girl offers herself to him, wants to marry and love him and comb
his hair, he asks himself, "Was I dumb or was she dumb?" For so many years
Richard had been looking for love, any love he could get; on the couch in the
prim little home "the light that shone out of this child's heart ... blinded me."

The year after *Black Boy* appeared Wright did an article for *Twice a Year*
in which he said (the italics are his):

> At the core of the personality of almost every delinquent child is
> found *emotional deprivation*, and this exists in a land where
> Negroes are traditionally regarded as possessing, as a gift of
> nature, a super-abundant fund of laughter, song, joy, and rhythm.

The sadness Richard Wright felt in Memphis in 1925, when Mrs. Moss
thrust her simple little Bess on him, was that here he could see for the first

time "the full degree to which my life at home had cut me off, not only from white people but from Negroes as well." The hunger had not been satisfied anywhere; it had stunted his growth. "My personality was lopsided." Hit too many times, "I felt that I had been slapped out of the human race." The whites would never take him in and the blacks had thrown him out. The price for standing up to his Uncle Tom had been even greater than he had thought it would be, for Uncle Tom kept all children away from him: "No matter how carefully I weighed my memories, I could recall no innocent intimacy, no games, no playing, none of the association that usually exists between young people living in the same house." The behavior of Uncle Tom and the other elders illustrates what Erik Erikson has said in *Young Man Luther*: "The most deadly of all possible sins is the mutilation of a child's spirit; for such mutilation undercuts the life principle of trust...."

Young Richard turned to the only thing that he had to trust. Books. Words. As money "melted into the bottomless hunger of the household" Richard "hungered for a different life." As he entered seventh grade, "my old hunger was still with me, and I lived on what I did not eat." Perhaps in books, in stories, he could find some food.

He is the only one in the community with that kind of hunger, and such a portrait could be violently misunderstood. *Time*'s reviewer (March 5, 1945) said that *Black Boy* was "the story of a man set apart from his own race by sensitivity and intellect, yet barred forever from the white race by the color of his skin." The assumption in the sentence, of course, is that poor Richard's "sensitivity and intellect" separate him "from his own race" because that race is incapable of the "sensitivity and intellect" which only whites can have. Richard, your whole trouble is that while on the outside you are black, inside you're really white like us. And when such white readers looked through the pages of *Black Boy* for portraits of "sensitive" or "intellectual" Negroes they would find only Richard. If Wright could say that the whites always thought of the blacks as "a variety of children," he did not provide much evidence for thinking the opposite. He seemed to join in, to accept the prejudice, saying:

> Our anger was like the anger of children, passing quickly from one petty grievance to another, from the memory of one slight wrong to another.

To say such things—and to show them over and over again in the portraits he drew of his family—opened Wright to charges not only from the unserious white reader but also from several black readers. Again he was facing the problem of *Native Son*, and facing it even more dangerously, for this was supposed to be fact, not fiction.

The virulent attack by W.E.B. Du Bois in the New York *Herald Tribune* (March 4, 1945) was formidable; here, after all, was another spokesman for the race. Du Bois's review is a curious document, and he seems unable to convince himself (or to admit to the reader) that the story is true. "The hero whom Wright draws, *and maybe it is himself,* is in his childhood a loathsome brat, foul-mouthed, and 'a drunkard'" (my emphasis). When Wright portrays the people around him he is not to be trusted because "the Negroes whom he paints have almost no redeeming qualities. Some work hard, some are sly, many are resentful; but there is none who is ambitious, successful, or really intelligent." Success, one gathers, is "a redeeming quality." Du Bois apparently felt that such a book could do nothing but damage, portraying to a mass white audience a picture of the Negro as a depraved being. It would confirm the prejudices that Du Bois himself had so long been working to tear down.

The most fiery objection would come many years later in an attack that far excels that of Du Bois in its appearance of elegance and its cultivated weariness of false definitions. When *Black Boy* first appeared Ralph Ellison praised it in "Richard Wright's Blues" for *Antioch Review* (June 1945). Ellison found the best things, the "fresh, human responses" in those passages that are probably the worst things in the book, the corn-pone lists of natural beauties that Wright felt compelled to put in here and there. These sections, which Ellison admired, could be written for high-school "voice of democracy" contests, colorless Americana.

> There was the breathlessly anxious fun of chasing and catching flitting fireflies on drowsy summer nights.
> There was the drenching hospitality in the pervading smell of sweet magnolias.
> There was the aura of limitless freedom distilled from the rolling sweep of tall green grass swaying and glinting in the wind and sun.
> There was the feeling of impersonal plenty when I saw a boll of cotton whose cup had split over and straggled its white fleece toward the earth.
> There was the pitying chuckle that bubbled in my throat when I watched a fat duck waddle across the back yard.

And so on. Wright has four of these little lists, and they add nothing to the book. One can hear them recited breathlessly into the microphone by Miss Alabama: "And somewhere in the back of my mind—" she wiggles in her swimsuit—."a voice whispered: *America.*" But this is what Ellison liked, at the time, and when his own taste became a little more secure he got on to more complicated errors. What so appalled him, as he looked out over the Hudson, was the conclusion Wright had drawn from his portraits of viciousness and destitution. In *Shadow and Act* Ellison quotes and then attacks a passage at the beginning of chapter two in *Black Boy*. Wright said that

> I used to mull over the strange absence of real kindness in Negroes, how unstable was our tenderness, how lacking in genuine passion we were, how void of great hope, how timid our joy, how bare our traditions, how hollow our memories, how lacking we were in those intangible sentiments that bind man to man, and how shallow was even our despair. After I had learned other ways of life I used to brood upon the unconscious irony of those who felt that Negroes led so passional an existence! I saw that what had been taken for our emotional strength was our negative confusions, our flights, our fears, our frenzy under pressure.

Ellison was moved to his essay partly by Irving Howe's estimate of Wright's importance in "Black Boys and Native Sons" (in which Howe had said that Ellison was "literary to a fault"). Ellison responded that just as "How Bigger Was Born" had been Wright's

> Jamesian preface to *Native Son*, the passage quoted above is his paraphrase of Henry James' catalogue of those items of a high civilization which were absent from American life during Hawthorne's day, and which seemed so necessary in order for the novelist to function. This, then, was Wright's list of those items of high humanity which he found missing among Negroes. Thank God, I have never been quite that literary.

Wright, said Ellison, was free to present himself as a hunger-crazed kid, desperate for values, but he should have had the grace and the sense not to project his troubles onto his people, and certainly not to do it in the name of literature.

But this is surely being "literary" On Ellison's part. The passage in *Black Boy* is by no stretch of the imagination comparable to James's list; that Ellison could think so (or say so, as a way of getting back at Howe) is a sign of desperate confusion. Wright was saying that in the terrible cultural bind of the South, the Negro's pain and desire to get out of that violence was all bottled up, constantly turning on other Negroes. In *Native Son* Bigger and his gang "had always robbed Negroes. They felt that it was much easier and safer to rob their own people, for they knew that white policemen never really searched diligently for Negroes who committed crimes against other Negroes." And in *Black Boy* young Richard "had seen many Negroes solve the problem of being black by transferring their hatred of themselves to others with a black skin and fighting them." He and his friend, Harrison, know they have been tricked into fighting each other so that the white men could enjoy it for sport: "The shame and anger we felt for having allowed ourselves to be duped crept into our blows and blood ran into our eyes, half blinding us. The hate we felt for the men whom we had tried to cheat went into the blows we threw at each other."

But that is only part of Wright's point in his passage on why the Negroes he knew in the South lacked what Ellison calls "high humanity." In *Black Boy* Wright, was trying to find a meaning in the unrelieved horror and shame. Ellison takes the passage out of context, ignoring the various ways Wright is trying to show us how this gross state came about. He refuses to dress up his Negroes in an imported Sunday best because he has a far larger task before him and he is far too seriously engaged to fall into the old error that if you write about the Negro, put him on stage or in a movie, he must always wear a coat and tie.

Wright's reflections on the Negro are crucially placed in *Black Boy*. Beginning chapter two, they follow the portrait of Wright's father which concluded chapter one. Wright had met his father for what was to be the last time, on Wright's return from his trip to Mexico in 1940. A quarter of a century had gone by now, since the father had run out on the family, and Wright's discovery of what the years had done to his father, and to himself, produced one of the very finest vignettes he would ever be able to do, a portrait that is almost unbearable in its sense of distance and waste and loss. The son confronts the ruin of his father "standing alone upon the red clay of a Mississippi plantation, a sharecropper, clad in ragged overalls, holding a muddy hoe in his gnarled, veined hands." Here Wright's prose is working at its very best: all the details are sharply done, there are no superfluous ones, and the language is almost entirely free of false phrases or unnecessary moralizing.

> When I tried to talk to him I realized that, though ties of blood made us kin, though I could see a shadow of my face in his face, though there was an echo of my voice in his voice, we were forever strangers, speaking a different language, living on vastly different planes of reality. That day a quarter of a century later

when I visited him on the *plantation*—he was standing against the sky, smiling toothlessly, his hair whitened, his body bent, his eyes glazed with dim recollection, his fearsome aspect of twenty-five years ago gone forever from him—I was overwhelmed to realize that he could never *understand* me or the scalding experiences that had swept me beyond his life and into an area of living that he could never know. I stood before him, poised, my mind aching as it embraced the simple nakedness of his life, feeling how completely his soul was imprisoned by the slow flow of the seasons, by wind and rain and sun, how fastened were his memories to a crude and raw past, how chained were his actions and emotions to the direct, animalistic impulses of his withering body....

From the white landowners above him there had not been handed to him a chance to learn the meaning of loyalty, of sentiment, of tradition. Joy was as unknown to him as was despair. As a creature of the earth, he endured, hearty, whole, seemingly indestructible, with no regrets and no hope. He asked easy, drawling questions about me, his other son, his wife, and he laughed, amused, when I informed him of their destinies.

The confrontation of these two men on the red Mississippi dirt is one which must have involved Wright in a great agony, for he was calling across irretrievable time to his father—the father that in *Black Boy* he associates with his dizzying hunger. They stand apart, talking softly, the son and the "endured, hearty, whole, seemingly indestructible" father whose whole life had been destruction—the "black peasant who had gone to the city seeking life, but who had failed in the city; a black peasant whose life had been hopelessly snarled in the city, and who had at last fled the city." And it is from the deep sadness of that encounter that Wright goes on to his list of what Negroes seemed to him to lack, how it all had been torn from them.

To say that Wright's passage is "Jamesian" is absurd. Wright is attempting to find the meaning he has presented in that horrid distance he felt from his father, trying to see why he could never have his father and his father never could fully have himself.

Wright continued his passage on the "absence" of redeeming culture in Negro life by saying that

Whenever I thought of the essential bleakness of black life in America, I knew that Negroes had never been allowed to catch the full spirit of Western civilization, that they lived somehow in it but not of it. And when I brooded upon the cultural barrenness of black life, I wondered if clean, positive tenderness, love, honor, loyalty, and the capacity to remember were native with man. I asked myself if these human qualities were not fostered, won, struggled and suffered for, preserved in ritual from one generation to another.

Wright's portraits of unbearable physical damage are in themselves terrifying, but they are also part of unbearable psychic damage. He is showing us that racism does not only oppress bodily; it is more fully corrosive, more fully damaging. Southern superstition maims the mind, stunts it, inhibits tenderness, never encourages the "human qualities" that must be fostered if they are to survive. To say otherwise would be essentially unserious, intellectually and morally.

Wright chose as the epigraph for his work a passage from the Book of Job: "They meet with darkness in the daytime, And they grope at noonday as in the night." The burden of *Black Boy* is to show how the blindness of the communities, black and white, came about. After the elder brother of one of his chums had been shot, Richard sat on the front porch, brooding in "a temporary paralysis of will and impulse." He thought of the white world as "something whose horror and blood might descend upon me at any moment" and he was "compelled to give my entire imagination over to it, an act which blocked the springs of thought and feeling in me." The extraordinary power and ferocity of the white world does not allow the Negro community any sense of freedom for the rituals of communal life, does not allow men and women to acknowledge their humanity by all those ceremonies through which one learns, acquires, and continues responses that give us any liberating sense of ourselves.

When Uncle Hoskins is killed, "fear drowned out grief." And, Wright shows us, if people are never given time for grief, they will be unlikely to grieve. Hoskins was dead, but "there was no funeral. There was no music. There was no period of mourning. There were no flowers." None of those tokens with which a culture makes peace with its dead are allowed—there is too much danger that the white man will "kill all his kinfolks!" The fact was that "Uncle Hoskins had simply been plucked from our midst and we, figuratively, had fallen on our faces to avoid looking into that white-hot face of terror that we knew loomed somewhere above us." Terror produces terror, brutality goes on into brutality. When young Richard tries to "understand" what it all means and why the black community had not fought back, "I asked my mother, and the fear that was in her made her slap me into silence." In such a world it is impossible to talk about "culture" because the greatest energy in that world makes culture unavailable, makes mother slap child reflexively.

> Shocked, frightened, alone without their husbands or friends, my mother and Aunt Maggie lost faith in themselves, and, after much debate and hesitation, they decided to return home to Granny and rest, think, map out new plans for living.

The phrases in the above sentence all carry a sharp charge, for we realize that those words we use—"lost faith in themselves," "much debate and hesitation," "return home to Granny," and the incredible sense of how utterly helpless they are in "map out new plans for living"—all these figures of speech are so utterly inadequate to the controlling emotion. This is *A Death in the Family* where the family has nothing to do but run for its life.

Richard imitates the reflex where it does not apply. Grandpa dies, not because whites have lynched him but because he has finally reached the end of old age. When Richard is sent to Uncle Tom's house with the news, he behaves as if it were a repetition of the Uncle Hoskins incident, running "every inch of the two miles" and bounding up the steps and into the room where his uncle is sleeping. Richard runs to the bed, shakes his uncle awake:

> "Uncle Tom, Granny says to come at once. Grandpa's dead."
> He stared at me for a long time.
> "You certainly are a prize fool," he said quietly. "Don't you know that that's no way to tell a person that his father's dead?"
> I stared at him, baffled, panting.

Richard is "baffled" because he is only repeating the haste and frenzy of that other death he had seen. No "prize fool," he has only learned the lesson that the culture had taught him..

Wright knew and showed how "the culture of one black household was ... transmitted to another black household, and folk tradition was handed from group to group." But he also saw how feeble that tradition was when the white world broke savagely in. He knew also how defective and how destructive any such "folk culture" would be in a land where those who exchanged it had no adequate education. In this sense Richard found himself to be one of the more fortunate children, for when he accompanied an insurance agent out onto the Delta plantation

> I had been pitying myself for not having books to read, and now I saw children who had never read a book. Their chronic shyness made me

seem bold and city-wise; a black mother would try to lure her brood into the room to shake hands with me and they would linger at the jamb of the door, peering at me with one eye, giggling hysterically.

And when in Memphis he told Mrs. Moss he was from Jackson she said, "You act mighty bright to be from there." She thought Jackson Negroes "just stand with their heads down, with one foot on top of the other and you have to guess at what they're trying to say."

Ignorant sickness infects the family's spiritual life: the oppressive brutalities of a Calvinist Christianity. When Richard first thought of bigotry in Memphis, he did not think of whites. "I discovered that all human beings were not mean and driving, were not bigots like the members of my family." His Granny and his Aunt Addie said "they were dead to the world, and those of their blood who lived in that world were therefore dead to them." And, of course, they are "dead" to the world, incapable of any lively, open response to it.

> Granny and Aunt Addie quarreled and fought not only with me, but with each other over minor points of religious doctrine, or over some imagined infraction of what they chose to call their moral code. Wherever I found religion in my life I found strife, the attempt of one individual or group to rule another in the name of God.

In all of this Wright is gathering the material and providing the insights through which we can see the nature of the black community's disease. What the white man gives—and takes away—continually enslaves and thwarts the possibility that a black person can look toward anyone, white or black, with confidence.

Jean Paul Sartre wrote:

> The order is given to reduce the inhabitants of the annexed country to the level of superior monkeys in order to justify the settler's treatment of them as beasts of burden. Violence in the colonies does not only have for its aim the keeping of these enslaved men at arm's length; it seeks to dehumanise them. Everything will be done to wipe out their traditions ... and to destroy their culture without giving them ours. Sheer physical fatigue will stupefy them. Starved and ill, if they have any spirit left, fear will finish the job....

Black Boy shows us this—the effect of having all culture wiped out, all paths to culture blockaded; Wright presents again and again the stupefying condition brought about not only in his own person but in those around him by the sheer physical fatigue as each day the family stumbles through the hours, starved, ill, numb. "I was already so conditioned toward my relatives that when I passed them I actually had a nervous tic in my muscles." All terror spins toward the center, and families fall apart twitching.

Yet an odd feature of those portraits is that so often they are etched in comedy. They are pathetic, endlessly hurt, but few in the family are merely passive—at least not passive when they have a Richard to intimidate; they loom up with ferocious energy into ghastly tragicomic figures of twisted power. Granny is one of Wright's greatest portraits and she inhabits a reality that we associate with a Dickensian grotesque. Just as Miss Havisham continually points her finger at Pip commanding, "Play" ("so that I may have the pleasure of observing"), so Granny continually points her finger at Richard commanding, "Sin" ("so that I may have the pleasure of beating the Hell out of you"). Granny is a Negro whose skin is white, a Christian who is continually sadistic. "Granny bore the standard for God, but she was always fighting." Wherever she turns she spreads destruction with a power that is entirely frightening! "Granny finally charged Ella with telling me things that I should not know and Ella, weeping and distraught, packed her things and moved." So utterly white is this black Granny that Richard enjoys going to town to watch the "baffled stares" of the whites who see one of their own color leading an "undeniably Negro" boy through the stores. Granny hurts herself by hitting too hard; her greatest discomfort comes when she lashes out at Richard, misses, and "the force of her blow was so strong that she fell down the steps, headlong, her aged body wedged in a narrow space between the fence and the bottom step." Grandpa has to tear the fence down to rescue her. We feel a certain clean joy when young Richard tells her, at the bath, to kiss his ass; it is an assault on her whole contorted world—this woman who seems incapable of kissing anything, incapable of admitting asses exist. When Richard tells her, she "seemed to have gone out of her mind," first becoming "terribly still" and then shrieking around the house for almighty vengeance.

Grandpa's voice is very quiet. He is in many ways Granny's opposite, her natural mate, as he quietly endures his own colossal illusion "that the war between the states would be resumed." Year in and year out he keeps "his Civil War rifle loaded in a corner" and his "blue uniform of the Union Army neatly folded." Grandpa is conspicuous by his silence, his hate all the more overpowering because it is inarticulate: "I never heard him speak of white people; I think he hated them too much to talk of them." And, as with Granny, Grandpa becomes a figure of grotesque comedy, unkillable delusion and will. He writes the War Department, asking for the back pay he will never get because the white officer who had signed him out was Swedish, recording "Richard Wilson" as "Richard Vinson." For decades Grandpa and Washington exchange letters that Grandpa cannot read or write but has to have someone else in the community take care of. His story is one of mighty exasperation and endurance:

> He would name persons long dead, citing their ages and descriptions, reconstructing battles in which he had fought, naming towns, rivers, creeks, roads, cities, villages, citing the names and numbers of regiments and companies with which he had fought, giving the exact day and the exact hour of the day of certain occurrences, and send it all to the War Department in Washington.

And when nothing comes of it, he can only hiss, "It's them goddamn rebels." Around the neighborhood he goes, having to hear his rejections read so many times that at last he believes and commits them to his indefatigable memory.

Grandpa and Granny are the comic-tragic extensions of Richard's own mother and father. The men appear slight and quiet, ruined and enduring. The women are filled with a savage Christianity expressing itself in countless slaps and quarrels. But the portrait of the mother is a good deal more than that, the most complicated and the richest in the book. When Du Bois objected that "toward his mother he never expresses love or affection" he acknowledged that Wright continually presents her as the one who beats him. And Ralph K. White in a "Value Analysis" of *Black Boy* for the *Journal of Abnormal and Social Psychology* (October 1947) could contend that Wright "disapproves" of his mother "87 per cent." Whatever that means, and however one does such a thing, Wright's feelings about his mother are rather more complicated.

The book begins with the boy almost dying under the whip of his mother. While she repeatedly beats him into senselessness, Richard could still say, "I had always felt a certain warmth with my mother" for it was she who first "taught me to read, told me stories." And when Richard defies Granny and Aunt Addie, his mother, tottering in and out of sanity, smiled and "rose and hobbled to me on her paralytic legs and kissed me." Richard saw how stroke after stroke, days of hurt in which she wanted only to die, had paralyzed her. His mother's agony touched everything, "gathering to itself all the poverty, the ignorance, the helplessness; the painful, baffling, hunger-ridden days and hours; the restless moving, the futile seeking, the uncertainty, the fear, the dread; the meaningless pain and the endless suffering." She becomes the central representative figure for the Negro community in *Black Boy*, embodying all its pain and making its quick, crippled gestures toward release. Richard so identifies with her and with her wounds that

> a somberness of spirit that I was never to lose settled over me during the slow years of my mother's unrelieved suffering, a somberness that was to make me stand apart and look upon excessive joy with suspicion, that was to make me self-conscious....

And there is great pathos (which Du Bois could not see, or did not want to admit, and which Ellison found "literary") in the way Richard's mother becomes, like the community, half-crazed with her deprivation.

All these figures and scenes are Wright's effort to take oppression with a seriousness that can expose the full damage. Wright knew that all the evil could not be laid to a man. He refused to create a "white villain." Simon Legree in *Uncle Tom's Cabin* is essentially a fantasy of assimilationism because Mrs. Stowe tries to place in one degraded figure an evil that is pervasive throughout the society. Simon Legree tempts us to think about racism as if it were a personal failure like drunkenness or wife beating. In *Black Boy* we see no villains; we do not even see a series of villains. We see men utterly helpless; varieties of foulness, stunt minds. The villain in *Black Boy* is the depraved consciousness of the white community which has dwarfed itself into a snarling thing.

Fifteen years later, at the Reverend Clayton Williams's American Church in Paris, Wright delivered an address that summarized the portraits of the Southern whites he had presented in *Black Boy*: "Slavery and half-slavery destroyed them as men. You can't burn and castrate the sons of your own fathers and rape the brown daughters who are really your sisters without becoming mad...."

When young Richard works at a white table he marvels at the cruelty of white people toward each other, their compulsive obscenity, their reflexive meanness. Negroes think of the people on the other sides of the tracks as "the white death." And everywhere we look—to Reynolds and Pease in the optical factory, to the white watchman at the hotel, to the storekeepers who cut up the Negro woman, to the men in Memphis who try to get niggers to stab each other for their sport—Wright shows the white world being crushed under "a burden of anxiety and compulsive cruelty." A half-decent white man cannot believe that his workers have beaten Richard and keeps asking "which one" it was. But *Black Boy* shows us it is no "one." Wright discovers that "they did not seem to be individual men, but part of a huge, implacable, elemental design toward which hate was futile." Years later, in his famous speech, "The Ballot or the Bullet," Malcolm X was to say explicitly what Wright's portrait presents implicitly, that black Americans dealing with the white man are "dealing with a man whose bias and prejudice are making him lose his mind, his intelligence, every day." And in this regard *Black Boy* is a book that should upset its white readers far more radically than it often seems to. To be on the side of Richard is to be on the side of life. Of course. It is only when we contend with the death all around him do we see what is centrally important: utter, total sickness. And, seeing that, one can begin to see the dimensions of Wright's indictment.

Reviewers, black and white, objected to the terms of *Black Boy*, for once again Richard Wright was awakening racism as a "beast in the skull." And now he was saying that when the beast took life he took it on all sides, black and white indiscriminately; in the Southern world from which Wright had come, the clawmarks were on everyone. The culture was bleeding to death.

Commenting on *Black Boy* in *Partisan Review* (Summer 1945) Elizabeth Hardwick said that

> in some ways it is a catalogue of all the neurotic compulsions the human being can endure. We have, among other things, pyromania, childhood drunkenness, anal eroticism, somnambulism, and several incidents that threaten to end in family killings.

In this world corroded by hurt, young Richard constantly endures what seem like the vicious and fantastic plots of a deformed mind. "I was a drunkard in my sixth year," he tells us.

> I staggered along the pavements, drunk, repeating obscenities to the horror of the women I passed and to the amusement of the men en route to their homes from work.

He was a chronic sleepwalker and "one night I found myself standing in the back yard. The moon was shining bright as day." Throughout the narrative we see him repeatedly paralyzed: on his first day, at school "frightened speechless" so that "other children had to identify me, tell the teacher my name and address," then again much later at another school he cannot write his name and "I realized how utterly I was failing and I grew weak and leaned my hot forehead against the cold blackboard" and again at the orphanage office unable to blot envelopes, and even in his early jobs, at the drugstore, unable to respond to orders, he freezes. "My sustained expectation of violence had exhausted me." When Wright would later describe the typical neurosis of the American Negro he would call it "The state of exaggeration"; in his own childhood it is a state of utter immobility.

All life was "like living in a dream, the reality of which might change at any moment." Richard carries around with him a horrid sense of guilt and terror: he burns the house down, kills the stray kitten, gets robbed of the grocery money; he "had the choice of being beaten at home or away from home." His brother says to him, "You did bad," and that is what everybody keeps telling him as he grows up. When he sets fire to the house, he can only see the flames for a moment before he sees "the image of my grandmother lying helplessly upon her bed and there were yellow flames in her black hair." And his mother says, "You didn't stand by that kitten, so why should I stand by you?" So often the words that spill helplessly from his mouth become "something he ought to be killed for." When he peeks into the whore house "evidently I had done something terrible." He concludes that "my life had somehow been full of a nameless wrong, an unatonable guilt."

That the boy could become a writer (or that he could survive with some sanity intact) was almost impossible. On the flyleaf of the first edition of the book we are told, "Remember, reader, that this is the story of an American! American, too, was the hope." That is, here was a story of terrific damage but here was also a story of a humble boy who made it: from log cabin to Honest Abe and from pickaninny to Negro Author. *Black Boy* was redeemed by its myth of eventual triumph. Perhaps it is a myth, but it shows not that any black boy can be a writer (as any poor white boy can be President Honest Abe). We see that a black boy, even in the South, can still be alive at nineteen. The myth of Honest Abe was that a system gave a man the opportunities to go from the bottom to the top of our society; Lincoln's ultimate majesty proved our system worked. The myth of *Black Boy* said that a system had not worked. Wright's wholeness showed the system missed him.

In *Soul on Ice* Eldridge Cleaver is proud to point out that there is no trace of "self-effacing love for his oppressors" in *Native Son*. And, one should add, there is no trace of it in *Black Boy*; though the autobiography does not center, as does the novel, on an act of violence against The Man, the life story itself in an aggressive act, a response not in the patience of "self-effacing" love but in the controlled urgency of masculine pride. To be sure, young Richard does not emerge as a big "bad" man, and he hardly seems to be a candidate for any representative role of "black manhood." Yet that fact raises the crucial question of what Wright is trying to accomplish in *Black Boy*. The answer, I think, involves the quiet, careful terms of self-definition, an insistence on the demands of a genuinely creative ego facing odds of intolerable force. And in this sense the Black Boy may be even harder to face than the Native Son. He is surely less liable to slogans. For all its sustained violence and horrors, there is a certain deep quiet to *Black Boy*. The pride that finally rises up out of its pages does not involve flamboyant acts of destruction. It is a spare, survivor's integrity, poised on the edge of despair. The book comes after Wright had shed the "Bigger" in him, and while there is no relaxing of rage against the system there is an insistence on a sustaining settlement. Which is not to be confused with peace.

Richard's survival was his danger; what most often got him into trouble finally got him out: words. What he says to Granny in the bath, what he writes on all the windows, what he shouts into Uncle Tom's ear, all these are the words he is beaten for. When he first turned to printed words he wanted magic symbols of his own distorted world, a reflection of the violence all around him. "I vowed that as soon as I was old enough I would buy all the novels there were and read them to feed that thirst for violence that was in me, for intrigue, for plotting, for secrecy, for bloody murders." He sought ghastly tales of Bluebeard "hanging his wives by their hair in dark closets" and mad scientists who would lure his victims to a room so that a great machine could suck all the air out and the "victims would die, turning red, blue, then black." Richard said, "This was what I wanted, tales like this." Granny is quite right in her assessment of it as "that Devil stuff." When Richard turns his own hand to composition he begins with "The Voodoo of Hell's Half-Acre." Art imitates life.

But to say that Richard Wright turned to books that would imitate his world is merely to describe a deprived child's hunger for gory fantasy. The magic of words was not a mere reflection of the violence of his world in Bluebeards and mad scientists; words became triumph over that world. Words are the boy's assertion, his way of making the world recognize his existence. Knowing can come to him only out of suffering, and it is all he has to defend himself against that suffering. Words are blood kin to the deprivation they master. Perception stays pain.

Words held for the boy the same thrill that numbers did when he first learned to count, dancing on his bed in his nightclothes, over and over again attaining one hundred. It is the joy of having the pieces come together (as they never came together in his life). Bertrand Russell has remarked that as a child his discovery of Euclid filled him with the pleasure which we usually confine to romantic love. For Richard Wright the discovery of words sent him into ecstasies of control and desire.

Although fear and hunger are the central feelings, there is a third that appears throughout the narrative, and it is vitally important to the characterization (and ultimate victory) of young Richard. That feeling is the shock of surprise. Each time brutality descends on him Richard is, simply, astonished. He cannot learn, cannot toughen himself, cannot get used to it. When Claude Brown and Malcolm X wrote their life stories they presented pictures of depraved worlds, but they also presented themselves as boys "well adjusted" to their worlds. They knew the name of the game. Young Richard never develops the reflexes for easy survival, never seems ready for what comes. His intelligence is large but profoundly unaware, unready. After years of it he still awakens each morning as if this were a first visit. And so he is continually "asking myself what on earth was the matter with me, why it was I never seemed to do things as people expected them to be done." A lady asks him "seriously," "Do you steal?" He laughs aloud because he assumed the lady thought of him as a person: "Lady, if I was a thief, I'd never tell anybody." He is plagued all through his job-hunting days: employers do not want him, do not like the look in his eyes. "Why don't you laugh and talk like the other niggers?" Constantly in trouble for it, "I had to keep remembering what others took for granted; I had to think out what others felt." It was only with the greatest slowness that "I learned to play the dual role which every Negro must play if he wants to eat and live." He refused to give up his mind to the insanity of the compromisers around him.

Words hold it together. Books are dignity, manhood. At the end of the story, when he asks why he had the determination to get out of the Southern darkness, where he had caught "a sense of freedom" in a world where no one had ever asked him to believe in himself, he concludes, "it had been only through books." But he knows that his belief in them "had risen more out of a sense of desperation than from any abiding conviction of their ultimate value." Books satisfied the sense of hunger that he had, the desire for wholeness.

Young Richard continually pesters his mother for names, how did we get them, what do they mean. He wants "just to know" and his mother responds, "but for what?" He cannot say. "I could think of no rational or practical reason why my father should try to find out who his father's father was." When he grew to manhood he could think of the reasons. In *Black Boy* he set out on the voyage into knowledge; summoning his best intelligence, he hoped to find meaning and perhaps even some redemption in the chamber of horrors where secrets lie among wounds.

The last word of the first chapter is "knowing." It saved Wright from being like his father, a man who was ruined by not knowing. As "knowing" concludes all the horrors that Wright presents in his opening chapter, so the book itself is an act of "knowing," impelled by the author's "conviction that the meaning of living came only when one was struggling to wring meaning out of meaningless suffering." *Black Boy* is finally about the realms of the mind, about how the mind is hopelessly conditioned and how it also has a frantic strength to resist conditioning. Wright's ability to come out of it all, and to write about it, is as clear as the world which spent all its energy to see that he never would do it.

CLAUDIA C. TATE

Black Boy:
Richard Wright's "Tragic Sense of Life"

Richard Wright's friends and critics alike persistently remark that Wright actually did not experience a childhood like that depicted in his autobiography, *Black Boy*. They contend that his childhood was not characterized by the incessant hunger, the beatings and the suffering, and the general bleakness of life that he ascribed to young Richard. Nor did Richard's childhood characterize a quality of life experienced by the majority of Wright's Black contemporaries. His implying that it did incited controversy, especially in reference to one particular passage from the text:

(After I had outlived the shocks of childhood, after the habit of reflection had been born in me, I used to mull over the strange absence of real kindness in Negroes, how unstable was our tenderness, how lacking in genuine passion we were, how hollow our memories, how lacking we were in those intangible sentiments that bind man to man, and how shallow was even our despair. After I had learned other ways of life I used to brood upon the unconscious irony of those who felt that Negroes led so passional an existence! I saw that what had been taken for our emotional strength was our negative confusion, our flight, our fears, our frenzy under pressure.

From *Black American Literature Forum* Vol. 10, No. 4 (Winter 1976). © 1976 *African American Review*.

(Whenever I thought of the essential bleakness of black life in America, I knew that Negroes had never been allowed to catch the full spirit of Western civilization, that they lived somehow in it but not of it. And when I brooded upon the cultural barrenness of black life, I wondered if clean, positive tenderness, love, honor, loyalty, and the capacity to remember were native with man. I asked myself if these human qualities were not fostered, won, struggled and suffered for, preserved in ritual from one generation to another.)[1]

It would be presumptuous of me to assume that I could account for the bleakness that Wright imposed upon the record of his childhood and youth. No one has this privilege, perhaps not even the author himself;[2] however, in pondering about the discrepancy between the facts of Wright's life and its written account in *Black Boy*, which was in manuscript in 1943,[3] one does well to note that in 1937 Wright read *The Tragic Sense of Life* by Miguel de Unamuno.[4] The influence of this work on Wright's thinking may bear some responsibility for the tragic tone, vision and attitude with which Wright invested his autobiography in an attempt to describe and explain the growth of his consciousness.

In *The Tragic Sense of Life* Unamuno postulates that all human existence is tragic in its essential and fundamental nature, that "... there is something for lack of a better name, we will call the tragic sense of life, which carries with it a whole conception of life and of the universe, a whole philosophy more or less conscious."[5] Unamuno's survey of human existence reveals the ubiquity of suffering from which he concludes that life is a perpetual struggle without even a hope for victory, and that the anguish which results from this struggle is the condition of all men. Accordingly, man's plight is that he should bear without relief the burden of physical and emotional distress, a struggle which is not without significant consequence. Suffering engenders consciousness, an acute awareness of both one's personal character and external reality:

> Suffering is the path of consciousness, and by it living beings arrive at the possession of self-consciousness. For to possess consciousness of oneself, to possess personality, is to know oneself and to feel oneself distinct from other beings, and this feeling of distinction is only reached through an act of collision, through suffering more or less severe, through the sense of one's own limits. Consciousness of oneself is simply consciousness of one's own limitations. (Unamuno, p. 140)

Consciousness is not inherent in the essential character of man; on the contrary, it is a psychological state which must be determined by experiencing distress and subsequently reflecting upon it. Particularly important to this thesis is Unamuno's insistence that life must not be subject to rational reflection and evaluation alone in order to assess its meaningfulness. He subscribes to the belief "that the real, the really real, is irrational, that reason builds upon irrationalities" (Unamuno, p. 5). Therefore, "... it is not enough to think about our destiny: it must be felt" (Unamuno, p. 16). Man must feel his life with his entire being (his heart, his mind, his senses) in order to reveal and evaluate the fundamental meaning of his existence. In this respect, Unamuno posits a qualitative distinction between the integrity of reason (rational truths) and the integrity of feelings (irrational truths) with the implication that rational analysis and facts have severe limitations, especially when one is probing metaphysical questions. His appreciation for irrational truthfulness in conjunction with his principal proposition that suffering engenders consciousness is precisely what appears to have had some influence on the substantive quality of Wright's portrayal of his childhood and youth.

Black Boy depicts the boy Richard's attempts to establish himself as a distinct and fully conscious individual and, as such, is more a portrait of Wright's developing personality and growth of consciousness than it is an accurate record of his childhood experiences.[6] The book recalls in episodic fashion incidents which take the boy deeper into his quest for self-discovery. The raging brutality of racism and the deprivation of his home life, as depicted in *Black Boy*, are interwoven into an emblem of spiritual conflict which is metaphoric, rather than factual, of man's daily struggle to endure the pressures of existence. According to Unamuno, life at best is a struggle, tragic in nature, and Wright appears to have dramatized this struggle with the substance of his own life. In recalling the events of his childhood, Wright seems to have relied on the integrity of his feelings in order to describe the essence of his existence, its fundamental character and meaning, rather than rendering the events with factual detail alone. As a result, he altered incidents, invested them with exaggerated bleakness, brutality, and a sense of immense and tragic conflict, so as to depict the difficulty of his day to day struggle to survive with a vestige of humanity. In addition, he wove an intricate design of narrative patterns, motifs of silence, hunger and suffering, into the autobiography in order to create an added tragic dimension which enhances the brilliancy of his portrait of a small boy nurturing his budding personality.

The motif of silence conceptualizes the difficulty that Richard had in establishing himself as a distinct and fully conscious individual. Keeping silent had a special significance within the Black community; it indicated acceptance, submission to the conditions of life, especially those caused by racial practices. Throughout *Black Boy*, Richard is repeatedly told to be silent, but he finds that it is against his fundamental nature to withhold his expressed opinions. In his daily dealings with people, he reveals, often without thinking, the presence of his consciousness—and as a result disturbs every facet of the Southern social framework. He emphatically defies those who would silence him, and even blatantly declares his ambition to be a writer. Severe punishment does not thwart his precocious self-consciousness, but reaffirms his determination to refuse to accept his "place" in either his household or society.

At the age of six, as Wright recalls, Richard's father deserted his family leaving Richard to face many a hungry day during his childhood. In addition to describing literally his deprivation, hunger serves as a symbolic motif for depicting Richard's compelling need to nurture his growing consciousness. Insatiable hunger defines the breadth of his childhood longings for imaginative adventure and his unfulfilled need to expand his awareness of himself and his environment. His physical craving for food and his emotional yearnings often coincide, and this fusion gives added emphasis to the very real nature of his compelling desire to nourish his developing personality:

> I now saw a world leap to life before my eyes because I could explore it, and that meant not going home when school was out, but wandering, watching, asking, talking. Had I gone home to eat my plate of greens, Granny would not have allowed me out again, so the penalty I paid for roaming was to forfeit my food for twelve hours. I would eat mush at eight in the morning and greens at seven or later at night. To starve in order to learn about my environment was irrational, but so were my hungers. (*BB*, p. 111)

Physical hunger isolates his personal needs from those of others and, as a consequence, makes him aware that he is a distinct and conscious individual. Emotional and spiritual hunger motivate his ceaseless questions and maintain his awareness of mental distress:

> Hunger stole upon me so slowly that at first I was not aware of what hunger really meant. Hunger had always been more or less at my elbow when I played, but now I began to wake up at night to find hunger standing at my bedside, staring at me gauntly. The hunger I had known before this had been no grim, hostile stranger; it had been a normal hunger that had made me beg

constantly for bread, and when I ate a crust or two I was satisfied. But this new hunger baffled me, scared me, made me angry and insistent. (*BB*, p. 13)

In this respect, virtual starvation engenders his consciousness and forces upon him the daily burden of struggling in order to survive. Food satiates his physical hunger, while knowledge of himself and the world nourishes his mind. Most significant of all the references to hunger is Wright's usage of this motif to stress Richard's growing awareness of his confined spiritual existence which longs to exceed the boundaries of social conventions: "I now knew what being a Negro meant. I could endure the [physical] hunger. I had learned to live with hate. But to feel that there were feelings denied me, that the very breath of life itself was beyond my reach, that more than anything else hurt, wounded me. I had a new hunger" (*BB*, pp. 219–20). He realizes that the possibility for a meaningful life is obstructed by his environment, and this knowledge awakens in him a new desire, a new and insatiable hunger. He yearns to satisfy this hunger and trains his sensibilities to reach beyond the confines of his environment to grasp as much of this life as possible. He says that "not only had the southern whites not known [him], but, more important still, as [he] had lived in the South [he] had not had the chance to learn who [he] was." Richard feels with alarming urgency that he has to know who he is and who he can be, and this compulsion, this hunger, ultimately forces him to leave the South in order that he might face the possibility of discovering his own identity: "The pressure of southern living kept me from being the kind of person that I might have been. I had been what my surroundings had demanded, what my family—conforming to the dictates of the whites above them—had exacted of me, and what the whites had said that I must be" (*BB*, p. 227). *Black Boy* concludes with Wright mapping out Richard's journey north, which appears to be yet another quest within the microcosm of Richard's consciousness. Having developed sufficient self-awareness to know that he possesses a distinct and possibly meaningful existence, Richard feels an unwavering obligation to hold his destiny within his grasp and to design his future. His self-conscious desire to determine the fundamental quality of his existence is characteristic of man's inherent and essential nature and, as such, is Wright's expression of a legitimate existential imperative.

So ubiquitous is suffering that Wright made its expression not only the most overwhelming narrative element in *Black Boy*, but also the principal source of his tragic vision. He measured and defined the quality of his existence by degrees of personal and racial suffering, and dramatized them through the fabric of Richard's life. The mental anguish that Richard felt while witnessing his mother's excruciating pain, which resulted from several paralytic strokes, is not only a somewhat accurate account of an event in Wright's childhood but is also metaphoric for the human condition of inherent suffering, "the tragic sense of life." Richard observes:

> My mother's suffering grew into a symbol in my mind, gathering to itself all the poverty, the ignorance, the helplessness; the painful, baffling, hunger-ridden days and hours; the restless moving, the futile seeking, the uncertainty, the fear, the dread; the meaningless pain and the suffering. Her life set the emotional tone of my life, colored the men and women I was to meet in the future, conditioned my relation to events that had not yet happened, determined my attitude to situations and circumstances I had yet to face. A somberness of spirit that I was never to lose settled over me during the slow years of my mother's unrelieved suffering, a somberness that was to make me stand apart and look upon excessive joy with suspicion, that was to make me self-conscious, that was to make me keep forever on the move, as though to escape a nameless fate seeking to overtake me. At the age of twelve, before I had had one full year of formal schooling, I had a conception of life that no experience would ever erase, a predilection for what was real that no argument could ever gainsay, a sense of the world that was mine and mine alone, a conviction that the meaning of living came only when one was struggling to wring a meaning out of senseless suffering. (*BB*, p. 87)

Senseless suffering, perpetual hunger and raging brutality characterize the quality of Richard's existence and temper his personal struggle to define and qualify for himself a meaningful life. These painful experiences convince him that meaningfulness can not be an individual assertion alone, but a quality of life that must be "fostered, won, struggled and suffered for, preserved [each and every day] in ritual from one generation to another" (*BB*, p. 33). Life's inherent suffering teaches him to measure all of his future experiences against his "predilection for what [is] real" (*BB*, p. 87). This predilection which Wright undoubtedly felt during his own youth qualified the very real and fundamental nature of his future life—and determined the substantive quality of his autobiography. Although it is probably true that *Black Boy* contains many exaggerated and even fictitious incidents, the emotions that they excite within Richard truthfully adhere to Wright's emotional existence. The work describes with a great degree of accuracy Wright's psychological reality, the emotional and intellectual determinants of his visible life. This subjective but very real dimension of Wright's existence exceeds the limitations of factual descriptions and rational explanations. Richard, the youth in *Black Boy*, is Wright's acknowledgment of these limitations; he is the psychological self-portraiture of the slow and painstaking development of Wright's consciousness.

NOTES

1. *Black Boy* (New York: Harper, 1945), p. 33. Future references will appear parenthetically in the text.

2. Wright maintains this position in reference to *Native Son* in his supplementary essay, "How 'Bigger' Was Born," *Saturday Review of Literature*, 22 (June 1, 1940),3.

3. Michel Fabre, *The Unfinished Quest of Richard Wright* (New York: Morrow, 1973), p. 253.

4. Michel Fabre, "Richard Wright's First One Hundred Books," *CLA Journal*, 16 (1973), 473.

5. Miguel de Unamuno, *The Tragic Sense of Life* (New York: Dover, 1954), p. 17.

6. Hereafter the name Richard refers to the boy portrayed in *Black Boy* and the name Wright refers to the actual man.

CHARLES T. DAVIS

From Experience to Eloquence:
Richard Wright's Black Boy *as Art*

*N*ative Son[1] is the work for which Richard Wright is best known, but *Black Boy*,[2] an autobiography more or less, may be the achievement that offers the best demonstration of his art as a writer. This idea is not so startling given Wright's special talents—the eye of a skilled reporter, the sensibility of a revolutionary poet, alert to varied forms of injustice, and the sense of symbolic meaning carried by the rituals of ordinary life. The problem up to the present time is not the lack of attention the work has received. Like *Native Son, Black Boy* was selected by the Book-of-the-Month Club and was thus assured a wide distribution and a serious if somewhat skewed reading from many critics. In 1970 Stanley Hyman, in reviewing Wright's entire career, assigned *Black Boy* to a period in which Wright's "important writing" occurred—according to his definition, Wright's last years as a resident in America, from 1940 to 1945.[3] But *Black Boy* by itself failed to acquire as an original work of art the reputation it deserves.

It appears now, from the perspective of a generation, that a measure of distortion was unavoidable, given the political temper of the time. The history of the publication of the manuscript entitled *American Hunger*,[4] of which *Black Boy* was a part, encouraged a violent political response. It was well known that "I Tried to Be a Communist," which appeared in the August and September issues of the *Atlantic Monthly* in 1944,[5] were chapters of an

From *Chant of Saints: A Gathering of Afro-American Literature, Art, and Scholarship* Michael S. Harper and Robert B. Stepto, ed. © 1979 Michael S. Harper and Robert B. Stepto autobiographical record to be published the following year, even though they were excluded finally with the rest of the matter dealing with the years in Chicago and New York. When *Black Boy* did appear, knowing critics read the book in light of the much-publicized account of Wright's difficulties with the Communist party. Baldly put, the situation for the critic encouraged a form of outside intrusion, a case of knowing too much, of supplying a frame of reference which a reading of the basic text does not support. The board of the Book-of-the-Month Club or Edward Aswell or both,[6] in suggesting a restriction of autobiographical matter to the period before migration to Chicago, exercised a judgment that displayed something more than the good sense of successful editors; indeed, that judgment pointed up the artistic integrity of the work. Someone concluded accurately that the intensity of *Black Boy* came from a concentration upon one metaphor of oppression, the South, and prevented the diffusion of power that would be the consequence of the introduction of a second, the Communist party.

If the political reaction created one kind of distortion in the eye of the examiner, more normal literary expectations created another. *Black Boy* baffled W. E. B. Du Bois, the most impressive black intellectual of his time. His review in the New York *Herald Tribune* states his dilemma: "... if the book is meant to be a creative picture and a warning, even then, it misses its possible effectiveness because it is as a work of art so patently and terribly overdrawn."[7] By 1945 Du Bois had published three major works with outstanding autobiographical elements, one of which, *Dusk of Dawn*, was a fully developed autobiography of considerable intellectual distinction,[8] and he could not be accused of responding merely to a sense of affront to his middle-class sensibilities. Du Bois was not prepared to accept Wright's bleak Mississippi; he was appalled not so much by the condition of terror there as by a state of mind that denied the possibility of humanity for blacks and frustrated all black efforts to achieve satisfaction beyond the minimal requirements for life. After all, Du Bois had vivid memories of his experience as a young teacher in rural Tennessee, where he encountered aspiring, sensitive pupils who, though often defeated or betrayed by their environment, were not totally crushed by Southern oppression.[9] Moreover, Du Bois joined, no doubt, a group of critics of *Black Boy* best defined by Ralph Ellison as consisting of readers who complained that Wright had "omitted the development of his own sensibility."[10] But this is to define sensibility in a way generally understood by the nineteenth century, which is to hold that sensibility is an orderly accretion of the mind and heart within an environment recognizably human, and not to accept Wright's radical equation of the existence of sensibility with survival.

Du Bois did not doubt that autobiography could be art, though more naive critics might. He could not accept the principles of an art as austere as Wright's was, one in which many of the facts of Southern life, so familiar to him, were excluded and in which generalization had been carried to such extreme lengths. After all, the book's title was *Black Boy*, not "A Black Boy,"[11] with an appropriately limiting modifier. Viewed superficially, Richard's odyssey was unique primarily because it had a happy ending—the escape from the hell of the South, where, apparently, all of his black associates (he had no friends in the narrative) were destined to spend the rest of their days. Wright's generalizations about the dehumanizing relationships between whites and blacks and the almost equally unsatisfying connections between blacks and blacks shaped his South, and these assumptions Du Bois thought to be distorted. One sweeping statement by young Wright in Memphis, where he lived from his seventeenth to his nineteenth year and where he committed himself formally to becoming a writer,[12] would certainly extract from Du Bois an expression of disbelief, if not annoyance: "I knew of no Negroes who read the books I liked and I wondered if any Negroes ever thought of them. I knew that there were Negro doctors, lawyers, newspapermen, but I never saw any of them. When I read a Negro newspaper I never caught the faintest echo of my preoccupation in its pages."[13]

Not only Du Bois, but also other blacks, even those lacking the knowledge of black life in America which Du Bois had acquired from his surveys and research projects at Atlanta University,[14] would be appalled at Richard's confession of his cultural isolation. This is a moment when generalization approaches fiction, when we must say that a statement may be acceptable within its context, but that it is questionable as a fact standing on its own, as something that might be supported by the confessions of other black boys, especially those emerging from families with middle-class aspirations and pretensions like Wright's.

Editing the raw matter of life is necessary, of course, to write an autobiography with any claim to art. No one has described this activity better than Ellison has in his critical examination of *Black Boy*: "The function, the psychology, of artistic selectivity is to eliminate from an art form all those elements of experience which contain no compelling significance. Life is as the sea, art a ship in which man conquers life's crushing formlessness...."[15] What Ellison did not say is that such editing requires the use of controlling principles that are invariably fictional. This is to say that the organizing ideas are assumptions that are not strictly true according to the most objective criteria. Operating from a strict conception of the truth, we have every right to question the emotional basis for *The Education of Henry Adams*, an especially intense form of self-pity coming from the most widely cultivated

American of his time, who, nonetheless, constantly reminds us of his lack of preparation for the nineteenth century, not to mention the twentieth. And in *Black Boy* we are asked to accept Richard's cultural isolation as well as his vulnerability to all forms of deprivation—physical, emotional, social, and intellectual.

Some critics, carried off by the impact of *Black Boy*, tend to treat the autobiography as if it were fiction. They are influenced by the fact that much great modern fiction, Joyce's *Portrait of the Artist as a Young Man*, for example, is very close to life. And the tendency here is reinforced by the fact that the author himself, Wright, is a creator of fictions. Yielding so is a mistake because many of the incidents in *Black Boy* retain the sharp angularity of life, rather than fitting into the dramatic or symbolic patterns of fiction. Richard's setting fire to the "fluffy white curtains" (p. 4), and incidentally the house, is not the announcement of the birth of a pyromaniac or a revolutionary, but testimony primarily to the ingenuity of a small black boy in overcoming mundane tedium. We must say "primarily" because this irresponsible act suggests the profound distress and confusion an older Richard would bring to a family that relied heavily upon rigid attitudes toward religion, expected behavior, and an appropriate adjustment to Southern life. Richard's fire is not Bigger's rat at the beginning of *Native Son*, when the act of killing brings out pent-up violence in the young black man and foreshadows, perhaps, the events of Book Two, "Flight," when Bigger's position becomes that of the cornered rat.[16] Nor does Richard's immodest invitation to his grandmother during his bath (p. 49) offer disturbing witness of the emergence of a pornographer or a connoisseur of the erotic; rather, it points to something more general, the singular perversity in Richard that makes him resist family and the South. In *Black Boy* we exist in a world of limited probability that is not life exactly, because there is an order to be demonstrated, and it does not display the perfect design of a serious fiction. We occupy a gray area in between. The patterns are here on several levels. Though they may not be so clear and tight as to permit the critic to predict, they do govern the selection of materials, the rendering of special emphases, distortions, and the style.

We seldom raise questions about what is omitted from an autobiography, yet if we wish to discover pattern, we must begin with what we do not find. The seasonal metaphor in *Walden* (we move from spring to spring) becomes all the more important once we realize that Henry Thoreau lived on the shore of Walden Pond more than two years.[17] Franklin's few "errata"[18] point up the strong aridity of an autobiography that touches so little on the traumas of the heart. Franklin's education, his achievements in business and science, and his proposals for the benefit of society seem at times supported by an emotional sub-structure far too frail. But the purposes of both autobiographies—in *Walden*, to offer the model of a renewed life; in the *Autobiography of Benjamin Franklin*, to sketch a convincing design of a successful life in the new world, one that emphasizes the practical values that most Americans admired and many Europeans envied—were achieved in part because of the shrewdness in excluding truthful, though extraneous matter. So, too, *Black Boy* profits from rigorous and inspired editing.

One function of the omissions is to strengthen the impression in our minds of Richard's intense isolation. This is no mean achievement given the fact that Wright was born into a large family (on his mother's side, at least) which, despite differences in personality, cooperated in times of need. The father, because of his desertion of his mother, was early in Richard's mind, perhaps in the sentiments of other family members, too, an object of hate and scorn. There are no names in the early pages of *Black Boy*, not even that of Richard's brother, Leon Allan, just a little more than two years younger than Richard. When the names begin to appear in *Black Boy*, they tend to define the objects of adversary, often violently hostile relationships—Grandmother Wilson, Aunt Addle, Uncle Thomas. Two notable exceptions are Grandfather Wilson, an ineffectual man capable only of reliving his past as a soldier in the Civil War, and Richard's mother, Ella, a pathetically vulnerable woman of some original strength who, because of continuing illness, slipped gradually into a state of helplessness that became for Richard symbolic of his whole life as a black boy in the South.[19]

The admirable biography of Wright by Michel Fabre suggests another dimension for Richard's opponents in his embattled household. The climax of the violence in the family occurred with the confrontation with Uncle Tom, portrayed as a retired and defeated schoolteacher reduced at the time to earning a living by performing odd jobs as a carpenter. Richard resented the fact that he was the victim of Uncle Tom's frustrations, and he responded to orders from the older man by threatening him with razors in both hands and by spitting out hysterically, "You are not an example to me; you could never be.... You're a *warning*. Your life isn't so hot that you can tell me what to do.... Do you think that I want to grow up and weave the bottoms of chairs for people to sit in?" (p. 140). A footnote from Fabre adds more information about the humiliated uncle:

> The portrait of Uncle Thomas in *Black Boy* is exaggerated. After living with the Wilsons, he moved next door and became a real-estate broker. In 1938, he was a member of the Executive Committee of the Citizen's Civic League in Jackson and wrote a book on the word *Negro*, discussing the superiority complex of the Whites and its effects on the Blacks. At this time Richard put

him in contact with Doubleday publishers and the uncle and the nephew were completely reconciled.[20]

Wright includes in *Black Boy* a touching description of meeting his father again after a quarter-century. As the newly successful author looked at a strange black sharecropper in ragged overalls holding a muddy hoe, the old resentment for past neglect faded: "I forgave him and pitied him as my eyes looked past him to the unpainted wooden shack" (p. 30). But *Black Boy* contains no softening reconsiderations of Uncle Tom, or of Aunt Addie, who, like her brother, seems to have possessed some redeeming qualities,[21] or of Granny Wilson for that matter. Their stark portraits dominate the family and define a living space too narrow, too mean, and too filled with frustration and poverty for an imaginative youngster like Richard.

A growing boy, when denied the satisfactions of a loving home, looks for emotional support at school or at play, and if he is lucky, he finds something that moderates domestic discontent. But there is little compensation of this sort in *Black Boy*. The reality of the life away from the family seems to be less bleak than Wright represents it, though his schooling was retarded by early irregularity because of the family's frequent moves, and his play restricted, perhaps, because of the family's desperate need for money and Granny's Seventh Day Adventist scruples. Once again we are struck by the absence of names—of teachers like Lucy McCranie and Alice Burnett, who taught Richard at the Jim Hill School in Jackson and recognized his lively intelligence,[22] or Mary L. Morrison or the Reverend Otto B. Cobbins, Richard's instructors in the eighth and ninth grades of the Smith-Robinson School,[23] to whose dedication and competence, despite personal limitations, Wright paid tribute elsewhere.[24] There was no question about his marginal status in these institutions, since Richard stood regularly at the head of his class.

Black Boy is singularly devoid of references to rewarding peer associations. There is no mention of Dick Jordan, Joe Brown, Perry Booker, or Essie Lee Ward, friends of this period and so valued that Wright was in touch with several of them ten years later when he was living in Chicago.[25] The fact that a few of Wright's childhood associates did succeed in making their way to Chicago has an amount of interest in itself, serving, as well, to break the isolation that Wright has fabricated so well. Among the childhood activities that went unrecorded were the exploits of the Dick Wright clan, made up of a group of neighborhood boys who honored in the name of their society, no doubt, their most imaginative member. The clan included Dick Jordan, Perry Booker, Joe Brown, and also Frank Sims, a descendant of a black senator during the Reconstruction period, Blanche K. Bruce.[26] What is amply clear, then, is that Wright had a childhood more than a little touched by the usual rituals and preoccupations of middle-class boys growing up in America, but what is also apparent is that reference to them would modify our sense of Richard's deprived and disturbed emotional life, a necessity for the art of the autobiography, rather more important than any concern for absolute accuracy.

Wright has little to say directly about sex. Richard's most serious temptation for sexual adventure comes toward the end of *Black Boy* in Memphis, when he is taken in by the Moss family. Richard succeeds in resisting the opportunity to take advantage of a cozy arrangement with Bess, the daughter whom Mrs. Moss seeks to thrust upon him, with marriage as her ultimate objective (p. 185). There are some indirect references to frustrated, sublimated, or distorted forms of sexual energy—in Miss Simon, certainly, the tall, gaunt, mulatto woman who ran the orphan home where Richard was deposited for a period (pp. 25–28). And there were exposures to white women, all calculated to teach Richard the strength of the taboo prohibiting the thought (not to mention the fact) of black–white sexual relations in the South. But Richard never takes an aggressive interest in sex; the adventures that he stumbles into create traumas when they are serious and unavoidable, or are embarrassing when he can resist participation and control his reactions. Wright, indeed, seems to be even more discreet than Franklin was; by comparison, Claude Brown is a raving sensualist in *Manchild in the Promised Land*, though roughly the same period of growth is involved. It is strange that so little space is given to sexual episodes and fantasies in the record of the gradual maturing of an adolescent—unbelievable, given the preoccupations of the twentieth century. We face the problem of omission again. Wright deliberately seeks to deprive his hero, his younger self, of any substantial basis for sensual gratification located outside his developing imagination. The world that *Black Boy* presents is uniformly bleak, always ascetic, and potentially violent, and the posture of the isolated hero, cut off from family, peer, or community support, is rigidly defiant, without the softening effects of interludes of sexual indulgence.

Richard's immediate world, not that foreign country controlled by whites, is overwhelmingly feminine. Male contacts are gone, except for occasional encounters with uncles. The father has deserted his home, and the grandfather is lost in the memories of "The War." The uncles tend to make brief entrances and exits, following the pattern of Hoskins, quickly killed off by envious whites in Arkansas, or the unnamed new uncle, forced to flee because of unstated crimes against whites (pp. 48–49, 57–60). Thomas is the uncle who stays around somewhat longer than the others do, long enough to serve as the convenient object for Richard's mounting rebellion. The encounter with Uncle Tom is the culminating episode marking a defiance expressed earlier against a number of authority figures, all women— Richard's mother, Miss Simon, Grandmother Wilson, Aunt Addie. Women dominate in Richard's world, with the ultimate authority vested in Granny— near-white, uncompromising, unloving, and fanatical, daring Richard to desecrate her Seventh Day Adventist Sabbath. The only relief from feminine piety is the pathetic schoolteacher who, in a happy moment, tells an enraptured Richard about Bluebeard and his wives (p. 34). But even this delight, moved in part, no doubt, by Bluebeard's relentless war against females, is short-lived. Granny puts a stop to such sinning, not recognizing, of course, the working out of the law of compensation.

Richard's odyssey takes him from the black world to the white—from the problems of home and family to new and even more formidable difficulties. The movement is outward into the world, to confront an environment that is not controlled by Granny, though it provides much that contributes to an explanation of Granny's behavior. Richard's life among blacks emphasizes two kinds of struggle. One is simply the battle for physical existence, the need for food, clothing, shelter, and protection that is the overwhelming concern of the early pages of *Black Boy*. The second grows out of Richard's deeply felt desire to acquire his own male identity, a sense of self apart from a family that exerts increasing pressure upon this growing black boy to behave properly, to experience Christian conversion, and to accept guidance from his (mostly female) elders. Survival in two senses, then, is the dominant theme, one which does not change when he leaves the black community. The terms are the same though the landscape is new. Richard desperately seeks employment in white neighborhoods and in the downtown business districts in order to contribute to the support of his family. He discovers, when he does so, that the demand to accommodate becomes even more insistent and less flexible than that exerted by his own family.

The difference is that the stakes are higher. Richard thinks he must find a job, any job, to earn a living. This awareness represents a step beyond the simple dependence that moves a small boy to complain, "Mama, I'm hungry" (p. 13). If he does not find work, Richard feels that he has failed his family in an essential way and made its survival precarious. Though his independence in the black world leads to harsh sanctions—threats, bed without supper, whippings—he is not prepared for the infinitely greater severity of the white world. It is cruel, calculating, and sadistic. Richard never doubts that he will survive the lashings received from his mother, Granny, and assorted aunts and uncles, but he does question his ability to endure exposure to whites. The ways of white folks are capricious and almost uniformly malignant. Richard understands that the penalty for nonconformity, down to the way a black boy walks or holds his head, is not simply a sore body, but death. When Richard gives up a good job with an optical company, with a chance, according to his boss, to become something more than a menial worker, he does so because of the opposition exhibited by whites who think he aspires to do "white man's work." Richard confides to his boss when he leaves the factory: "I'm scared.... They would kill me" (p. 168).

From the woman who inquires of Richard, looking for yet another job, "Boy, do you steal?" (p. 128) to the two young men who attempt to arrange for Richard to fight another black boy for the amusement of an assembly of whites (pp. 209–10), we witness an unrelieved set of abuses. Certainly omission of some mitigating circumstances and artful distortion are involved in this bitter report. Richard is gradually introduced to a white world that grows progressively more dominant, divisive, and corrupting concerning the black life that serves it. Richard understands fully what is expected of him:

> I began to marvel at how smoothly the black boys acted out the roles that the white race had snapped out for them. Most of them were not conscious of living a special, separate, stunted way of life. Yet I know that in some period of their growing up—a period that they had no doubt forgotten—there had been developed in them a delicate, sensitive controlling mechanism that shut off their minds and emotions from all that the white race had said was taboo. (p. 172)

In Wright's South it was unthinkable for a black boy to aspire to become a lens-grinder, much less to harbor the ambition to become a writer. When Richard is thoughtless enough to reveal his true aim in life to one of his white employers, the response is predictable: "You'll never be a writer.... Who on earth put such ideas into your nigger head?" (p. 129). Given his difficulties in adjusting to an oppressive Southern system, Richard sustains his interest in writing through a monumental act of will. We are led to the inevitable conclusion that Richard must flee the South if he is to remain alive, and the desire to achieve an artistic career seems less important in light of the more basic concern for life itself.

We have every reason to suspect that the treatment of whites gains a certain strength from artistic deletion, too. Michael Fabre points out that Wright's relationship with a white family named Wall does not fit the pattern of abuse and brutal exploitation that emerges from the autobiography: "Although *Black Boy* was designed to describe the effects of racism on a black child, which meant omitting incidents tending to exonerate white persons in any way, there is no doubt that the Walls were liberal and generous employers. For almost two years Richard worked before and after class, earning three dollars a week bringing in firewood and doing the heavy cleaning."[27] Fabre adds, with reference especially to Mrs. Wall and her mother, "Since they respected his qualities as an individual, he sometimes submitted his problems and plans to them and soon considered their house a second home where he met with more understanding than from his own family."[28] This is not matter that reinforces a design displaying increasing difficulty for Richard as he moves outward and into contact with white society. Nor does it support Richard's growing conviction that his survival depends upon his escape from the South. The design of *Black Boy* offers an accelerating pattern of confrontations, taking into account both an increase in danger for Richard and a mounting seriousness in terms of society's estimate of his deviations. Like Big Boy, Richard must flee or die.

The narrator of *Black Boy* has three voices. The simplest records recollected events with clarity and a show of objectivity. We may be troubled by an insufficient context surrounding or an inadequate connection linking these episodes until we become aware of the suggestion of a psychological dimension for them. The incidents illustrate basic emotions: the discovery of fear and guilt, first, when fire destroys Richard's house; the experience of hate, directed this time toward the father, in killing the kitten; the satisfactions of violence, in defeating the teenage gang; the dangers of curiosity about the adult world, in Richard's early addiction to alcohol. The psyche of a child takes shape through exposure to a set of unusual traumas, and the child goes forth, as we have seen, into a world that becomes progressively more brutal and violent. Style in this way reinforces the first theme of the autobiography, survival.

It is in hearing the more complicated and lyrical second voice of the narrator that we sense for the first time another theme in the autobiography. This is the making of the artist. The world, we have been told, is cold, harsh, and cruel, a fact which makes all the more miraculous the emergence of a literary imagination destined to confront it. The bleak South, by some strange necessity, is forced to permit the blooming of a single rose. Wright expends upon the nourishment of this tender plant the care that he has given to describing the sterile soil from which it springs.

A third, didactic voice offers occasional explanations of the matter recorded by the other two. It comments at times upon the lack of love among blacks in the South, the distortions in human relationships involving blacks and whites, and corruption in the social and economic systems. At other times it advises us of the necessity for secrecy when a black boy harbors the ambition to write, and explains the difficulties which he confronts when he seeks to serve an apprenticeship to his art. Despite formidable opposition and the danger of complete isolation, this ambition lives and forces the growth of Richard's imaginative powers.

We do not begin simply with the statement of the intention to become an artist. We start, rather, as Joyce does in *A Portrait of the Artist*, with the sense experience that rests behind the word. Richard's memory offers rich testimony of the capacity to feel objects of nature, small and large. Not only these. We note that accompanying the record of sensations is the tendency to translate sensation into an appropriate emotion—melancholy, nostalgia, astonishment, disdain. All of the senses achieve recognition in Richard's memory, and all combine to emphasize memories of violent experiences: the killing of the chicken; the shocking movement of the snake; the awesome golden glow on a silent night (pp. 7–8).

Apart from this basic repository of sensation and image, we sense early in Richard two other qualities just as essential to the budding artist. One is detachment, the feeling of being different from others. In two worlds to which he is exposed, that of the family and then the more muddled arena of affairs, he rejects all efforts to moderate his apartness. Though conversion and subsequent baptism apparently point to joining the company of the saved, viewed in the conventional way, damnation is assured by the refusal to deliver the right kind of valedictory at the graduation exercises of his grammar school (p. 153). Barely passing one ritual, he flunks another. He maintains under pressure his status as an alien, so ultimately he will be free to exercise the imagination that faces the cold world.

The second quality is curiosity. His mother tells Richard that he asks too many questions. Our young hero is apparently undaunted by the fact that his insistent prying has led to one of the earliest addictions to alcohol recorded in literature. But another addiction is more serious, to the truth in the appearances about him. "Will you stop asking silly questions!" his mother commands (p. 42). About names, about color, about the relationship between the two. Curiosity constantly leads Richard to forbidden areas more menacing than the saloon, to the mysterious privileged province of whites in Mississippi and the equally mysterious restriction of the blacks.

A neat form of inversion is involved in the development of Richard's artistic talent. We note that the qualities supporting and sustaining the growing boy's imagination are just those preventing a successful adjustment to life in the South. To achieve a tolerable existence, not even a comfortable one, Richard must have firm relationships with the members of his family and with his neighbors and peers; to survive in the larger, white-dominated society he must accept without questioning the inflexible system of Southern mores and customs. Richard, rejecting these imperatives, responds to the demands of his own imagination.

Richard's sensations in nature anticipate a discovery just as valuable and far reaching. This is literature itself. Of the encounter with *Bluebeard* Richard says, "My sense of life deepened...." He recalls, further, a total emotional response, emphasized, no doubt, by the background of an unresponding family, and he realizes that he stands on the threshold of a "gateway to a forbidden and enchanting land" (p. 36). So, early, the opposition is clear. On the one hand is the bleak environment frowning upon any activity of the imagination, whether passive or active, and on the other a determined Richard who will not be turned aside. His reading would be done in secret, a clandestine activity abetted by delivering racist newspapers and borrowing the library card of a compliant white man. There is no evidence that he discussed his reading with anyone, black or white. In Memphis, when he was able to patronize second-hand bookstores and to buy magazines like *Harper's*, *Atlantic Monthly*, and *American Mercury*, his tastes reflected the shape of his early conditioning (p. 198). He admired the great liberators, the destroyers of provincial and private worlds like the one that oppressed him; Mencken in a *Book of Prefaces and Prejudices*; Sinclair Lewis in *Main Street* and *Babbitt*; Theodore Dreiser in *Sister Carrie* and *Jennie Gerhardt* (pp. 217–19).

It might be said that Richard has the loneliness of a naturalistic hero, of McTeague or of Carrie Meeber. Theirs are worlds in which no one talks to anyone else, worlds entirely given over to the expression of power. One person's drive pitted against that of another, and the consequence of the struggle has more to do with heredity or chemistry than with persuasion. Richard's behavior, much like that of a character created by Norris or Dreiser, though it is not governed by the tight probability of fiction, carries constantly the solemn and overwhelming weight of the universe. He cannot say "sir" without acquiescing to the ever-present power of the white man, and he cannot read Mencken without the satisfaction that he has triumphed over a hostile white South through subterfuge and trickery.

Richard's commitment to write precipitates confrontations. As we have seen, his honest admission of this aspiration to one white lady employer results in bitter ridicule, and Richard feels, despite the pressures of his situation, that his ego has been assaulted. His first publication, "The Voodoo of Hell's Half-Acre," is little more than the crude rendering of the stuff of *Flynn's Detective Weekly*, but Richard discovers that printing it is an act of defiance, further separating him from the world that surrounds him, both black and white (p. 146).

Richard does not intend to restrict his range to any half-acre, though his first is identified as "Hell." His province would be the real world around him. True, it is sometimes not to be distinguished from the subject area defined by his first literary effort. At a very young age Richard sees "elephants" moving across the land—not real "elephants," but convicts in a chain gang, and the child's awe is prompted by the unfortunate confusion of elephant and zebra (p. 52). An inauspicious beginning, perhaps, but the pattern of applying his imagination to his immediate surrounding is firmly set. Later, Richard says more soberly that he rejects religion because it ignores immediate reality. His faith, predictably, must be wedded to "common realities of life" (p. 100), anchored in the sensations of his body and in what his mind could grasp. This is, we see, an excellent credo for an artist, but a worthless one for a black boy growing to maturity in Mississippi.

Another piece of evidence announcing Richard's talent is the compulsion to make symbols of the details of his everyday experience. This faculty is early demonstrated in his tendency to generalize from sensational experience, to define an appropriate emotion to associate with his feelings. A more highly developed example is Richard's reaction to his mother's illness and sufferings, representative for him in later years of the poverty, the ignorance, the helplessness of black life in Mississippi. And it is based on the generalizing process that Richard is a black boy, any black boy experiencing childhood, adolescence, and early manhood in the South.

Richard leaves the South. He must, to survive as a man and to develop as an artist. By the time we reach the end of the narrative, these two drives have merged. We know, as well, that the South will never leave Richard, never depart from the rich imagination that developed despite monumental opposition. We have only the final promise that Richard will someday understand the region that has indelibly marked him.

Richard's ultimate liberation, and his ultimate triumph, will be the ability to face the dreadful experience in the South and to record it. At the end of *A Portrait of the Artist as a Young Man*, the facts of experience have become journal items for the artist.[29] At the conclusion of *Invisible Man*, Ellison's unnamed narrator can record the blues of his black life, with the accompaniment of extraordinary psychedelic effects. Stephen Dedalus is on his way to becoming an artist; Ellison's hero promises to climb out of his hole, half-prepared, at least, to return to mundane life.[30] The conclusion of *Black Boy* is less positive and more tentative. True, Richard has made it; he has whipped the devils of the South, black and white. But he has left us with a feeling that is less than happy. He has yet to become an artist. Then we realize with a start what we have read is not simply the statement of a promise, its background and its development, but its fulfillment. Wright has succeeded in reconstructing the reality that was for a long time perhaps too painful to order, and that reconstruction may be Wright's supreme artistic achievement, *Black Boy*.

Notes

1. (New York: Harper, 1940.) Dorothy Canfield Fisher in the introduction writes that the "novel plumbs blacker depths of human experience than American literature has yet had, comparable only to Dostoievski's revelation of human misery in wrongdoing" (p. x).

2. The full title is *Black Boy: A Record of Childhood and Youth* (New York: Harper, 1945). Dorothy Fisher in the introductory note calls Wright's work "the honest, dreadful, heartbreaking story of a Negro childhood and youth ..." (p. vii), without referring to its art or even its place in an American literary tradition.

3. "Life and Letters: Richard Wright Reappraised," *Atlantic Monthly*, 225 (March, 1970), 127–32.

4. *American Hunger* (New York: Harper & Row, Publishers) was published in 1977. It is not the whole autobiography but the second part, the continuation of *Black Boy*. Michel Fabre in the afterword provides an accurate brief history of the decision to publish only the first section in 1945. See pp. 143–44.

5. *Atlantic Monthly*, 174 (August, 1944), 61–70; (September, 1944), 48–56.

6. Fabre, "Afterword," *American Hunger*, pp. 143–44.

7. W. E. B. Du Bois, "Richard Wright Looks Back," *New York Herald Tribune*, March 4, 1945, sec. 5, p. 2.

8. The three are *The Souls of Black Folk: Essays and Sketches* (Chicago: A. C. McClurg, 1903), *Darkwater: Voices from Within the Veil* (New York: Harcourt, Brace, 1920), and *Dusk of Dawn: An Essay toward an Autobiography of a Race Concept* (New York: Harcourt, Brace, 1940).

9. Chapter IV, "Of the Meaning of Progress," in Du Bois, *The Souls of Black Folk*, pp. 60–74.

10. "Richard Wright's Blues," *Antioch Review*, 5 (June, 1945), 202. Reprinted in *Shadow and Act* (New York: Random House, 1964).

11. Wright wrote Edward Aswell, his editor at Harper's, on August 10, 1944, suggesting *Black Boy* as a title for the book. He added, for emphasis, that *Black Boy* was "not only a title but also a kind of heading to the whole general theme" (Fabre, "Afterword," *American Hunger*, p. 144).

12. Wright comments on this commitment in *Black Boy*: "I had once tried to write, had once reveled in feeling, had let my crude imagination roam, but the impulse to dream had been slowly beaten out of me by experience. Now it surged up again and I hungered for books, new ways of looking and seeing" (p. 218).

13. *Ibid.*, p. 220.

14. Between 1897 and 1915 Du Bois edited fifteen studies on the condition and status of blacks in America. These volumes represented the Proceedings of the Annual Conference on the Negro Problem, organized by Du Bois and held at Atlanta University.

15. Ellison, "Richard Wright's Blues."

16. *Native Son*, pp. 4–5.

17. Thoreau is precise about the length of his actual stay, despite the fact that the events of *Walden* fall within the design of a single year: "The present was my next experiment ... for convenience, putting the experience of two years into one." Henry David Thoreau, *Walden*, ed. Sherman Paul (Boston: Houghton Mifflin, 1957), p. 58.

18. Franklin refers in this way to his neglect of Miss Read, to whom he was engaged, during a period spent in London: "This was another of the great errata of my life...." "Autobiography" in Benjamin Franklin, *Autobiography and Other Writings*, ed. R. B. Nye (Boston: Houghton Mifflin, 1958), p. 38.

19. See Michel Fabre, *The Unfinished Quest of Richard Wright* (New York: William Morrow, 1973), pp. 1–17.

20. Fabre, *Unfinished Quest*, p. 533.

21. Another footnote by Fabre in *Unfinished Quest* suggests an additional dimension for Addie, who, "too, was not, spared in *Black Boy*. She reacted rather well to reading the book—she stated that if Richard wrote in that way, it was to support his family ..." (p. 533).

22. *Ibid.*, p. 39.

23. *Ibid.*, p. 48.

24. E. R. Embree describes, in *Thirteen Against the Odds* (New York: Viking, 1944), Wright's attitude toward his education in Jackson: "He [Wright] remembers the Smith-Robinson school with some gratitude. The teachers tried their best to pump learning into the pupils" (p. 27).

25. Fabre, *Unfinished Quest*, p. 39.

26. *Ibid.*, p. 43.

27. *Ibid.*, pp. 46–47.

28. *Ibid.*, p. 47.

29. See James Joyce, *A Portrait of the Artist as a Young Man* (New York: New American Library, 1955), pp. 195–96.

30. Ellison's narrator states his final position with some care: "Thus, having tried to give pattern to the chaos which lives within the pattern of your certainties, I must come out, I must emerge." *Invisible Man* (New York: New American Library, 1952), p. 502.

HORACE A. PORTER

The Horror and the Glory:
Richard Wright's Portrait of the Artist in
Black Boy *and* American Hunger

As the curtain falls on the final page of *American Hunger*, the continuation of Richard Wright's autobiography, *Black Boy*, he is alone in his "narrow room, watching the sun sink slowly in the chilly May sky." Having just been attacked by former Communist associates as he attempted to march in the May Day parade, he ruminates about his life. He concludes that all he has after living in both Mississippi and Chicago, are "words and a dim knowledge that my country has shown me no examples of how to live a human life." Wright ends his autobiography with the following words:

> I wanted to try to build a bridge of words between me and that world, oui side, that world which was so distant and elusive that it seemed unreal.
>
> I would hurl words into this darkness and wait for an echo, and if an echo sounded, no matter how faintly, I would send other words to tell, to march, to fight, to create a sense of the hunger for life that gnaws in us all, to keep alive in our hearts a sense of the inexpressibly human.[1]

American Hunger (1977) is the continuation of *Black Boy* (1945). Wright initially composed them as one book entitled *The Horror and the Glory*. Thus,

---

From *Richard Wright: A Collection of Critical Essays*, Richard Macksey and Frank E. Moorer, ed. © 1984 Horace A. Porter.

a reading of the two volumes as one continuous autobiography is crucial for a comprehensive understanding of his portrayal of himself as a young writer. Wright achieves remarkable poetic closure by bringing together at the end of *American Hunger* several interrelated themes which he elaborately spells out in *Black Boy*. The passage cited above illustrates his concern for words, his intense and troubling solitude, and his yearning to effect a revolution in the collective consciousness of America through the act of writing. In a sentence, the end of *American Hunger* is essentially the denouement of *Black Boy*.

Although critics have discussed the effect of Wright's early life on his writings, none has shown systematically how *Black Boy* (and to a lesser degree *American Hunger*) can be read primarily as a portrait of the artist as a young man. Consequently, I intend to demonstrate how the theme of words (with their transforming and redeeming power) is the nucleus around which ancillary themes swirl. Wright's incredible struggle to master words is inextricably bound to his defiant quest for individual existence and expression. To be sure, the fundamental nature of the experience is not peculiar to Wright. Many, if not most writers, are marked by their experience with words during childhood. It is no accident that, say, Jean Paul Sartre, a writer whom Wright eventually meets and admires, entitles his autobiography *Les Mots*. What one sees in Wright's autobiographies is how the behavior of his fanatically religious grandmother, the painful legacy of his father, the chronic suffering of his mother, and how his interactions with blacks and whites both in and outside his immediate community are all thematically connected to the way Wright uses words to succeed as a writer and as a man.

The first chapter of *Black Boy*, the first scene, foreshadows the major theme—the development of the young artist's sensibility—of the book. Wright begins his narrative by recounting how he set fire to his house when he was four years old. His is a conflagration sparked by an odd combination of boredom, curiosity, and imagination. One day Wright looks yearningly out into the empty street and dreams of running, playing, and shouting. First, he burns straws from a broom; then, his temporary pyromania getting the better of him, he wondered how "the long fluffy white curtains" would look if he lit them: "Red circles were eating into the white cloth; then a flare of flames shot out.... The fire soared to the ceiling.... Soon a sheet of yellow lit the room."[2] Then, most terrifying of all, Wright runs outside and hides in "a dark hollow of a brick chimney and balled [himself] into a tight knot."[3] Wright's aim in hiding under the burning house was to avoid the predictable whipping by his mother. Moreover, his four-year-old imagination is so preoccupied with the effect of his derring-do that he does not realize that his own life is on a burning line. Hiding beneath the house and thinking of the possible consequences of his actions—the death of family members—Wright states: "It seemed that I had been hiding for ages, and when the stomping and screaming died down, I felt lonely, cast forever out of life."[4]

Wright may not have been completely aware of the psychological import of his opening scene. For, it appears that we must interpret young Wright's act of arson for what it really may have been. Perhaps even at that early age he was trying to free himself from the tyranny of his father's house in which his fanatically religious grandmother ruled: "I saw the image of my grandmother lying helplessly upon her bed and there were yellow fumes in her black hair...."[5] The fact that young Wright has these thoughts while in "a dark hollow of a brick chimney ... balled ... into a tight knot," raises more profound psychological issues. Does this image represent a yearning to return to the womb? Does it constitute symbolic parricide? Does it symbolize the possibility of a new birth? When Wright sets his father's house aflame, he also makes an eloquent statement against the world the Southern slaveholders had made. Wright's later anxiety and guilt over having turned his back on his father's world drives him to write. His autobiography is an act of self-assertion and self-vindication in which he fearlessly confronts his father. Moreover, he demonstrates his love for his mother. And he pays homage to the anonymous, illiterate blacks whose world he fled.

In the process of moving away from his family and community, Wright began experiencing the problem (a consuming sense of loss and abandonment) that was to become central to his life and work. In certain primary respects, he was surely cognizant of the problem, but it operated on levels sufficiently profound as to be unfathomable later in his career. Numerous passages in *Black Boy* illustrate the phenomenon.

What has been characterized as ritual parricide comes readily to mind when Wright's father is awakened one day by the meowing of a stray cat his sons have found. Wright's father screams at him and his brother: "'Kill that damn thing!'" His father shouts, "'Do anything, but get it away from here!'" Ignoring the advice of his brother, Wright does exactly what his father suggests. He puts a rope around the cat's neck and hangs it. Why? Wright explains:

I had had my first triumph over my father. I had made him believe that I had taken his words literally. He could not punish me now without risking his authority. I was happy because I had at last found a way to throw criticism of him into his face. I had made him feel that, if he whipped me for killing the kitten, I would never give serious weight to his words again. I had made

him know that I felt he was cruel and I had done it without his
punishing me.[6]

Young Wright's cunning act of interpretation is the telling point here.
If one were dubious about the meaning of the son's act of arson, the passage
cited above demonstrates a full-blown hatred and contempt. But note how
Wright focuses on his father's words, how he attempts to neutralize his
father's psychological authority by a willful misinterpretation of his
statement.

At the end of the first chapter of *Black Boy*, Wright banishes his father
from the remaining pages of both volumes of his autobiography. His father
eventually deserts his mother and she struggles to support her two sons. On
one occasion when Wright and his mother pay his father and his "strange
woman" a visit in order to obtain money for food, Wright's father hands him
a nickel. Wright refuses to accept the nickel, his father laughs and puts the
nickel back in his pocket, stating, "'That's all I got.'" That image of his
father was indelibly etched in Wright's memory. Wright states that over the
years, his father's face would "surge up in my imagination so vivid and strong
that I felt I could reach out and touch it; I would stare at it, feeling that it
possessed some vital meaning which always eluded me."[7]

Wright does not see his father for "a quarter of a century" after that
encounter. His reunion with his father after a prolonged period leads to one
of the more poignant and profound meditations of the autobiography.
Staring at "the sharecropper, clad in ragged overalls, holding a muddy hoe in
his gnarled, veined hands," Wright sees his biological father, but he also sees
another man. The man standing before him is now both more and less than
his father:

> ... My mind and consciousness had become so greatly and
> violently altered that when I tried to talk to him I realized that,
> though ties of blood made us kin, though I could see a shadow of
> my face in his face, though there was an echo of my voice in his
> voice, we were forever strangers, speaking a different language,
> living on vastly different planes of reality.... I stood before him,
> pained, my mind aching as it embraced the simple nakedness of
> his life, feeling how completely his soul was imprisoned by the
> slow flow of the seasons, by wind and rain and sun, how fastened
> were his memories to a crude and raw past, how chained were his
> actions and emotions to the direct, animalistic impulses of his
> withering body ... I forgave him and pitied him as my eyes looked
> past him to the unpainted wooden shack. From far beyond the

horizon that bound this bleak plantation there had come to me through my living the knowledge that my father was a black peasant who had gone to the city seeking life, but who had failed in the city, and who at last fled the city—that same city which had lifted me in its burning arms and borne me toward alien and undreamed of shores of knowing.[8]

In the foregoing meditation, Wright depicts his father as a "sharecropper," a "black peasant," whose actions and emotions are "chained ... to the direct, animalistic impulses of his body." He and his father are "forever strangers, speaking a different language." Even in this passage which ostensibly has little to do with language, Wright reminds us that his ability to use and understand words has transformed him. His mind and consciousness have been "greatly and violently" altered. So Wright finally achieves the kind of authority he longed for as a kid. His father is no longer the threatening figure who told him to kill the kitten. From Wright's point of view, he has become something other; now, he is more phenomenon than person. Thus, Wright is simultaneously compassionate and dispassionate. On the one hand, he forgives his father; on the other, he clearly indicates that certain bonds between him and his father have been irreparably severed.

Wright's mother also plays an important role in this psychological scheme of reconciliation and vindication. Despite the fact that his mother whipped him until he was unconscious after he set the house afire, he expresses tenderness toward her throughout *Black Boy*; Wright informs the reader that his mother was the first person who taught him to read and told him stories. After Wright had hanged the kitten in order to triumph over his father, he explains that his mother, who is "more imaginative, retaliated with an assault upon my sensibilities that crushed me with the moral horror involved in taking a life."[9] His mother makes him bury the kitten that night and makes him pray.

Wright's mother not only instructs him in the high moral values of civilized society, but she also teaches him how to survive in a hostile and impoverished environment. She teaches him "the ethics of living Jim Crow." She frequently whips him because she knows that certain small gestures of self-pride and assertion would lead readily to brutality or death. Thus, if Wright's mother's arm is sometimes the arm of the oppressive social order, that same arm is, ironically, the tender, loving arm of the parent, nurturing and protecting her young. She instructs him in those traditions of black life that are sustaining—the necessity of learning to persevere, the ability to maintain grace under pressure, the practice of containing one's pain. Small wonder that Wright sees in his mother's suffering and in her will to live in spite of her rapidly declining health, a symbol of the numerous ills and injustices of the society in which they both live.

> My mother's suffering grew into a symbol in my mind, gathering to itself all the poverty, the ignorance, the helplessness; the painful, baffling, hunger-ridden days and hours; the restless moving, the futile seeking, the uncertainty, the fear, the dread; the meaningless pain and the endless suffering. Her life set the emotional tone of my life, colored the men and women I was to meet in the future, conditioned my relation to events that had not yet happened.... A somberness of spirit that I was never to lose settled over me during the slow years of my mother's unrelieved suffering, a somberness that was to make me stand apart and look upon excessive joy with suspicion, that was to make me self-conscious, that was to make me keep forever on the move, as though to escape a nameless face seeking to overtake me.[10]

Wright, the loving son, feels powerless before the seemingly vast impersonal forces which break his mother's spirit and ruin her health. His mother's life becomes a psychological and emotional charge to him; the "vital meaning" inherent in her suffering is the unstated psychological instruction to dedicate his life to the amelioration of the ills and injustices of society in whatever manner he finds appropriate and effective. Had Wright become indifferent toward the symbol of suffering his mother's life represents, his indifference would have been in effect psychological and moral betrayal of the first order. However, his reflections on his mother's suffering profoundly changes his whole attitude at the tender age of twelve. The spirit he catches sharpens the edges of his inchoate, artistic sensibility. We witness the writer's personality assuming self-conscious definition:

> The spirit I had caught gave me insight into the suffering of others, ... made me sit for hours while others told me of their lives.... It made me love burrowing into psychology, into realistic and naturalistic fiction and art.... It directed my loyalties to the side of men in rebellion; it made me love talk that sought answers to questions that could help nobody, that could only keep alive in me that enthralling sense of wonder and awe in the face of the drama of human feeling which is hidden by the external drama of life.[11]

Furthermore, the symbol of Wright's mother's suffering gives him hope. Long before he leaves the South he dreams of going North in order to "do something to redeem my being alive":

> I dreamed of going North and writing books, novels. The North symbolized to me all that I had not felt and seen; it had no relation whatever to what actually existed. Yet, by imagining a place where everything was possible, I kept hope alive in me. But where had I got this notion of doing something in the future, of going away from home and accomplishing something that would be recognized by others? I had, of course, read my Horatio Alger stories, and I knew my Get-Rich-Quick Wallingford series from cover to cover, though I had sense enough not to hope to get rich … yet I felt I had to go somewhere and do something to redeem my being alive.[12]

Note that Wright considers the writing of books or novels as the activity which would give his life meaning—"redeem my being alive."

In the preceding pages, we discuss the subtle psychological question of Wright's relationship to his parents. The task now is to demonstrate specifically how Wright uses words to remove himself from the oppressive community which tries to stifle his imagination. Over the years, Wright becomes increasingly defiant and articulate. And the members of his Southern community become suspicious of his goals and motives.

Words lead to Wright's salvation and to his redemption. From the first pages of *Black Boy*, the reader witnesses Wright at the tender, impressionable age of six becoming a messenger of the obscene. One day a black man drags Wright, who is peering curiously through the doors of a saloon, inside. The unscrupulous and ignorant adults give him liquor and send obscene messages by him back and forth to one another. Wright goes from one persons to the next shouting various obscenities in tune to the savage glee and laughter of the crowd. Surely, the incident makes Wright, inquisitive as he is, wonder about the odd effects of his words.

He later learns his first lesson on the power of the written word. Returning home after his first day of school during which he had learned "all the four-letter words describing physiological and sex functions," from a group of older boys, he decides to display his newly acquired knowledge. Wright goes from window to window in his neighborhood and writes the words in huge soap letters. A woman stops him and drives him home. That night the same woman informs his mother of what Wright calls his "inspirational scribblings." As punishment, she takes him out into the night with a pail of water and a towel and demands that he erase the words he had written: "'Now scrub until that word's gone,' she ordered."

This comical incident may appear insignificant on the surface. Furthermore, one cannot know the nature or the degree of the psychological effect the incident had on Wright. However, it seems reasonable to assume that it had a significant psychological impact. As Wright presents it, it is the first occasion on which words he writes are publicly censored; the first incident during which family members and neighbors become angry, if amused, because of words he writes. Wright states: "Neighbors gathered, giggling, muttering words of pity and astonishment, asking my mother how on earth I could have learned so much so quickly. I scrubbed at the four-letter soap words and grew blind with anger."[13]

Wright's first written words are not the only words to get him in trouble. His first exposure to imaginative literature also causes a scene. One day a young school teacher, who boards with his grandmother, read to him *Bluebeard and His Seven Wives*. Wright describes the effect that the story has on him in visionary terms: "The tale made the world around me, throb, live. As she spoke reality changed, the look of things altered, and the world became peopled with magical presences. My sense of life deepened and the feel of things was different, somehow. Enchanted and enthralled...."[14]

Wright's visionary, enchanted state does not last. His grandmother screams "'you stop that you evil gal!' ... 'I want none of that devil stuff in my house!'" When Wright insists that he likes the story and wants to hear what happened, his grandmother tells him, "'you're going to burn in hell....'" Wright reacts strongly to this incident. He promises himself that when he is old enough, he "would buy all the novels there were and read them." Not knowing the end of the tale fills Wright with "a sense of emptiness and loss." He states that the tale struck "a profoundly responsive chord" in him:

> So profoundly responsive a chord had the tale struck in me that the threats of my mother and grandmother had no effect whatsoever. They read my insistence as mere obstinacy, as foolishness, something that would quickly pass; and they had no notion how desperately serious the tale had made me. They could not have known that Ella's whispered story of deception and murder had been the first experience in my life that had elicited from me a total emotional response. No words or punishment could have possibly made me doubt. I had tasted what to me was life, and I would have more of it somehow, some way....[15]

This passage dramatizes one of the central conflicts of Wright's autobiography. It shows, on the one hand, Wright's literary precocity and illustrates on the other how his days with his grandmother led to one psychological scrimmage after another. The grandmother loathes what she considers to be Wright's impertinence. No matter, given Wright's thirst for knowledge, his longing to achieve a self-conscious, independent manhood, his intense desire to live in a world elsewhere, he proves to be extremely vigilant in his fight against those, including his grandmother, his uncle, his aunt, and his high school principal, whom he calls his "tribal" oppressors. To Wright, theirs is at worst the path to poverty and ignorance and at best a path to what Mann's Tonio Kröger calls "the blisses of the commonplace." Wrights wants neither.

Reflecting on his grandmother's insistence that he join the church and walk in the path of righteousness (as she sees it), Wright states: "We young men had been trapped by the community, the tribe in which we lived and which we were a part. The tribe for its own safety was a asking us to be at one with it..."[16] Moreover, commenting on how the community views anyone who chooses not to have his soul saved, Wright asserts:

> This business of saving souls had no ethics; every human relationship was shamelessly exploited. In essence, the tribe was asking us whether we shared its feeling; if we refused to join the church, it was equivalent to saying no, to placing ourselves in the position of moral monsters.[17]

It is important to keep in mind that Wright's mother is an exception. To be sure, she shares many of the views of the community, but out of love, she aids Wright in his attempt to escape the tribe. Speaking of his mother after the Bluebeard incident, Wright says: "I burned to learn to read novels and I tortured my mother into telling me the meaning of every strange word I saw, not because the word itself had any value, but because it was the gateway to a forbidden and enchanting land."[18]

Against the wishes of the community, Wright continues to read and develop as a young writer. His first real triumph comes when the editor of the local Negro newspaper accepts one of Wright's stories, "The Voodoo of Hell's Half-Acre." The plot of the story involves a villain who wants a widow's home. After the story is published, no one, excepting the newspaper editor, gives any encouragement. His grandmother calls it "'the devil's work'"; his high school principal objects to his use of "hell" in the story's title; even his mother feels that his writing will make people feel that he is "weak minded." His classmates do not believe that he has written the story:

> They were convinced that I had not told them the truth. We had never had any instruction in literary matters at school; the

literature of the nation of the Negro had never been mentioned. My schoolmates could not understand why I had called it *The Voodoo of Hell's Half-Acre*. The mood out of which a story was written was the most alien thing conceivable to them. They looked at me with new eyes, and a distance, a suspiciousness came between us. If I had thought anything in writing the story, I had thought that perhaps it would make me more acceptable to them, and now it was cutting me off from them more completely than ever.[19]

Herein, Wright identifies another problem which menaces him throughout his writing life. The problem is the young artist's radical disassociation of sensibility from that of the group. In this regard, he is reminiscent of the young artist heroes of Mann and Joyce, of Tonio Kröger and Stephen Daedalus. However, Wright's plight as a young artist is significantly different in a crucial way. His is not simply the inability to experience, by dint of his, poetic sensibility, "the blisses of the commonplace." Not only is Wright pitted against his immediate family and community, the tribe, as he calls them. He must also fight against the prejudices of the larger society.

Wright wrote "The Voodoo of Hell's Half-Acre" when he was fifteen. He concludes:

Had I been conscious of the full extent to which I was pushing against the current of my environment, I would have been frightened altogether out of my attempts at writing....

I was building up in me a dream which the entire educational system of the South had been rigged to stifle. I was feeling the very thing that the state of Mississippi had spent millions of dollars to make sure that I would never feel; I was becoming aware of the thing that the Jim Crow laws had been drafted and passed to keep out of my consciousness; I was acting on impulses that Southern senators in the nation's capital had striven to keep out of Negro life....[20]

A telling example which brilliantly demonstrates what Wright means in the passage cited above involves his love for words and books once again. When Wright is nineteen, he reads an editorial in the Memphis *Commercial Appeal* which calls H. L. Mencken a fool. Wright knows that Mencken is the editor of the *American Mercury* and he wonders what Mencken has done to deserve such scorn. How can he find out about Mencken? Since blacks are denied the right to use the public libraries, he is not permitted to check out books. But Wright proves both ingenious and cunning.

He looks around among his co-workers at the optical company where he is employed and chooses the white person—a Mr. Falk—who he thinks might be sympathetic. The man is an Irish Catholic, "a pope lover" as the white Southerners say. Wright had gotten books from the library for him several times, and wisely figures that since he too is hated, he might be somewhat sympathetic. Wright's imagination and courage pays of Although somewhat skeptical about Wright's curious request from the outset, Mr. Falk eventually gives Wright his card, warning him of the risk involved and swearing him to secrecy. Wright promises that he will write the kind of notes Mr. Falk usually writes and that he will sign Falk's name.

Since Wright does not know the title of any of Mencken's books, he carefully composes what he considers a foolproof note: "*Dear Madam: Will you please let this nigger have some books by H. L. Mencken.*"[21] The librarian returns with Mencken's *A Book of Prefaces and Prejudices*. His reading of Mencken provides him with a formidable reading list: Anatole France, Joseph Conrad, Sinclair Lewis, Sherwood Anderson, Dostoevski, George Moore, Flaubert, Maupassant, Tolstoy, Frank Harris, Twain, Hardy, Crane, Zola, Norris, Gorky, Bergson, Ibsen, Shaw, Dumas, Poe, Mann, Dreiser, Eliot, Gide, Stendhal, and others. Wright starts reading many of the writers Mencken mentions. Moreover, the general effect of his reading was to make him more obsessive about it: "Reading grew into a passion.... Reading was like a drug, a dope."[22]

Mencken provides Wright with far more than a convenient reading list of some of the greater masters. He becomes an example to Wright—perhaps an idol—both in matters of style and vocational perspective or stance:

> I opened *A Book of Prefaces* and began to read. I was jarred and shocked by the style, the clear, clean, sweeping sentences. Why did he write like that? And how did one write like that? I pictured the man as a raging demon, slashing with his pen, consumed with hate, denouncing everything American, extolling everything European or German, laughing at the weaknesses of people, mocking God, authority. What was this? I stood up, trying to realize what reality lay behind the meaning of the words.... Yes, this man was fighting, fighting with words. He was using words as a weapon, using them as one would use a club. Could words be weapons? Well, yes, for here they were. Then, maybe, perhaps, I could use them as a weapon.[23]

A few months after reading Mencken, Wright finds the convenient opportunity to flee to the North. He closes *Black Boy* on an optimistic note.

American Hunger opens with Wright's arrival in Chicago and with the din of that windy city entering his consciousness, mocking his treasured fantasies. Wright had envisioned Chicago as a city of refuge. However, his first years are "long years of semi-starvation." He works as a dishwasher, part-time post office clerk, life insurance salesman, and laboratory custodian. Since none of these jobs lasts long, finding adequate food and shelter becomes extremely difficult. At one point, Wright shares a windowless rear room with his mother and younger brother. But good luck occasionally comes in the guise of ill. Many of the experiences he has while working odd jobs supplies revelations which subsequently form the core of his best fiction. Wright probably would not have written *Native Son* if he had not seen and felt Bigger Thomas's rage.

The first half of *American Hunger* is primarily devoted to a sociopsychological portrayal of Wright's life and work among the black and white poor. Wright shows how ignorance and racial discrimination fuel prejudice and self-hatred. He gives us glimpses of *les miserables*, who are corrupted, exploited, and destroyed. While working as an insurance salesman, Wright himself aids in the swindling of the black poor. Yet we are aware throughout that his is a form of predatory desperation. His is the hard choice between honesty and starvation.

Communists dominate the second half of *American Hunger*. As Wright tells his story, he has strong reservations about the party from the outset and gets involved indirectly. He becomes a member of the party primarily because he is a writer and he leaves it for the same reason. Lacking intellectual communion and meaningful social contacts, he joins Chicago's John Reed Club. The members enthusiastically welcome him, and he is immediately given a writing assignment for *Left Front*. After only two months and due to internal rivalry, Wright is elected Executive Secretary of the club. He humbly declines the nomination at first, but, after some insistent prodding, reluctantly accepts the position. thus, though not a Communist, he heads one of the party's leading cultural organizations. Given his independence of mind, however, he raises too many troubling questions for party, officials and they soon begin to wage a war against him. They try to harness his imagination and whip it down the official ideological path. But Wright is already at work on the stories of his first book, *Uncle Tom's Children*. He writes: "Must I discard my plot ideas and seek new ones? No. I could not. My writing was my way of seeing, my way of living, my way of feeling, and who could change his sight, his notion of direction, his senses?"[24]

Wright dwells rather tediously on the Communist party in the six brief chapters of *American Hunger*. However, he does devote limited space to the story of how he "managed to keep humanly alive through transfusions from books" and the story of how he learned his craft: "working nights I spent my days in experimental writing, filling endless pages with stream-of-consciousness Negro dialect, trying to depict the dwellers of the Black Belt as I felt and saw them."[25] And ever conscious of the need to refine his craft, Wright moved into other realms. He read Stein's *Three Lives*, Crane's *The Red Badge of Courage*, and Dostoevski's *The Possessed*. He strove to achieve the "dazzling magic" of Proust's prose in *A Remembrance of Things Past*: "I spent hours and days pounding out disconnected sentences for the sheer love of words.... I strove to master words, to make them disappear, to make them important by making them new, to make them melt into a rising spiral of emotional stimuli, each feeding and reinforcing the other, and all ending in an emotional climax that would drench the reader with a sense of a new world. That was the single aim of my living."[26] Finally Wright was able to redeem himself with words. They moved him from Mississippi to Chicago to New York and eventually made Paris his home town. Using words, he hurled himself at the boundary lines of his existence. Goethe's saying that "Man can find no better retreat from the world than art, and man can find no stronger link with the world than art" sums up the conundrum of Wright's life.

NOTES

"The Horror and the Glory: Richard Wright's Portrait of the Artist in *Black Boy* and *American Hunger* by Horace A. Porter. Printed by permission of the author.

1. Richard Wright, *American Hunger* (New York, 1977), 135. It is unfortunate that *American Hunger* is such a late arrival. Its chief value is that it brings together for the first time in book form the second half of Wright's original autobiography, most of which was published in essay form in the *Atlantic Monthly* (August and September 1944), in the anthology *Cross Section* (1945), and in the September 1945 issue of *Mademoiselle*. Therefore, *American Hunger* is hardly new and surely not a lost literary treasure and fortuitously blown into public view by heaven's four winds. In any case, whatever the reason for its belated, posthumous publication, it has been effectively robbed of its capacity to affect significantly the public's mind. For despite the power of *Black Boy* and *Native Son*, they are now part and parcel of a bygone era. For a thorough discussion of this matter, see Jerry W. Ward, "Richard Wright's Hunger," *Virginia Quarterly Review* (Winter, 1978), 148–153.

2. Richard Wright, *Black Boy* (New York, 1945), 4.

3. *Ibid.*, 4.

4. *Ibid.*, 5.

5. *Ibid.*, 5.

6. *Ibid.*, 10–11.

7. *Ibid.*, 30.

8. *Ibid.*, 34–31.

9. *Ibid.*, 11.

10. *Ibid.*, 87.
11. *Ibid.*, 87.
12. *Ibid.*, 1–17.
13. *Ibid.*, 22.
14. *Ibid.*, 34.
15. *Ibid.*, 36.
16. *Ibid.*, 134.
17. *Ibid.*, 134.
18. *Ibid.*, 135.
19. *Ibid.*, 146.
20. *Ibid.*, 148.
21. *Ibid.*, 216.
22. *Ibid.*, 218–19.
23. *Ibid.*, 218.
24. Richard Wright, *American Hunger* (New York, 1977), 93.
25. *Ibid.*, 24.
26. *Ibid.*, 25.

YOSHINOBU HAKUTANI

Creation of the Self in
Richard Wright's Black Boy

I

Black Boy is generally acclaimed not only as the finest autobiography written by a black author but as one of the greatest autobiographies ever written in America. Critics, however, are not in agreement on what kind of autobiography it is. W. E. B. Du Bois, for instance, wondered about the authenticity of the book, saying, "The [sub]title, 'A Record of Childhood and Youth,' makes one at first think that the story is autobiographical. It probably is, at least in part. But mainly it is probably intended to be fiction or fictionalized biography. At any rate the reader must regard it as creative writing rather than simply a record of life."[1] Yet even if one regards the book as a creative work rather than an actual record of life, and despite its felicities of language, *Black Boy*, Du Bois felt, falls short of its possible effectiveness because it is "so patently and terribly overdrawn."[2] Those who are not impressed by the book criticize the excessive emphasis on violence, meanness, and despair in Wright's work. Moreover, they are not convinced of the authenticity of *Black Boy* as an autobiography because they feel that the world, bad as it is, cannot be so bad as Wright says it is.

Even those who are convinced of its authenticity do not necessarily consider it a higher accomplishment than *Native Son*. When the book appeared, many distinguished writers became its advocates: Sinclair Lewis,

From *Black American Literature Forum* Vol. 19, No. 2 (Summer 1985). © 1985 African American Review.

William Faulkner, Gertrude Stein, Henry Miller, Ralph Ellison, Lionel Trilling. Among them Faulkner, who perhaps knew black life in the South as well as anyone, wrote to Wright that he was deeply moved by *Black Boy*, but commented that what is said in it is better said in *Native Son*. "The good lasting stuff," Faulkner wrote, "comes out of one individual's imagination and sensitivity to and comprehension of the sufferings of Everyman, Anyman, not out of the memory of his own grief."[3] This response by a fellow novelist suggests that *Black Boy* suffers as a work of art since Wright's method here is less impersonal than it is in a novel like *Native Son*. To Faulkner, art cannot be created when too much is made of one's own life; dealing with impersonal forces of nature and society in such a novel as *Native Son* requires a sense of detachment. For this reason Faulkner said, "I hope you will keep on saying it, but I hope you will say it as an artist, as in *Native Son*."[4]

Faulkner's evaluation is based on the assumption that *Black Boy* is an autobiography. But the narrator of the book takes such an impersonal attitude that the book as a whole may not sound like a usual autobiography. As Du Bois has noted, there is a genuine paucity of personal love or affection expressed toward Wright's mother in *Black Boy*.[5] The young Wright amply expresses his awe and wonder at his suffering mother: He is unable to understand the reason that she was deserted by her husband, broken by paralysis, and overwhelmed by every unimaginable circumstance she had to face. His reaction, as a narrator, is intellectual rather than personal. By contrast, in Theodore Dreiser's autobiography of his youth, *Dawn*, the narrator's wonder at his equally suffering mother is tinged with personal sorrow and sympathy. In short, Wright's intention in *Black Boy* seems to have been to portray his experience with naturalistic objectivity, rather than from a personal point of view.

A literary naturalist is expected to establish a milieu taken from life and, into it, project characters who then act in accordance with that milieu. The naturalist must record, without comment or interpretation, what actually happens. If Wright regarded himself as a fictional persona in *Black Boy*, he would be less concerned with either his own life or his own point of view. The focus of his interest in the book would be on the events that occurred outside of his life. It is understandable, then, that Wright's account of his own life would not be entirely authentic. One might even suspect that Wright's self-portrait would abound with fictional accounts, and, indeed, many differences between *Black Boy* and his life have been pointed out. One reviewer's objection to the book as autobiography is based on discrepancies found between Wright's accounts in the book and "The Ethics of Living Jim Crow."[6] For example, *Black Boy* describes a fight between Wright and a group of white boys in which he was injured behind the ear and later ushered to a doctor by his mother, whereas in his "Ethics of Living Jim Crow," Wright relates that "a kind neighbor saw me and rushed me to a doctor, who took three stitches in my neck." Also in *Black Boy* Wright often refers to his mother as a cook "in the white folks' kitchen" and describes her as less intellectual than she really was.[7] In fact, Ella Wilson, his mother, before her marriage to his father, was well educated for a black woman and taught school. Edwin R. Embree, who intimately knew Wright's youth and early literary career, testifies that "his mother, light brown, good looking, possessed of a few years of book learning, got jobs a few months as a teacher at $25.00 a month."[8]

These alterations, however, are not a major reason for calling *Black Boy* a fictionalized biography. Even though parts of the book are fictional, it is nevertheless autobiographical and should not be equated with a novel. No one for a moment can overlook the fact that it portrays Wright himself, and if it concerns others, their lives are necessarily intertwined with his. But the most important distinction *Black Boy* bears as autobiography is Wright's intention to use the young self as a mask. The attitudes and sentiments expressed by the young Wright are not totally his own but represent the responses of those he called "the voiceless Negro boys" of the South.[9] Such a technique makes *Black Boy* a unique autobiography just as a similar technique makes *Native Son* a unique novel (Wright tells us that Bigger Thomas is a conscious composite portrait of numerous individual blacks he has known in his life[10]).

II

The uniqueness of Wright's autobiography can be explained in another way. Since he is a spokesman for the voiceless black youths of the South he had known in his life, he must be objective and scientific in his observations. Thus *Black Boy*, though not intended as such, is a convincing sociological study. Like sociology, it not only analyzes a social problem but offers a solution to the problem it treats. Wright's purpose is to study the way in which black life in the South was determined by its environment, and, to borrow Zola's words, his desire is to "disengage the determinism of human and social phenomena so that we may one day control and direct these phenomena."[11] Wright is constantly trying to make his investigation systematic and unbiased. He is concerned with the specific social forces in the environment of a black boy: white racism, black society, and his own family.

James Baldwin has accused Wright of his belief that "in Negro life there exists no tradition, no field of manners, no possibility of ritual or intercourse, such as may, for example, sustain the Jew even after he has left his father's house."[12] Unlike Baldwin, who grew up in a highly religious black community in Harlem, Wright in the deep South witnessed "the essential bleakness of black life in America" (p. 33). The central issue, however, is whether such human traits as, in Wright's words, "tenderness, love, honor, loyalty, and the capacity to remember" are innate in the Negro tradition, as Baldwin says, or are "fostered, won, struggled and suffered for," as Wright believed (p. 33). Elsewhere Wright tells us that he "wrote the book to tell a series of incidents strung through my childhood, but the main desire was to render a judgment on my environment .... That judgment was this: the environment the South creates is too small to nourish human beings, especially Negro human beings."[13] Wright, therefore, squarely places the burden of proof upon white society, contending with enough justification given in *Black Boy* that the absence of these human qualities in black people stemmed from years of white oppression.

To Wright, the effect of white oppression in the South was most visible in the black communities of the Mississippi Delta. By the time he became fourteen he was able to read and write well enough to obtain a job, in which he assisted an illiterate black insurance salesman. On his daily rounds to the shacks and plantations in the area, he was appalled by the pervasiveness of segregated life: "I saw a bare, bleak pool of black life and I hated it; the people were alike, their homes were alike, and their farms were alike" (p. 120). Such observations later infuriated not only white segregationists but many black citizens, who wrote letters to the FBI and denounced *Black Boy*. Letters called him "a black Nazi" and "one of the biggest spreaders of race hatred." Another black protester complained: "I am an American Negro and proud of it because we colored people in America have come a long way in the last seventy years .... We colored people don't mind the truth but we do hate lies or anything that disturb[s] our peace of mind."[14]

What had, at first, disturbed Wright was not the failure of many blacks and whites alike to see the facts of racism, but their inability to recognize malice in the minds of white racists. *Black Boy* recounts an incident in which Wright was once wrongfully accused of addressing a white employee at an optical company without using the title "Mr." Another white employee later corroborated the accusation by telling Wright: "'Didn't you call him *Pease*? If you say you didn't, I'll rip your gut string loose with this f—k-g bar, you black granny dodger! You can't call a white man a liar and get away with it!'" (p. 166). Consequently Wright was forced to leave his job. Resenting a black man's obtaining what they considered a white man's occupation, these white men deliberately created a falsehood to deny Wright a livelihood.

In retrospect, however, Wright realizes that such grudges as white men held against black men did not seem to derive from the white men themselves. He theorizes that they were not acting as individual men, but as "part of a huge, implacable, elemental design toward which hate was futile" (p. 170). Wright's autobiography does not for one moment concern itself with the theme of evil, as romantic fiction or tragic drama sometimes does.[15] *Black Boy* is intended as a sociological document rather than a novel; what such a document shows is the fact that the oppressors are as much victims of the elemental design of racism as are the oppressed. The center of Wright's interest, then, rests on deciphering this design.

In *Black Boy* Wright is continually at pains to show that white people have a preconceived notion of a Negro's place in the South: He serves them, he is likely to steal, and he cannot read or write. The tabooed subjects that Southerners refused to discuss with black men included "American white women; the Ku Klux Klan; France, and how Negro soldiers fared while there; Frenchwomen; Jack Johnson; the entire northern part of the United States; the Civil War; Abraham Lincoln; U. S. Grant; General Sherman; Catholics; the Pope; Jews; the Republican Party; slavery; social equality; Communism; Socialism; the 13th, 14th, and 15th Amendments of the Constitution" (p. 202). Sex and religion were the most accepted subjects, for they were the topics that did not require positive knowledge or self-assertion on the part of the black man. White men did not mind black men's talking about sex as long as it was not interracial. Sex was considered purely biological, and like religion it would not call for the will power of an individual. Although blacks were physically free, the South had replaced traditional slavery with a system by which their freedom of speech and movement was closely monitored and restricted. The culprit was not any individual white man; it was the complicity of white society that had allowed the design of slavery to renew itself in the twentieth-century South.

What underlies this new design of slavery? Most significantly, black men are classified as animals, a mentality inherited from the old days of slavery. Not only are black people considered to be white men's servants, but they are expected to entertain them as though blacks were animals in the zoo. Crimes perpetrated on fellow blacks are not condemned as such. Wright cites an incident in which his foreman at a company he worked for instigated antagonism between Wright and a black employee at another company so that they would try to stab each other. Wright, avoiding the trap, agreed instead to fight a boxing match to satisfy the white employees' whim. "'I suppose,'" Wright reasoned, "'it's fun for white men to see niggers fight.... To white men we're like dogs or cocks'" (pp. 207–208). Even killing among black men would not prick the white men's consciences. Such an attitude echoes that of the white public at the trial of Bigger Thomas for the murder of Bessie Mears, his black girlfriend, in *Native Son*.

Another degrading assumption white men hold about black men is that, since they are treated as animals, they are not supposed to possess intellectual capabilities. The reason for the young Wright's losing employment is often related to his intelligence, which poses a threat to the white man's sense of superiority. Wright points out, for instance, that some black men tried to organize themselves and petitioned their white employers for higher wages and better working conditions. But he correctly observes that such a movement was swiftly avenged by further restrictions and brutality. Throughout the book Wright continues to demonstrate the fact that Southern whites would rather have blacks who stole goods and property than blacks who were conscious, however vaguely, of the worth of their own intelligence and humanity. For Wright, racism induces black deceit and encourages black irresponsibility. Ironically, blacks are rewarded in the degree that they can make the whites feel safe and maintain their moral superiority.

Needless to say, the forces of racism have devastating effects on black life. Critics, both black and white, have complained that Wright in *Black Boy* lacks racial pride. It is true that he is critical of the black community in the South, but it is not true that he places the blame on the black community itself. His intention is to show that a racist system produced the way of life that was forced on black people. In terms of social determinism, *Black Boy* provides a literary experiment to demonstrate uniformity in Negro behavior under the influence of social forces.[16]

Most black people, he admits, do adjust to their environment for survival. But in doing so they lose individuality, self-respect, and dignity. This is perhaps the reason that Benjamin Davis, Jr., a black leftist critic, attacked Wright's portrayal of the Southern black community: "*Black Boy* says some wholly unacceptable things about the Negro's capacity for genuine emotion."[17] To Wright, however, it is the circumstances in which Negroes find themselves that cause the personalities to warp, and this in turn results in various forms of hypocritical and erratic behavior. The most striking example of this appears in an incident with an elevator boy the young Wright encountered in Memphis. The black boy, who professed that "he was proud of his race and indignant about its wrongs," never hesitated to expose his buttocks for a white man to kick so he could solicit a quarter from the white man. Wright tells us he felt "no anger or hatred, only disgust and loathing," and that he confronted this youth:

"How in God's name can you do that?"

"I needed a quarter and I got it," he said soberly, proudly.

"But a quarter can't pay you for what he did to you," I said.

"Listen, nigger," he said to me, "my ass is tough and quarters is scarce." (p. 200)

About white men's sexual exploitation of black women, Wright is as much critical of black women as of white men, because black women expect and readily condone white men's behavior. Once a black maid who had been slapped playfully on her buttocks by a white nightwatchman told the indignant Wright who had witnessed the incident: "'They never get any further with us than that, if we don't want 'em to'" (p. 174).

Understandably such portraits of black men and women made some readers feel that Wright unduly deprived black people of their personal honor and dignity. For Ralph Ellison, Wright's autobiography lacks "high humanity," especially among its blacks. As Dan McCall correctly argues, however, "Wright is trying to show us how this gross state came about. He refuses to dress up his Negroes in an imported Sunday best because he has a far larger task before him."[18] Wright explains:

I began to marvel at how smoothly the black buys acted out the roles that the white race had mapped out for them. Most of them were not conscious of living a special, separated, stunted way of life. Yet I knew that in some period of their growing up—a period that they had no doubt forgotten—there had been developed in them a delicate, sensitive controlling mechanism that shut off their mind and emotions from all that the white race had said was taboo. (p. 172)

One of the remarkable insights *Black Boy* offers is that social determinism takes its heaviest toll in Wright's family life. One would assume that if black boys are mistreated in society at large, they would at least be protected in their family. But in Wright's early childhood his father deserted his wife and children; not only did Wright become a casualty of the broken family, but his father himself was a victim of the racial system in the deep South. Wright observes about his father: "From the white landowners above him there had not been handed to him a chance to learn the meaning of loyalty, of sentiment, of tradition" (p. 30).

Consequently, the young Wright was subjected to the crushing blow of family antagonisms.[19] His grandmother's Seventh-Day-Adventist doctrine as practiced at home epitomizes this hostility and strife. Wright saw "more violent quarrels in our deeply religious home than in the home of a gangster, burglar, or a prostitute .... The naked will to power seemed always to walk in the wake of a hymn" (p. 119). While Granny held on to the helm of the family, several of Wright's uncles also attempted to administer their authority. One of them, enraged by Wright's impolite mannerisms, scolded his nephew for not acting as "the backward black boys act on the plantations"; he was ordered "to grin, hang my head, and mumble apologetically when I was spoken to" (p. 138). It seems as though black adults, subjected to racism in white society, in turn felt compelled to rule their children at home. The black adults had grown up in the world in which they were permitted no missteps in a white-dominated society. The fact that Wright's worst punishments, such as those he has given by his mother for setting fire to his grandmother's house, were inflicted by his closest relatives suggests how completely black life was dominated by white racism.

III

Despite the naturalistic philosophy that underlies Wright's vision of black life, the miracle of *Black Boy* is that its hero, by the time he left for Chicago, had not become the patient, humorous, subservient black man of the white myth. Nor did he end up as either the degraded, grinning, and perpetually frustrated Negro or a murderer like Bigger Thomas of *Native Son*. Throughout the book Wright is at great pains to create a manhood as a direct challenge to the overwhelming forces of society. *Black Boy* reveals how self-creation can be thwarted and mauled, but unlike James Farrell's *Studs Lonigan* or Dreiser's *An American Tragedy*, the hero's spirit remains unbroken. Most importantly, however, what distinguishes *Black Boy* from any other naturalistic work is that it is the story of a man estranged from his own race by sensitivity and intellect, yet segregated from the white race by the color of his skin.

Finding himself in no-man's-land, the young Wright attempted to create his own world. Although *Black Boy* is predominantly a portrayal of Southern society, it is also a self-portrait. Despite the devastating effects of the society upon his own life, he came to the conclusion that anything was "possible, likely, feasible, because I wanted everything to be possible" (p. 64). Early in the book he rationalizes this passion for ego: "Because I had no power to make things happen outside of me in the objective world, I made things happen within. Because my environment was bare and bleak, I endowed it with unlimited potentialities, redeemed it for the sake of my own hungry and cloudy yearning" (p. 64).

About this process of self-creation, critics have charged that he deliberately degrades black life to dramatize the emergence of the self as a hero.[20] But given his life as we know it today, one can scarcely deny the authenticity of the events recounted in the book, nor are the episodes about racism unbelievable or unconvincing. Although Du Bois argues that "the suffering of others is put down simply as a measure of his own suffering and resentment,"[21] it is understandable that Wright did so in order to make his own life representative of the voiceless black boys, as well as to indicate that they too are capable of self-creation.

Whether or not our hero is too selfish and proud an achiever to be credible can be judged by how convincingly his maturation is portrayed. In his early childhood Wright acquired a hatred for white people, not based on his own experience, but derived from other Negro children. Like any child, black or white, Wright had his vision circumscribed by blinders and colored glasses. As he grew older, however, he realized that the roots of racial hatred did not exist in any individuals, but stemmed from an inherited system. The white race was as much its victim as the black race. From this vantage point, he took social determinism to be a threat to his autonomy and began to wage a battle. By the time he was nineteen, he became aware that his life experiences "had shaped me to live by my own feelings and thoughts" (p. 221).

It was the crushing effects of environment and temperament that Wright learned so well from his immediate relatives. When he was a young boy, one of his uncles was murdered by his white business competitors; his grandmother was a religious fanatic. The greatest blow to his childhood came from his own father, who succumbed to the temptation of sex and alcohol. When he saw his father again a quarter of a century later, he realized that, "though ties of blood made us kin, though I could see a shadow of my face in his face, though there was an echo of my voice in his voice, we were forever strangers, speaking a different language, living on vastly distant planes of reality" (p. 30). Not only is Wright denying the influence of heredity on his own character, but he is distinguishing two men subjected to the same environment. His father, Wright concludes, "was a black peasant who had gone to the city seeking life, but ... whose life had been hopelessly snarled in the city, and who had at last fled the city—that same city which had lifted me in its burning arms and borne me toward alien and undreamed—of shores of knowing" (p. 31).

What, then, were the forces in his life that young Wright had learned to ward off in his struggle for independence? Throughout his youth he witnessed how deeply superstitious religion had trapped the minds and hearts of black people. As a child he was impressed with the elders at church for the inspiring language of their sermons: "a gospel clogged with images of vast lakes of eternal fire, of seas vanishing, of valleys of dry bones, ... of the lame walking; a salvation that teemed with fantastic beasts having multiple heads and horns and eyes and feet" (p. 89). But such sensations departed quickly once he left the church and saw the bright sunshine with the crowded people pouring into the streets. To him none of these religious ideas and images seemed to have anything to do with his life. He knew not only that religion had a capacity to mesmerize people in the black community, but also that it was used by "one individual or group to rule another in the name of God" (p. 119).

As some critics have noted, *Black Boy* is relatively free from the hero's references to his own sexual awakening.[22] Sex in *Black Boy* is treated much like religion, for Wright knew during his adolescent years that one could be easily victimized by sexual forces. The only time sexual attraction is mentioned is in connection with a church service in which Wright, at twelve, was infatuated with the elder's wife. The fact that the woman is depicted in grotesquely physical terms rather than spiritual and felicitous images ("a black imp with two horns; ... a scaly, naked body; wet, sticky fingers; moist, sensual lips; and lascivious eyes") suggests that he is indeed debasing his sexual attraction (p. 98). That he could easily fend off such biological forces can be contrasted with Fishbelly Tucker's unsuccessful struggle with his sexual problems in *The Long Dream*. In that novel, sex is dealt with in its sordid context; the hero's ritual of initiation into manhood is performed in a house of prostitution.

Although *Black Boy* is strung with a series of episodes that illustrates various forms of racial oppression, the center of attention lies in our hero's transcendence of that oppression. Racial oppression is caused not only by the external forces of society but by the internal problems of the oppressed. "Some," Wright admits, "may escape the general plight and grow up, but it is a matter of luck."[23] To the hero of *Black Boy*, most of them were victims of racial prejudice, failures in the battle for survival. No small wonder an anonymous reviewer, calling *Black Boy* "the most ferocious exercise in misanthropy since Jonathan Swift," was appalled by the hatred Wright expresses toward both whites and blacks.[24] Obviously, the reader misunderstood Wright's intention, for the book is not meant to be a satire like *Gulliver's Travels*, in which the narrator assails and loathes every conceivable human vice and depravity. Rather, *Black Boy* is Wright's honest attempt to refute a naturalistic philosophy of life. Our hero is a catalyst in accomplishing this task.

In "Blueprint for Negro Writing," Wright asserts that "theme for Negro writers will rise from understanding the meaning of their being transplanted from a 'savage' to a 'civilized' culture in all its social, political, economic, and emotional implications."[25] In *Black Boy*, his chief aim is to show how this youth, whom the South called a "nigger," surmounted his obstacles in the civilized culture. The most painful stance he took in this struggle was to be an intense individualist; he created selfhood and exerted his will at the risk of annihilation. In scene after scene both the black and the white community kept piling crushing circumstances upon him, but no matter how unbearably they were pressed down on him, he refused to give in. Only under such pressure can one discover one's self. For others, this process of creation might have been aided by chance, but for him "it should be a matter of plan." And himself an exemplar, Wright defined the mission as "a matter of saving the citizens of our country for our country."[26]

One could be puzzled by this youth's individuality and fortitude if the seed of manhood had not been sown in the child. Despite a critic's disclaimer to the contrary, *Black Boy* contains ample evidence for the child's precocity and independence.[27] Wright's earlier self is presented even to the point of betraying his vanity: When he moved to his grandmother's house after his family was deserted by his father, he took pride in telling the timid children of the new neighborhood about his train ride, his cruise on the *Kate Adams* on the Mississippi River, and his escape from the orphanage (p. 33). Moreover, the young child is presented as a rebel who refuses to compromise with the dictates of society and family. Once he was dismayed to find out that the man who had beaten a black boy was not the boy's father. Though Wright was told by his mother that he was "'too young to understand,'" he responded with a resolution: "'I'm not going to let anybody beat me'" (p. 21). This youthful attitude gave rise to an even more awesome resolution, of which he later became capable when he heard the story of a black woman who had avenged her husband's murder. According to the rumor, when she was granted permission to claim her husband's body for burial, she took with her a shotgun wrapped in a white sheet and, while kneeling down before the white executioners, shot four of them—a tale that served as the exact prototype of "Bright and Morning Star." *Black Boy* records the young Wright's belligerency:

> I resolved that I would emulate the black woman if I were ever faced with a white mob; I would conceal a weapon, pretend that I had been crushed by the wrong done to one of my loved ones; then, just when they thought I had accepted their cruelty as the law of my life, I would let go with my gun and kill as many of them as possible before they killed me. The story of the woman's deception gave form and meaning to confused defensive feelings that had long been sleeping in me. (p. 65)

Becoming a rebel inevitably led to being a misfit. In Wright's life, however, it is his innate character that allowed this to happen. How self-assertive the young Wright was can be best demonstrated in a comparison between him and his playmates. Although he identified himself with a mistreated group, there was a crucial difference between him and other black children. They constantly complained about the petty wrongs they suffered, but they had no desire to question the larger issues of racial oppression. Their attitude resembles that of the young Fishbelly in *The Long Dream*; just like his father before him, Fishbelly servilely worships the powerful white people. He falls in love with the values of the white world because such demeanor can offer him material rewards and make his manhood easier and less painful to achieve. The young Wright, on the other hand, found among the black boys no sympathy for his inquiring mind. As a result he was forced to contemplate such questions for himself.

As early as twelve years old, Wright held "a sense of the world that was mine and mine alone, a notion as to what life meant that no education could ever alter, a conviction that the meaning of living came only when one was struggling to wring a meaning out of meaningless suffering" (pp. 87–88). His decision to leave the South seven years later, the final action of our hero, was based upon such conviction, as if the seed of manhood had already been in the child. Without mental companionship to rely on, however, he withdrew and turned inward like the anti-hero of an existentialist novel. In his recoil he had once again discovered that the revelation of all truths must come through the action and anguish of the self. It was at this point in his ordeal that he came in contact with the works of American realists such as H. L. Mencken, Theodore Dreiser, and Sherwood Anderson. It was their ideas, he tells us, that literally delivered his brooding sensibility to a brighter horizon, a vision that ... America could be shaped nearer to the hearts of those who lived in it" (p. 227). It was also at this time that he decided to head North to discover for himself that man could live with dignity and determine his own destiny. Because he knew he could not make the world, he sought to make things happen within him and caught a sense of freedom; in so doing he discovered the new world.

NOTES

1. "Richard Wright Looks Back," *New York Herald Tribune Book Review*, 4 Mar. 1945, p. 2.

2. *Ibid.*

3. "Letter to Richard Wright," in *Richard Wright: Impressions and Perspectives*, ed. David Ray and Robert M. Farnsworth (Ann Arbor: Univ. of Michigan Press, 1973), p. 143.

4. *Ibid.*

5. Richard Wright Looks Back," p. 2.

6. See Beatrice M. Murphy, *Pulse*, 3 (Apr. 1945), 32–33.

7. Richard Wright, *Black Boy: A Record of Childhood and Youth* (New York: Harper & Brothers, 1945), p. 17. Later references are to this edition and indicated in parentheses.

8. See "Richard Wright: Native Son," in *13 Against the Odds* (New York: Viking, 1944), pp. 25–26.

9. See "The Handiest Truth to Me to Plow Up Was in My Own Life," *P.M. Magazine*, 4 Apr. 1945, p. 3.

10. "How 'Bigger' Was Born," in *Native Son* (1940; rpt. New York: Harper & Row, 1966), p. xii.

11. "The Experimental Novel," in *Documents of Modern Literary Realism*, ed. George J. Becker (Princeton: Princeton Univ. Press, 1963), p. 181.

12. *Notes of a Native Son* (1955; rpt. New York: Bantam Books, 1968), 28.

13. "The Handiest Truth," p. 3.

14. See Addison Gayle, *Richard Wright: Ordeal of a Native Son* (Garden City, NY: Anchor Press/ Doubleday, 1980), pp. 173–74. According to Gayle, Senator Bilbo of Mississippi condemned *Black Boy* on the floor of the U.S. Senate on June 7, 1945, as "the dirtiest, filthiest, lousiest, most obscene piece of writing that I have ever seen in print ... it is so filthy and dirty.... it comes from a Negro, and you cannot expect any better from a person of his type" (p. 173).

15. In general I agree with Dan McCall, who says: "Wright knew that all the evil could not be laid to a man. He refused to create a 'white villain.' ... In *Black Boy* we see no villains; we do not even see a series of villains. We see men utterly helpless; varieties of foulness, stunted minds" (*The Example of Richard Wright* [New York: Harcourt, 1969], p. 128).

16. Edward Margolies observes: "Wright traps the reader in a stereotyped response— the same stereotyped response that Wright is fighting throughout the book: that is, that all Negroes are alike and react alike" (*The Art of Richard Wright* [Carbondale: Southern Illinois Univ. Press, 1969], p. 19).

17. "Some Impressions of *Black Boy*," *Daily Worker*, 1 Apr. 1945, p. 9.

18. *The Example of Richard Wright*, pp. 118–19.

19. Black Boy as autobiography can be closely compared with Angelo Herndon's *Let Me Live* (1937). Both writers depict the forces of segregation that had devastating effects on their educations and job opportunities. Both describe poverty and hunger in the plights of their families. But, while Wright grew up without his father and with his bedridden mother and hostile relatives, Herndon could rely on the traditional family loyalty—a father with trust and confidence in his son and a warmhearted, loving mother.

20. W. E. B. Du Bois writes: "After this sordid, shadowy picture we gradually come upon the solution. The hero is interested in himself, is self-centered to the exclusion of everybody and everything else" ("Richard Wright Looks Back," p. 2). John M. Reilly also argues that Wright "will not risk telling experiences inconsistent in any way with his image of himself as an alienated peasant youth in rebellion against the hostile Southern caste system .... Wright suppresses his connections with the bourgeoisie. Had he mentioned these connections, Wright might have modified the picture of a bleak and hostile environment, but there is no question of falsification" ("Self-Portraits by Richard Wright," *Colorado Quarterly*, 22 [Summer 1971], 34).

21. "Richard Wright Looks Back," p. 2.

22. Edward Margolies considers sex in *Black Boy* in terms of "violence (the dangers inherent in relationships with white prostitutes); bravado (adolescent boys speaking of their prowess); adultery (his father's abandonment of his wife for another woman); obscenities (which Wright learned at the age of six); or condescension and rejection

(Wright's fending off the daughter of his landlady in Memphis because she was incapable of understanding the depths of his sensibilities)" (*The Art of Richard Wright*, pp. 17–18). Katherine Fishburn maintains that *The Long Dream* has more detail and a much more thorough treatment of a young black's sexual maturation than *Black Boy* (*Richard Wright's Hero: The Faces of a Rebel-Victim* [Metuchen, NJ: Scarecrow, 1977], p. 14).

23. "The Handiest Truth," p. 3.

24. *Newark Evening News*, 17 Mar. 1945.

25. In *Richard Wright Reader*, ed. Ellen Wright and Michel Fabre (New York; Harper & Row, 1978), p. 47.

26. "The Handiest Truth," p. 3.

27. Reviewer F. K. Richter observed that *Black Boy* is an unconscious demonstration of Aristotle's entelechy, that manhood resides in childhood. But he maintains that because Wright fails to provide indispensable factors that made the child grow, "the book loses some of its value as autobiography and non-fiction and takes on, however slightly, a quality of fiction" (*Negro Story*, 1 [May–June 1945], 93–95).

KENETH KINNAMON

Call and Response:
Intertextuality in Two Autobiographical Works
by Richard Wright and Maya Angelou

In his provocative account of Afro-American literary criticism from the 1940s to the present, Houston A. Baker, Jr., traces three stages of development: integrationism, the "Black Aesthetic," and the "Reconstruction of Instruction." As his major representative of the first stage, "the dominant critical perspective on Afro-American literature during the late 1950s and early 1960s," Baker makes a strange choice—Richard Wright, in the 1957 version of "The Literature of the Negro in the United States." According to Baker, Wright, sanguine because of the Supreme Court school desegregation decision of 1954, believed that the leveling of racial barriers in American society would lead to a homogenous American literature in which minority writers would be absorbed into the mainstream of cultural expression. Even the verbal and musical folk forms of the black masses would eventually disappear with the inevitable triumph of democratic pluralism in the social order.[1] Actually, Wright's essay is not basically an optimistic statement of integrationist poetics. It is, rather, a document in the proletarian-protest stage of Afro-American literature and literary criticism that dominated the Thirties and Forties, constituting the stage immediately preceding Baker's first stage.[2] The proletarian-protest stage anticipates elements of all three of Baker's stages. Like the integrationist stage it postulates a fundamental unity of human experience transcending racial and

From *Studies in Black American Literature: Belief vs. Theory in Black American Literary Criticism*, Joe Weixlmann and Chester J. Fontenot, ed. © 1986 Keneth Kinnamon.

national (but not economic) boundaries. Its commitment to an engaged literature is as fierce as that of the Black Aestheticians. And in "Blueprint for Negro Writing,"[3] at least, it advocates a sophisticated modern literary sensibility, as does the Stepto-Gates school. What it does not do is examine the special perspective of black women writers, a failing shared by the following three stages. This deficiency seems particularly conspicuous now that good women writers are so abundant and female critics are beginning to assess their achievement in relation to the total Afro-American literary tradition.

Despite its unfortunate effort at social disengagement, to my mind the most illuminating effort to provide a theoretical framework for the interpretation of Afro-American literature is Robert B. Stepto's *From Behind the Veil: A Study of Afro-American Narrative* (Urbana: University of Illinois Press, 1979). In this seminal work Stepto argues that the central myth of black culture in America is "the quest for freedom and literacy." Shaped by the historical circumstances of slavery and enforced illiteracy, this myth exists in the culture prior to any literary expression of it. Once this "pregeneric myth" is consciously articulated, it begins to take generic shape, especially as autobiography or fiction. The resulting narrative texts interact with each other in complex ways that constitute a specifically Afro-American literary tradition and history. In his book Stepto explores this intertextual tradition, dividing it into what he designates "The Call" and "The Response." In "The Call," he treats four slave narratives (by Bibb, Northup, Douglass, and Brown), *Up From Slavery*, and *The Souls of Black Folk*. To this call he discusses the twentieth century response of *The Autobiography of an Ex-Coloured Man*, *Black Boy*, and *Invisible Man*. All would agree that, of these nine works, those by Douglass, Washington, Du Bois, Johnson, Wright, and Ellison are classics of Afro-American literature, but notice that all of these authors are not only men, but race men, spokesmen, political activists. By way of complementing Stepto's somewhat narrow if sharp focus, I propose here to examine some intertextual elements in *Black Boy* and *I Know Why the Caged Bird Sings* to ascertain how gender may affect genre in these two autobiographical quests for freedom and literacy and, in Angelou's case, community as well.

In many ways these two accounts of mainly Southern childhoods are strikingly similar. Both narratives cover a period of fourteen years from earliest childhood memories to late adolescence: 1913 to 1927 (age four to eighteen) in Wright's case, 1931 to 1945 (age three to seventeen) in Angelou's case. Both Wright and Marguerite Johnson (Angelou's given name) are products of broken homes, children passed back and forth among parents and other relatives. Both have unpleasant confrontations with their fathers' mistresses. Both spend part of their childhoods in urban ghettoes (Memphis and St. Louis) as well as Southern small towns. Both suffer physical mistreatment by relatives. Both are humiliated by white employers. Lethal white violence comes close to both while they are living in Arkansas. Each child is subjected by a domineering grandmother to rigorous religious indoctrination, but each maintains a skeptical independence of spirit. From the trauma or tedium of their surroundings, both turn to reading as an escape. Both excel in school, Wright graduating as valedictorian from the eighth grade of Smith-Robinson School in Jackson, Mississippi, and Johnson as salutatorian of Lafayette County Training School in Stamps, Arkansas, fifteen years later.

In addition to these general similarities, some highly specific resemblances suggest more than mere coincidence or common cultural background. In *Black Boy* Wright recalls an incident in Memphis involving a preacher invited to Sunday dinner, the main course being "a huge platter of golden-brown fried chicken." Before the boy can finish his soup the preacher is picking out "choice pieces": "My growing hate of the preacher finally became more important than God or religion and I could no longer contain myself. I leaped up from the table, knowing that I should be ashamed of what I was doing, but unable to stop, and screamed, running blindly from the room. 'That preacher's going to eat *all* the chicken!' I bawled."[4] The gluttonous preacher's counterpart in *I Know Why the Caged Bird Sings* is Reverend Howard Thomas, whose "crime that tipped the scale and made our hate not only just but imperative was his actions at the dinner table. He ate the biggest, brownest and best parts of the chicken at every Sunday meal."[5] Wright's literary imagination was first kindled by the story of Bluebeard. As a child Angelou also learned of Bluebeard. A later common literary interest was Horatio Alger, who nurtured Wright's dreams of opportunities denied in the South. To Marguerite Johnson, however, Alger was a reminder that one of her dreams would be permanently deferred: "I read more than ever, and wished my soul that I had been born a boy. Horatio Alger was the greatest writer in the world. His heroes were always good, always won, and were always boys. I could have developed the first two virtues, but becoming a boy was sure to be difficult, if not impossible" (p. 74). One is tempted to think that Angelou had Wright specifically in mind in this passage, but even if she did not, her text provides an instructive gloss on Wright's, pointing out that sexism as well as racism circumscribes opportunity.

Other parallel passages provide additional intertextual clues to a basic difference in perspective on childhood experiences. One of the numerous relatives with whom young Richard could not get along was Aunt Addie, his teacher in a Seventh-Day Adventist school in Jackson. After a bitter confrontation in which the twelve-year-old boy threatens his aunt with a knife, she finds occasion for revenge:

> I continued at the church school, despite Aunt Addie's never calling upon me to recite or go to the blackboard. Consequently I stopped studying. I spent my time playing with the boys and found that the only games they knew were brutal ones. Baseball, marbles, boxing, running were tabooed recreations, the Devil's work; instead they played a wildcat game called popping-the-whip, a seemingly innocent diversion whose excitement came only in spurts, but spurts that could hurl one to the edge of death itself. Whenever we were discovered standing idle on the school grounds, Aunt Addie would suggest that we pop-the-whip. It would have been safer for our bodies and saner for our souls had she urged us to shoot craps.
>
> One day at noon Aunt Addie ordered us to pop-the-whip. I had never played the game before and I fell in with good faith. We formed a long line, each boy taking hold of another boy's hand until we were stretched out like a long string of human beads. Although I did not know it, I was on the tip end of the human whip. The leading boy, the handle of the whip, started off at a trot, weaving to the left and to the right, increasing speed until the whip of flesh was curving at breakneck gallop. I clutched the hand of the boy next to me with all the strength I had, sensing that if I did not hold on I would be tossed off. The whip grew taut as human flesh and bone could bear and I felt that my arm was being torn from its socket. Suddenly my breath left me. I was swung in a small, sharp arc. The whip was now being popped and I could hold on no more; the momentum of the whip flung me off my feet into the air, like a bit of leather being flicked off a horsewhip, and I hurtled headlong through space and landed in a ditch. I rolled over, stunned, head bruised and bleeding. Aunt Addie was laughing, the first and only time I ever saw her laugh on God's holy ground. (pp. 96–97)

In Stamps pop-the-whip was considerably less dangerous: "And when he [Maya's brother Bailey] was on the tail of the pop the whip, he would twirl off the end like a top, spinning, falling, laughing, finally stopping just before my heart beat its last, and then he was back in the game, still laughing" (p. 23). Now pop-the-whip is not among the gentlest of childhood activities, but surely it is less potentially deadly than Wright makes it out, surely it is closer to Angelou's exciting but essentially joyous pastime. With his unremittingly bleak view of black community in the South, Wright presents the game as sadistic punishment inflicted by a hateful aunt. In Angelou's corrective it becomes a ritual of ebullient youthful bravado by her "pretty Black brother" who was also her "unshakable God" and her "Kingdom Come" (p. 23).

Another pair of passages shows the same difference. Both Wright's Grandmother Wilson and Johnson's Grandmother Henderson ranked cleanliness close to godliness. On one occasion Wright remembers his grandmother bathing him:

> I went to her, walking sheepishly and nakedly across the floor. She snatched the towel from my hand and began to scrub my ears, my face, my neck.
> "Bend over," she ordered.
> I stooped and she scrubbed my anus. My mind was in a sort of daze, midway between daydreaming and thinking. Then, before I knew it, words—words whose meaning I did not fully know— had slipped out of my mouth.
> "When you get through, kiss back there," I said, the words rolling softly but unpremeditatedly. (p. 36)

Naturally the response to this call is a severe beating. Angelou treats a similar situation with humor:

> "Thou shall not be dirty" and "Thou shall not be impudent" were the two commandments of Grandmother Henderson upon which hung our total salvation.
> Each night in the bitterest winter we were forced to wash faces, arms, necks, legs and feet before going to bed. She used to add, with a smirk that unprofane people can't control when venturing into profanity, "and wash as far as possible, then wash possible." (p. 26)

No children like to scrub or be scrubbed, but Wright uses the occasion to dramatize hostility between himself and his family, while Angelou's purpose is to portray cleanliness as a bonding ritual in black culture: "Everyone I knew respected these customary laws, except for the powhitetrash children" (p. 27).

In *Black Boy* the autobiographical persona defines himself *against* his environment, as much against his family and the surrounding black culture as against the overt hostility of white racism. Like the fictional persona

Bigger Thomas, the protagonist of *Black Boy* is an archetypal rebel who rejects all social norms. In the opening scene he sets his family's house on fire, eliciting a traumatically severe whipping from his mother. His father "was always a stranger to me, always alien and remote" (p. 9). Young Richard subverts his paternal authority by a disingenuous literalism in the cat-killing episode. At the end of the first chapter he recalls his last meeting with his father in 1940, providing an exaggerated geriatric description complete with toothless mouth, white hair, bent body, glazed eyes, gnarled hands.[6] His father was a brutalized "black peasant," "a creature of the earth" without loyalty, sentiment, tradition, joy, or despair—all in contrast to his son, who lives "on a vastly different plane of reality," who speaks a different language, and who has traveled to "undreamed-of shores of knowing" (pp. 30, 31). Wright's symbolic effort to bury his father corresponds to a persistent attempt to come into his own by opposing or ignoring all members of his family, who consistently try to stifle his articulation of his individuality, to inhibit his quest for freedom. Shouting joyously at the sight of a free-flying bird outside his window, Richard is rebuked in the opening scene by his younger brother with the words "'You better hush.'" His mother immediately steps in to reinforce the message: "'You stop that yelling, you hear?'" (p. 3). These are the first words spoken to Richard in *Black Boy*, but they reverberate in other mouths throughout the work. His brother plays an exceedingly minor role before being sent to Detroit to live with an aunt. His mother is presented more sympathetically than are other members of the family, but even she functions as a harsh disciplinarian striving to suppress her son's dangerous individualism. His grandmother and other relatives join this effort, leading often to violent arguments in which Richard threatens them with knife or razor blade.

Outside the family the boy's relations to other black children are marked by fights on the street and in the schoolyard described with the same hyperbolic violence employed in the pop-the-whip episode. In the classroom he has to struggle against a paralyzing shyness that renders him almost mute and unable to write his own name: "I sat with my ears and neck burning, hearing the pupils whisper about me, hating myself, hating them; I sat still as stone and a storm of emotion surged through me" (p. 67). In describing his contacts with the general black community Wright emphasizes brutalization and degradation, as in his account of saloons in Memphis or in this paragraph on life in West Helena:

> We rented one half of a double corner house in front of which ran a stagnant ditch carrying sewage. The neighborhood swarmed with rats, cats, dogs, fortunetellers, cripples, blind men,

whores, salesmen, rent collectors, and children. In front of our flat was a huge roundhouse where locomotives were cleaned and repaired. There was an eternal hissing of steam, the deep grunting of steel engines, and the tolling of bells. Smoke obscured the vision and cinders drifted into the house, into our beds, into our kitchen, into our food; and a tar-like smell was always in the air. (p. 52)

Richard learns about sex voyeuristically by peeping at the whores at work in the other half of the duplex in the Arkansas town, as he had earlier watched the exposed rears of privies in Memphis. When he does manage to establish some degree of rapport with other boys, "the touchstone of fraternity was my feeling toward white people, how much hostility I held toward them, what degrees of value and honor I assigned to race" (p. 68). But as the reader of "Big Boy Leaves Home," *The Long Dream*, or biographies of Wright knows, in *Black Boy* the author minimizes the important role his friendship with peers actually played in his adolescent life. Religion is also rejected, whether the peripheral Seventh-Day Adventism of his grandmother or the mainstream black Methodism of his mother. So estranged and isolated from the nurturing matrices of black culture, an estrangement as much willed from within as imposed from without, Wright was able to utter this famous indictment:

(After I had outlived the shocks of childhood, after the habit of reflection had been born in me, I used to mull over the strange absence of real kindness in Negroes, how unstable was our tenderness, how lacking in genuine passion we were, how void of great hope, how timid our joy, how bare our traditions, how hollow our memories, how lacking we were in those intangible sentiments that bind man to man, and how shallow was even our despair. After I had learned other ways of life I used to brood upon the unconscious irony of those who felt that Negroes led so passional an existence! I saw that what had been taken for our emotional strength was our negative confusions, our flights, our fears, our frenzy under pressure.

(Whenever I thought of the essential bleakness of black life in America, I knew that Negroes had never been allowed to catch the full spirit of Western civilization, that they lived somehow in it but not of it. And when I brooded upon the cultural barrenness of black life, I wondered if clean, positive tenderness, love, honor, loyalty, and the capacity to remember were native with man. I asked myself if these human qualities were not fostered, won, struggled and suffered for, preserved in ritual form from one generation to another.) (p. 33)

In part this passage attempts to shame whites by showing them what their racism has wrought, but in a more crucial way it defines Wright's individualistic alienation from all sense of community, that permanent spiritual malaise that is both the key biographical fact and the ideological center of his art.

With Maya Angelou the case is quite otherwise. If she never experienced the physical hunger that characterized much of Wright's childhood, he was not raped at the age of eight. Yet here youthful response to rejection and outrage is to embrace community, not to seek alienation. *I Know Why the Caged Bird Sings* is a celebration of black culture, by no means uncritical, but essentially a celebration. Toward her family, young Marguerite is depicted as loving, whether or not her love is merited. She idolizes her slightly older brother Bailey. Her Grandmother Henderson is presented not only as the matrifocal center of her family but as the leader of the black community in Stamps, strong, competent, religious, skilled in her ability to coexist with Jim Crow while maintaining her personal dignity. She is a repository of racial values, and her store is the secular center of her community. Crippled Uncle Willie could have been presented as a Sherwood Anderson grotesque, but Angelou recalls feeling close to him even if he was, like Grandmother Henderson, a stern disciplinarian. Angelou would seem to have every reason to share Wright's bitterness about parental neglect, but she does not. When her father shows up in Stamps she is impressed by his appearance, his proper speech, and his city ways. Her mother beggars description: "To describe my mother would be to write about a hurricane in its perfect power. Or the climbing, falling colors of a rainbow.... My mother's beauty literally assailed me" (p. 58). Absorbed in their own separate lives, her parents neglect or reject her repeatedly, but she is more awed by their persons and their personalities than she is resentful. Her maternal family in St. Louis is also impressive in its worldly way, so different in its emphasis on pleasure and politics from the religious rectitude of the paternal family in Stamps.[7] Even Mr. Freeman, her mother's live-in boyfriend who first abuses and then rapes the child, is presented with more compassion than rancor.

Afflicted with guilt after Freeman is killed by her uncles, Marguerite lapses into an almost catatonic silence, providing an excuse to her mother to send her back to Stamps. Southern passivity provides a good therapeutic environment for the child, especially when she is taken under the wing of an elegant, intelligent black woman named Mrs. Bertha Flowers, who treats her to cookies, Dickens, and good advice. Better dressed and better read than anyone else in the community, she nevertheless maintains good relations with all and urges Marguerite not to neglect the wisdom of the folk as she pursues literary interests: "She said that I must always be intolerant of ignorance but understanding of illiteracy. That some people, unable to go to school, were more educated and even more intelligent than college professors. She encouraged me to listen carefully to what country people called mother wit. That in those homely sayings was couched the collective wisdom of generations" (p. 97). In contrast to Wright's grandmother, who banished from her house the schoolteacher Ella for telling the story of Bluebeard to Richard, Grandmother Henderson is quite friendly with "Sister" Flowers, both women secure in their sense of self and their mutual respect.

Angelou also recalls favorably the larger rituals of black community. Religious exercises, whether in a church or in a tent revival meeting, provide a festive atmosphere for Marguerite and Bailey. Racial euphoria pervades the black quarter of Stamps after a Joe Louis victory in a prizefight broadcast on Uncle Willie's radio to a crowd crammed into the store.[8] A summer fish fry, the delicious feeling of terror while listening to ghost stories, the excitement of pre-graduation activities—these are some of the pleasures of growing up black so amply present in *I Know Why the Caged Bird Sings* and so conspicuously absent in *Black Boy*.

A comparison of the graduation exercises in the two works is particularly instructive. Marguerite is showered with affectionate attention and gifts, and not only from her family and immediate circle of friends: "Uncle Willie and Momma [her Grandmother Henderson] had sent away for a Mickey Mouse watch like Bailey's. Louise gave me four embroidered handkerchiefs. (I gave her three crocheted doilies.) Mrs. Sneed, the minister's wife, made me an undershirt to wear for graduation, and nearly every customer gave me a nickel or maybe even a dime with the instruction 'Keep on moving to higher ground,' or some such encouragement" (p. 169). Richard feels more and more isolated as graduation nears: "My loneliness became organic. I felt walled in and I grew irritable. I associated less and less with my classmates" (p. 152). Refusing to use a speech prepared for him by the school principal, he resists peer and family pressure, as well as the implicit promise of a teaching job, in order to maintain his sense of individual integrity. Giving his own speech, he rejects utterly the communal ceremony implicit in the occasion:

> On the night of graduation I was nervous and tense; I rose and faced the audience and my speech rolled out. When my voice

stopped there was some applause. I did not care if they liked it or
not; I was through. Immediately, even before I left the platform,
I tried to shunt all memory of the event from me. A few of my
classmates managed to shake my hand as I pushed toward the
door, seeking the street. Somebody invited me to a party and I did
not accept. I did not want to see any of them again. I walked
home, saying to myself: The hell with it! With almost seventeen
years of baffled living behind me, I faced the world in 1925. (p.
156)

The valedictorian of Marguerite's class accepts the help of a teacher in
writing his speech, but before he mounts the podium a white politician
delivers the Washingtonian message that "we were maids and farmers,
handymen and washerwomen, and anything higher that we aspired to was
farcical and presumptuous" (pp. 175–176). But this ritual of racial
humiliation is immediately followed by a ritual of racial survival and
solidarity. After giving his speech, the valedictorian improvises by singing
"Lift Ev'ry Voice and Sing" with renewed meaning, joined by all present, the
white man having left. From shame the collective emotion is transformed by
the song of a black poet to pride: "We were on top again. As always, again.
We survived. The depths had been icy and dark, but now a bright sun spoke
to our souls. I was no longer simply a member of the proud graduating class
of 1940; I was a proud member of the wonderful, beautiful Negro race" (p.
179). Unlike Wright, Angelou stresses the intimate relation of the black
creator to the black audience. Gathering his material from the stuff of the
black experience, with its suffering and its survival, James Weldon Johnson
transmutes the experience into art, giving it back to the people to aid them
to travel the stony road, to fortify their spirit by reminding them of their
capacity to endure. The episode is a paradigm of Angelou's own artistic
endeavor in *I Know Why the Caged Birds Sings*.

It is important to recognize that Angelou's Southern environment is as
grievously afflicted by white racism as Wright's. Just as young Richard is
tormented by whites, so is Marguerite by her employer Mrs. Cullinan, who
calls her out of her name, or by Dentist Lincoln, who owes Grandmother
Henderson money but will not treat the child's toothache because " '... my
policy is I'd rather stick my hand in a dog's mouth than in a nigger's' " (p.
184). White violence comes dangerously close to both Uncle Willie and
Bailey. Indeed, the town is quintessentially Southern in its racial attitudes,
comparable to Wright's Elaine or West Helena or Jackson: "Stamps,
Arkansas, was Chitlin' Switch, Georgia; Hang 'Em High, Alabama; Don't
Let the Sun Set on You Here, Nigger, Mississippi; or any other name just as

descriptive. People in Stamps used to say that the whites in our town were so prejudiced that a Negro couldn't buy vanilla ice cream. Except on July Fourth. Other days he had to be satisfied with chocolate" (p. 47). It is not that Angelou de-emphasizes the racist assault on Black personality and community; it is just that she shows with respect if not always agreement the defensive and compensatory cultural patterns developed to survive in such an environment. This is Maya Angelou's response in *I Know Why the Caged Bird Sings* to the call of *Black Boy*.

One hesitates to generalize on the basis of a single book by one woman writer, but a quick recall of such writers as Linda Brent, Zora Neale Hurston, Gwendolyn Brooks, Margaret Walker, Paule Marshall, Sonia Sanchez, Toni Morrison, Sherley Anne Williams, Nikki Giovanni, Carolyn M. Rodgers, Ntozake Shange, Alice Walker, Gayl Jones, and numerous others suggests that, more than male writers, women are concerned with such themes as community, sexism (especially sexual exploitation), and relations with family and friends. They seem correspondingly less interested in individual rebellion, alienation, and success against the odds. A theory which can encompass both visions, adding community to the myth of freedom and literacy, accommodating *I Know Why the Caged Bird Sings* as easily as *Black Boy*, may follow the stages delineated by Houston Baker and become the primary contribution of the present decade to Afro-American literary criticism.

NOTES

1. "Generational Shifts and the Recent Criticism of Afro-American Literature," *Black American Literature Forum*, 15 (1981), 3–4.

2. Baker seems unaware that "The Literature of the Negro in the United States" in its first version was a lecture Wright delivered in 1945, closer in time and temper to "Blueprint for Negro Writing" (1937) than to the late Fifties. The concluding pages of the essay in Wright's *White Man, Listen!* (Garden City, New York: Doubleday, 1957), pp. 105–150, mentioning the Supreme Court decision, are an addendum for the benefit of European audiences to the lecture first published as "Littérature noire américaine," *Les Temps Modernes*, No. 35 (August, 1948), pp. 193–220. Baker's treatment of Wright here contains other examples of chronological and interpretative confusion.

3. Richard Wright, "Blueprint for Negro Writing," *New Challenge*, 2 (Fall, 1937), 53–65.

4. *Black Boy* (New York: Harper, 1945), p. 23. Subsequent parenthetical page citations in the text are to this edition,

5. *I Know Why the Caged Bird Sings* (New York: Random House, 1969), pp. 33–34. Subsequent parenthetical page citations in the text are to this edition.

6. The extent of the exaggeration is evident from the photographs Wright took of his father at the time, which reveal an erect, black-haired, rather youthful appearance for a man in his early sixties. See Constance Webb, *Richard Wright: A Biography* (New York:

Putnam, 1968), following p. 128, and Michel Fabre, *The Unfinished Quest of Richard Wright* (New York: Morrow, 1973), pp. 19, 205. Wright's "description" of his father actually corresponds much more closely to a photograph of a sharecropper in Wright's *12 Million Black Voices* (New York: Viking, 1941), p. 23.

7. George E. Kent discusses this contrast with his customary acuity in "Maya Angelou's *I Know Why the Caged Bird Sings* and Black Autobiographical Tradition," *Kansas Quarterly*, 7, No. 3 (1975), 72–78.

8. Wright did share the racial pride in Joe Louis. See "Joe Louis Uncovers Dynamite," *New Masses*, 18 (8 October, 1935), 18–19; "High Tide in Harlem," *New Masses*, 28 (5 July 1938), 18–20; *Lawd Today* (New York: Walker, 1963), p. 52; and "King Joe," *New Letters*, 38 (1971), 42–45.

DONALD B. GIBSON

Richard Wright's Black Boy and the Trauma of Autobiographical Rebirth

T he stuff of Richard Wright's *Black Boy* originates from his experience of life in the South, in Mississippi, Arkansas, and Tennessee. The shape of the work, however, derives from Wright's experience in the North; for the autobiography's retrospective character allowed Wright to imagine that his early experience was preparing him to be the person he found himself to be after he had been in Chicago and New York for some years. It is from that perspective that the earlier events of his life are narrated, and it is because of that perspective that Wright chooses what events from his past to relate and how to relate them.

It is also because of the perspective from which the autobiography is written that there are several inconsistencies between his own account and that of Michel Fabre in his definitive biography. For example, in his actual life as a youth Wright had several close friends, but his *Black Boy* describes none of these relationships. The sense we get of his family's actual social standing in their community as told in the biography is not revealed in the autobiography. These discrepancies exist because Wright conceived his experience from his birth to the time he composed *Black Boy* as a description of one who from his very earliest times was a strong individualist. Hence his very first memory, the memory of setting fire to his family's house, is of an act of defiance and exertion of individual will. That he sets the house on fire

From *Callaloo* No. 28 (Summer 1986). © 1986 Charles H. Rowell.

is not entirely an accident, for he seems old enough to know what is going to happen if he puts flame to the "fluffy white curtains" which he has specifically been forbidden by his parents to touch. His description of the act begins the autobiography because it is to him emblematic of his essential character: he is the strong individualist capable initially of defying parental authority at the cost nearly of death ("my mother had come close to killing me" 6), and eventually of defying the authority of the whole southern institutional scheme. Significantly enough the beating he receives at the beginning of the autobiography is administered by his mother, and the instrument with which he is chastised is not a switch, but a "tree limb" (6). He is in a fevered and hysterical state for several days, suggesting that the beating was rather severe. That initial scene tells us not only that he is strong enough even at four years of age to defy parental authority, but, as well, it indicates intense emotional disruption of the ordinarily sympathetic bond between parent and child, especially mother and child. Whether in actual fact his life was in danger or whether his reaction was a hysterical reaction to the extraordinarily harsh beating he received at the hands of his mother, the fact is that he felt as though his mother, whom the child expected to protect, nourish, and sustain his life, came close to expressing the most extreme form of rejection—infanticide. The whole of the autobiography's first chapter is centered around the failure of his parents to fulfill the parental role. It begins by illustrating how the mother has failed him, and it ends by showing how the father has failed him and failed in life as well. Clearly Wright's father, the logic goes, was not a good model to emulate. Each section of the first chapter reveals another facet of Wright's parents' failing him or his assuming himself functions originally belonging to them. The point is that failing to find the necessary support and sustaining function in adults or in a community, he had to rely upon himself—to cultivate those qualities in himself, to become self-reliant, a strong individualist. That is why in the book Wright differs from every other black person who appears in that world. And that is why he is able to resist efforts on the parts of black and white alike to make him conform to an inimical scheme of values.

Following the section describing his recuperation from the beating is the Thoreauvian catalogue of experiences, largely sensational (of the senses), deriving from his contact with nature. The interesting aspect of the catalogue is that Wright himself, at a very early age presumedly, interprets the meaning of his observations directly and not through any medium. "Each event spoke with a cryptic tongue" (7) and he, alone and unaided by any higher or more developed intelligence, is able to read as they "slowly revealed their coded meanings" (7). He is only able to read and understand because he assumes the authority of the interpreter. He assumes that authority because the preceding scene has taught him that he must rely upon himself, not only for protection from death, but for understanding of meaning as well. No reliable authority is available to tell him what experience means; hence he must discover it himself. He might have learned this from reading Thoreau and Emerson, but I think he learned it from his own understanding of his particular experience. Perhaps if one shares a somewhat common attitude toward authority as Wright and Thoreau did, both hating external authority, one may well come to the conclusion that if the meaning of nature is be ascertained, it must be understood directly by the individual and not as determined by the authoritative interpretation of some external medium.

The next section of the first chapter, the boat trip to Memphis, reveals a similar message. One cannot rely upon external interpreters of experience, even if those interpreters are one's parents. Richard asks his mother perfectly reasonable questions about the trip, but her answers are predetermined by her fixed sense that the world is as it is without cause or reason. (She feels no necessity to answer his questions.) Hence her answers do not make sense. It is not reasonable that the name of the boat is the *Kate Adams* because "that's the boat's name" (8), nor does it make sense that the whistle blows "when the captain wants it to blow" (8). Such "knowledge" one cannot depend upon. One can, however, depend upon the knowledge of one's own senses: "Solace came when I wandered about the boat and gazed at Negroes throwing dice, drinking whisky, playing cards, lolling on boxes, eating, talking, and singing" (9). What is true about the trip is not what the authoritative voice of Richard's mother tells him, but what he discovers through his own perception. The text following likewise reveals the unreliability of parents and therefore parental authority and the necessity to challenge, resist, and finally reject parental authority by rejecting—for perfectly good reason—the parents.

The burden of the whole of the first chapter of *Black Boy* is a recital of examples of parental rejection providing an explanation and a justification for Wright's individualism. Once the individual severs himself from his family life, his disaffection from the community may likely follow. Wright's logic proceeds along these lines: he explains his individualism, his separateness, by reference to the character of his early life. "How could I have turned out differently?" his narration asks. It tells us that there is no way he could have been different; no way he could have done otherwise than to cut himself off from community. His parents fail him utterly. The greatness of the narration of the autobiography lies in Wright's dual awareness of the nature of the failure: it is personal; it is social. It has to do with the personalities of his parents; it has to do with the situation of black people in the South during the time. *Black Boy* is at once an explanation and defense of Wright's separateness from a black community and a strong protest against the plight of all the black boys and girls, men and women subjected in his words, to "the ethics of living Jim Crow."

Though Richard Wright's mother has good and positive qualities to recommend her as parent (ample evidence of this exists later on in the text) those qualities are not evident in the first chapter of the autobiography. Instead we are apprised of her limitations. We have already spoken of her nearly beating Richard to death; we later see how he associates in his mind his hunger with his mother's failure to perform one of the basic parental functions, to nourish. Throughout the autobiography Wright refers time and time again to his hunger for food, his constant want of nourishment. His criticism and censure of his mother is implicit and probably barely on the verge of consciousness. His story about the minister who comes to Sunday dinner is revealing, for the underlying dynamic of the scene indicates deeper meaning than the folk and darky humor implied about black ministers and fried chicken. The anecdote has two essential meanings: 1) Richard's mother has allowed the intrusion into his life of the authority of an adult male who is not his parent; 2) she has given that figure access to the food denied Richard. It is significant that the final point of the story is that Richard ends up not only with none of the fried chicken, a rare dish indeed, but with no dinner at all. The authority of the preacher over his mother and the authority of the mother over him combine to keep him hungry. The underlying logic runs: if I am to be fed, I must personally assume authority.

Wright's mother's rejection of him (again it is rejection because the action is perceived by Wright as such, whether or not it *in fact* was) is apparent during the scene in which she forces him to confront the gang of boys who take the money he has been given to purchase food. Her motive was undoubtedly a good one. The point is, however, that she finally bars him from the shelter of the house. Whether her method of teaching is sound is not the issue. Rather Wright's perception of the meaning of the event is the question at hand. He is rejected: "She slammed the door and I heard the key turn in the lock. I shook with fright. I was alone upon the dark hostile streets and gangs were after me" (16). He wins that night "the right to the streets of Memphis" (16). That right also allowed him the questionable privilege to go to the saloons where he is made drunk and taught to curse. As a direct result of his mother's "lesson," of winning "the right to the streets of Memphis," he roams every day further and further from home begging money and drink.

But an even greater rejection, because it is an explicit and clear rejection, is his mother's placing him and his brother in an orphan's home. He does not explicitly blame his mother since he understands that "she had no choice" (25). Yet when she breaks off her nightly visits, Richard begins to distrust her: "I was rapidly learning to distrust everything and everybody" (26). The dynamic of the situation is that his mother has placed him away from herself; though he knows, intellectually, the reasons, the intellectualization cannot take precedence over the feelings. Hence, "Dread and distrust had already become a daily part of my being and my memory grew sharp, my senses more impressionable; I began to be aware of myself as a distinct personality striving against others" (26). The situation is made worse because hunger and fear reside in the orphan's home as well as outside. His decision to run away reflects the thrust toward individualism. Had he run away in order to draw upon the resources of a community, to find sustenance among people with whom he identified because of common heritage, circumstance or situation, that would be one thing. As it is, he runs away into the general society, into nothing. The reason he can imagine this is because in life he ran away to nothing—not to something. In the first chapter of *Black Boy* he tells us how his father let him down too.

That Richard's father has disappointed and failed to support him in general is particularly born out by his association of his experience of the orphan's home with his relation with his father. His mother puts him in the position of having to accept his situation at the orphan's home or to seek his father's help.

> Again I was faced with choices I did not like, but I finally agreed. After all, my hate for my father was not so great and urgent as my hate for the orphans' home. (28)

Richard's "first triumph over his father" (11) occurs when he pretends to take literally the father's command that he kill an annoyingly noisy cat. Richard's victory consists in his applying an intrepid logic to his father's unreasoned and emotional outburst demanding the death of the cat. He believes he has thoroughly outwitted him. "I had made him believe that I taken his words literally. He could not punish me now without risking his authority. I was happy because I had at last found a way to throw my criticism of him into his face" (11). The triumph, however, quickly backfires, for immediately afterwards we learn that Richard feels a deeper and more persistent hunger for food than he had ever felt before, and this new hunger occurs because his father is no longer present (though Richard does not immediately make the connection). He must certainly feel that his father disappears because of his own striking out against him. The mother's mocking attempt to deal with the situation (a situation of is own creation as he sees it), if you are hungry, "jump up and catch a kungry" (13), simply compounds his sense of parental alienation and confirms his conviction of parental rejection. If your father lets you down, the logic goes, and if your mother can't take care of you thereafter, then you have to take care of yourself—to figure out how you can survive independent of others.

After the section detailing his experiences at the orphanage, where he becomes acutely aware of the extent of his parents' mistreatment of him—his mother, whatever the justification, abandons him to the fear and hunger which the orphanage experience brings; his father, having abandoned the family, fails to prevent such a turn of events—Richard describes his last meeting with his father after he has grown up and returned to Mississippi some twenty-five years later. Again the function of the episode renders poignantly Richard's acute sense that his father has failed in a very basic way to perform the parental function. This scene follows and reiterates the message of the orphan's home episode. When Richard is told that he must accompany his mother to his father's dwelling in order to ask for money for the family to return to Arkansas, his father is living with a "strange" woman who thinks Richard is "cute" and tells his father to give him a nickel. Reacting to the humiliation of the scene to him and his mother, Richard tells the strange woman that she "ought to be dead" (29)—along with his father, no doubt, for participating in the grotesque game—and refuses the repeated offer of the nickel. The father of course denies money for the trip. When he has left his father's room, he tells us, thus delivering a mighty judgment against his father, "I had the feeling that I had had to do with something unclean" (30).

Richard's final judgment of his father is rendered in the last episode of chapter one. He describes briefly his father's life and character as he finds them to be many years after the scene with his father and the strange woman has occurred. His description chronicles the extent of his estrangement.

A quarter of a century was to elapse between the time when I saw my father sitting with the strange woman and the time when I was to see him again, standing alone upon the red clay of a Mississippi plantation, a sharecropper, clad in ragged overalls, holding a muddy hoe in his gnarled, veined hands—a quarter of a century during which my mind and consciousness had become so greatly and violently altered that when I tried to talk to him I realized that though ties of blood made us kin, though there was an echo of my voice in his voice, we were forever strangers speaking a different language, living on vastly different planes of reality. (30)

The connection between the two points in time is obvious. The earlier episode shapes and colors the latter as Wright attempts to account for the sense of estrangement and alienation from community which he felt when he wrote *Black Boy*. The chapter has had mostly to do with parental rejection of the child; it ends with the child's rejection of the parent (and by extension "parents"). The final lines tell of how he succeeds where his father has failed. He becomes the parent.

> From far beyond the horizons that bound this bleak plantation there had come to me through my living the knowledge that my father was a black peasant who had gone to the city seeking life, but who had failed in the city; a black peasant whose life had been hopelessly snarled in the city, and who had at last fled the city—that same city which had lifted me in its burning arms and borne me toward alien and undreamed-of shores of knowing. (31)

The relation which Wright establishes between his own personal experience and his generalized social views is clearly indicated (however unconsciously) in the famous passage occurring near the beginning of the second chapter where he bemoans what he sees as the shortcomings of black people which have come to be because of racism and segregation.

> After I had outlived the shocks of childhood, after the habit of reflection had been born in me, I used to mull over the strange absence of real kindness in Negroes, how unstable was our tenderness, how lacking in genuine passion we were, how void of great hope, how timid our joy, how bare our traditions, how hollow our memories, how lacking we were in those intangible sentiments that bind man to man, and how shallow was even our despair .... Whenever I thought of the essential bleakness of black life in America, I knew that Negroes had never been allowed to catch the full spirit of Western civilization, that they lived somehow in it but not of it. (33)

If we look back to the conclusion of the first chapter, the coda which focuses on his father and his final alienation from him, we will find that the terms he uses to describe his father just a few paragraphs before are remarkably similar to the generalized observation about black people.

> From the white landowners to above him there had not been handed to him a chance to learn the meaning of loyalty, of

sentiment, of tradition. Joy was as unknown to him as was despair. And a creature of the earth, he endured, hearty, whole, seemingly indestructible, with no regrets and no hope. He asked easy, drawling questions about me, his other son, his wife, and he laughed, amused, when I informed him of their destinies. (30)

The fact that the generalized comment of the second chapter is parenthetical suggests that its relation to its context may be associational, that it does not necessarily follow strictly logically from what precedes it nor does it lead logically into what follows. The genesis of the unconscious associations of "father" and "orphans' home" is clear enough. His response to his escape from the home prompts the generalized comment which turns out then to be a judgment of his father, the implication being that it his father had caught the "full spirit of Western civilization," then he would not have been abandoned by him and would not ever have needed to be in the home.

The first chapter is, then, the autobiography's introduction. The remainder of the book fills in the details of the outline implied there, apprising us of the distance between Richard and everyone else in his environment. Even his brother is depicted as a shadowy figure, one who cannot be relied upon for support and protection from the untrustworthy children and adults, white and black, known and unknown, who people his world. Relatives, those who would ordinarily form the core of community, are enemies, at first potentially then actually so. Richard's relatives in their attempt to exert authority over him coerce, beat, or threaten him in a manner not entirely different from the way the white world menaces him if he does not give in to its demand that he submit to its authority. We learn finally that Wright resists the attempt of the white South to thrust identity and an alien sense of actuality on him by having learned to resist authority within the confines of his own family and community. Thus Richard Wright explains where he came from; how he got to be who he was at the time he wrote *Black Boy*.

WORKS CITED

Wright, Richard. *Black Boy: A Record of Childhood and Youth*. New York: Harper & Brothers, 1945.

ELIZABETH J. CINER

Richard Wright's Struggle with Fathers

Be your own father ...
—*Invisible Man*

I

"If I were asked what is the one, over-all symbol or image gained from my living that most nearly represents what I feel to be the essence of American life," Richard Wright wrote in 1942, "I'd say it is that of a man struggling mightily ... for self-possession" ("Why I Selected" 448). The struggle of the individual for self-possession, which is a struggle to be fully human and free, is the strongest unifying element in Wright's work. In his earliest published book, *Uncle Tom's Children*, Wright depicts ways in which black Americans are not externally free, writing about characters whose freedom to grow, live, work, and change is limited by whites. But already in that work he has begun to wonder about the possibility of achieving internal psychological freedom, especially for people who are oppressed. Although external freedom (or his characters' lack of it) continues to be a significant theme in Wright's work, by the time he publishes *Black Boy* in 1945 he has shifted his focus from the one to the other.

For Wright, internal freedom is contingent upon one's ability to make uncoerced choices. The internally free person is a self-assertive, self-

From *Richard Wright: Myths and Realities*, C. James Trotman, ed. © 1988 C. James Trotman.

117

controlled individual operating autonomously in the world. Not someone known by others ("The white South said it knew 'niggers,' and I was what the white South called a 'nigger,' Wright writes in *Black Boy* 283), not an object owned by another, the self-possessed person is his own master. And knowing who he is, the self-possessed person can look critically at (is not overwhelmed by) the society in which he finds himself, often taking the initiative needed to transform that society. To borrow language from Richard Shaull's introduction to *Pedagogy of the Oppressed*, the world for the free man is not, as it is for the slave, a "static and closed order, a *given* reality which man must accept and to which he must adjust" but rather "it is a problem to be worked on and solved" (12–13).

The form the struggle for self-possession most often takes in Wright's work is a struggle to achieve adulthood (or manhood, since all but one of Wright's protagonists are male), and there are both personal and historical reasons for this. Keneth Kinnamon isolates "four basic facts of Wright's youth—his racial status, his poverty, the disruption of his family, and his faulty education," all of which he claims "left ineradicable scars [on Wright's] psyche and deeply influenced his thought" as well as providing "much of the subject matter of his early writings" (4). Kinnamon's four basic facts, however, are aspects of a more general autobiographical fact which is that Wright saw himself as locked in combat with his family. Sometimes literally and more often metaphorically, Wright believed family members tried to beat and train out of him "a kind of consciousness, a mode of being that the way of life about [him] had said could not be, must not be" (187). In the autobiography Wright sees his relatives as enemies who, if they could, would choke off his desire to know, to do, to be, starving him not only physically but also intellectually, emotionally and spiritually.

Wright was clearest about his feelings towards his family in discussions on the autobiography. When he said, for instance, "I wrote the book to tell a series of incidents stringing through my childhood, but the main desire was to render a judgement on my environment" ("The Author" m3), he meant *his* environment. So little of the autobiography concerns itself with the white South that an understanding of Wright's critique of racism and of the white racist South depends on understanding not only what they, the whites, "do" to Richard, but also what his family does to Richard. Having accepted (for whatever reasons) the terms of racism, "the static and closed order," family members become accomplices of and agents for the State. Attempting to access the degree to which racism could and did damage human beings, Wright is not interested in cherishing but in exposing what lay at the heart of his own upbringing, the attempts of his family to prevent him from ever growing up.

Of course if Wright's family did not want him to be adult as he defined it, neither did the larger society. As Addison Gayle, Jr. points out, by the time of the Civil War, a "language system" had already evolved in America which "serve[d] the twin purposes of rationalizing slavery and binding the slave mentally to the slavocracy" (32). Both the rationalizing and the binding depended to a large degree on an analogy that equated black men and women with children. "Not content with merely enslaving black men, Americans undertook the task of stripping them of all semblance of humanity … reducing the man to the status of child" (4). The rationalizations were pristine in their simplicity: If black slaves were overgrown children, then white slave owners could pretend that no real loss of freedom had occurred; they were merely beneficent parents whose wayward children required constant supervision. Those slaves who did assert themselves, who were neither loyal nor tractable, who seemed indifferent or hostile to "parental" authority and guidance, were not men and women rebelling, convinced they were complete human beings whose rights even whites must respect, but rather boys and girls who had not yet learned their lessons, or dangerous beasts, savage children in grownups' bodies. Black people from this vantage point might be biologically adult, but they were not mature morally, intellectually, or socially. By definition, if you were black, you could not possibly act like an adult, and whites worked hard to make this definition a reality, punishing and redefining all acts of self-assertion.

Although clearly the legend sketched here is but one of a number of potent legends created about blacks by whites, it is one that, given his feelings about his own family, appealed to Wright. In some ways, this is what is most obvious about Wright's work. Throughout the fiction characters are blocked from reaching maturity. When they act like adults—when they try to protect their families, for instance, or improve their farms, or advance in their jobs—their actions are interpreted by whites as trying to "act white." The titles of Wright's first three published works, *Uncle Tom's Children*, *Native Son*, and *Black Boy*, contain references to non-adults; only posthumously do we find anything so positive as the title *Eight Men*, and even in that work the manhood of all but one of the characters is at issue. Black males are perpetually "boys" in the eyes of "the Man" in Wright's world. And to be a boy is to be a "non-man," says Wright, a being "that knew vaguely that it was human but felt that it was not" (*Black Boy* 213).

II

While it is certainly true, as Donald B. Gibson asserts, that the "burden of the whole of the first chapter of *Black Boy* is a recital of examples of parental rejection providing an explanation and a justification for Wright's individualism" (493–494), it is also true that while his family rejects him, Richard simultaneously rejects them. Moreover, this dual rejection serves Richard: Resisting his family not only teaches him in a general way to resist white racists (Gibson 497–498), it also provides a specific map for him, a way out of the fate he feels awaits him. Richard does not want anyone to dominate him—black, white, parent, teacher, relative, boss, or priest. Committed to ordering his life by his own feelings, he rejects his uncles, the school principal, and Shorty. Above all others, though, he rejects his father and his grandmother, the two people who in their opposite but to Richard equally unacceptable reactions to racism, threaten him the most. The one, his grandmother, finds solace in a stern religion she tries to impose on Richard; the other, his father, deserts his family, finding release in alcohol and adultery. Throughout the autobiography Richard acts and reacts in ways which show him trying to be very different from these two potential role models. In the end, by becoming an author, Richard succeeds.

While the autobiography opens with an attack on his grandmother, it is with Richard's father that much of the first long chapter is concerned. Mr. Wright is "forbidding," the "lawgiver in the family," a giant in front of whom Richard is awestruck. When Richard's family moves to Memphis, Richard, afraid to go into the strange city streets alone, is confined to home where he must be quiet while his father (a night porter) sleeps. One morning Richard finds himself forced to quiet a kitten whose mewing provokes his father. "'Kill the damn thing ... Do anything, but get it away from here'" (17), his father commands. Immediately resentful, Richard hangs the kitten and so, Wright tells us, enjoys his "first triumph" (18) over his father.

When Richard had hanged the kitten, his mother had warned him "'That kitten's going to get you ...'" (18), a warning Richard shrugged off, saying "'That kitten can't even breathe now'" (18). But Richard learns he is wrong: "My mother's words," he reports, "made it live again in my mind" (20). Victim here of another's language, Richard experiences words as weapons, as surely as he will experience them fourteen years later when reading Mencken. As a final gesture, his mother forces him into a prayer of forgiveness—"Dear God, our father, forgive me, for I knew not what I was doing"—which perhaps for the first time links biological and spiritual fathers. Subsequent episodes will cement the connection: When Richard complains of hunger, his mother insists that he will have to wait for God to send food because his father is gone; a preacher, "God's representative," a man also used to having his "own way" (33), eats all the fried chicken while Richard labors unsuccessfully to finish his soup. Fathers, spiritual or biological, Richard's experience leads him to believe, satisfy their own appetites at the expense of their children.

With his father gone, Richard's mother sends him out to buy the groceries. Richard sets out "proud" and feeling "like a grownup" (13). When he is robbed and beaten (and forced out of the house by his mother), he compensates for his youth and small size, arming himself with a big stick, defending himself first against the boys who stole from him and then against their parents who "rushed into the streets and threatened [him]: They had never seen such frenzy. For the first time in my life I shouted at grownups, telling them I would give them the same if they bothered me." Richard's victory here is a multiple one. Supplanting his father as provider of food, he triumphs over him a second time and more decisively. At the same time he triumphs over his own fear. Where Richard had been "afraid to go into the city streets alone" (16) now he has "won" for himself the "right to the streets of Memphis" (25).

Once free from fear, Richard quickly familiarizes himself with the adult world which has captured his father, showing himself to be his father's son. Far from home, the boy frequents a saloon, learns to drink, and is taught to proposition women. At the age of six, "[f]or a penny or a nickel I would repeat to anyone whatever was whispered to me," encouraged by the responses he got. "In my foggy, tipsy state, the reaction of the men and women to my mysterious words enthralled me. I ran from person to person, laughing, hiccoughing, spewing out filth that made them bend double with glee" (29). Given his inclinations, why Wright does not follow in his father's footsteps is one of the mysteries of the text. Perhaps his mother's beatings are effective. Perhaps when the effects of the alcohol wear off what Richard remembers from these experiences is not the comfort of the drink but the power of his socially unacceptable language.

Richard sees his father one last time in boyhood, at the home of his father's mistress. He recoils from the encounter for reasons he cannot make clear to himself:

> We left. I had the feeling that I had had to do with something unclean. Many times in the years after that the image of my father and the strange woman, their faces lit by the dancing flames, would surge up in my imagination so vivid and strong that I felt I could reach out and touch it; I would stare at it, feeling that it possessed some vital meaning which always eluded me. (42)

According to Albert Stone, the fire "represents the sexual passion which separates and unites father, mother, and mistress and which likewise includes the child who, looking into the coals, sees himself an unconscious participant in the sexual drama" (131). But as a child, all Richard knows is that he is on one side of a room, his father is on the other, between them is "a bright fire that blazed in a grate" (40), and the gap between them is not as wide as Richard would have it be. Even not knowing what other life is possible for him, Richard instinctively rejects the narrow and degraded life his father has chosen.

Carl Brignano claims that Wright was searching for a father and that the search "was a real one," although symbolically the search expresses itself as "a search for Negro dignity, economic opportunity, and social acceptance in a racially integrated South" (6). More to the point perhaps, Wright appears to be searching for a way to be a father, a person in power if not over others than at least over himself. His father's fire attracts Richard, but his father's life, finally, does not. Wright is emphatic on this point in the chapter's final paragraphs:

> A quarter of a century was to elapse between the time when I saw my father sitting with the strange woman and the time I was to see him again ... a sharecropper, clad in ragged overalls, holding a muddy hoe in his gnarled, veined hands—a quarter of a century during which my mind and consciousness had become so greatly and violently altered that when I tried to talk to him I realized that, though ties of blood made us kin, though I could see a shadow of my face in his face, though there was an echo of my voice in his voice, we were forever strangers, speaking a different language, living on vastly distant planes of reality. (42)

Whatever Wright has become it is not his father. From this point in the narrative, the older Wright drops out, his ghost, so to speak, emerging at the end of *Black Boy* to haunt Richard when he returns to Memphis as a young man. Memphis, for Wright, is the city his father "had gone to ... seeking life" (43). But his father "had failed in the city; a black peasant whose life had been hopelessly snarled in the city, and who had at last fled the city" (43), that same city in whose "burning arms" Richard is "lifted" and "borne ... toward alien and undreamed-of shores of knowing" (43).

With Richard's father out of the picture, his grandmother becomes head of the family and the authority figure Richard must contend with on a day-to-day basis. She is a religious woman, a fanatic Seventh Day Adventist, according to Wright, and from the very beginning her religiousness conflicts with Richard's free expression: "I was dreaming of running and playing and shouting," the first paragraph of the autobiography goes, "but the vivid image of Granny's old, white, wrinkled, grim face, framed by a halo of tumbling black hair ... made me afraid" (9). Richard finally gets out of the house by burning it down, and, while Richard is not labelled a Devil proper until the scenes which come at the end of the second chapter, there is an unmistakably diabolical aspect to his "play" in the opening scene; at least part of him clearly wants to see his grandmother lying helpless upon her bed, "yellow flames" instead of that halo in her hair. The motivation behind Richard's act, his characterization of Granny as an awe-inspiring figure lying somewhere above him, and his attraction to fire, all raise the question of Richard's own affiliation with Satan. Richard is first fascinated by the liveliness of the fire; as a result of his play with it, he falls into a fever and feels his body on fire. Perhaps, in his misbehavior, he finds a way to incorporate this living vital element within him. But if Richard is a devil, then he is one in the romantic sense, a rebel and heretic defying not lawful authority but tyrannical oppression. Not unlike Prometheus, Richard steals fire and uses it in ways objected to strenuously by those in authority.

After his father's desertion, Richard, his brother, and his mother return to Granny's house. There Richard meets the young schoolteacher Ella who boards with the family. When he asks her about the books she reads, Ella, who knows Granny forbids novels, attempts to placate Richard by closing her book and whispering to him *Bluebeard and His Seven Wives*. Richard is "enchanted and enthralled" by the story. "My imagination blazed" (47), Wright writes. But just as Ella is about to finish, "when my interest was keenest, when I was lost to the world around me" (47), Granny steps out on the porch and puts an end to the story, telling Ella, "'I want none of that Devil stuff in my house!'" (47), warning Richard, "'You're going to burn in hell'" (48).

The story is indeed the Devil's stuff, about Bluebeard, a satanic figure if ever there was one, and it is precisely the story Richard wants to hear: "Ella's whispered story of deception and murder had been the rust experience in my life that had elicited from me a total emotional response" (48). Richard's life is given symbolic form through the story; deprived of it he is deprived of a way to come to grips with his life through literature. But as the subsequent scene shows, Richard not only empathizes with Bluebeard's wives but also with Bluebeard who through deception and violence achieves his unlawful desires. Within days, Richard mounts an ingenious attack on Granny, this one a symbolic and linguistic assault.

Richard and his brother are taking baths in two tubs of water under the watchful eyes of Granny. Splashing water, flinging suds at one another, they ignore Granny's scolding until she puts down her knitting and calls Richard to her:

"Bend over," she ordered.

I stooped and she scrubbed my anus. My mind was in a sort of daze, midway between daydreaming and thinking. Then, before I knew it, words—words whose meaning I did not fully know— had slipped out of my mouth.

"When you get through, kiss back there," I said, the words rolling softly but unpremeditately. (49)

Pandemonium ensues. With eyes "blazing," Granny shoves Richard from her and beats him with a towel she is holding. Naked, he runs screaming from the house as his mother hurries from her bed. Granny, close to hysterics, reports on what "that black little Devil" (50) has done, and Richard's mother takes up both towel and chase.

Much in the form of this scene looks back to the opening scene of the autobiography; its content, though, derives from Richard's early experiences with language: words like "enthralled" and "dazed" recall his saloon experiences while "soap" and "scrub" attach themselves to an episode which involved Richard scribbling obscene words on windows with a soap cake. None of the characters makes any of these connections. Granny's explanation holds sway: She "said emphatically that she knew who had ruined me," Richard reports, "that she knew I learned about 'foul practices' from reading Ella's books."

Granny, who distrusts stories because they are fictions and hence lies is wrong about Ella and foul practices only in fact. Fictionally speaking Granny is right; stories can be the Devil's work and this one has been, providing Richard with what he needed to attack Granny for interfering with his pleasure in hearing the story. While Richard called the story one of deception and murder, it is also a story of sexual perversion, of foul practices.

When Richard says that Granny "knew who had ruined" him by teaching him "foul practices," the implication is clearly sexual, and Wright is effecting a comic reversal with Ella becoming the seducer and Richard the one seduced. The language of the Bluebeard scene itself is sexual feelings well up, things seem to throb, Richard feels his body ablaze with excitement. Referring back to the word-play Richard indulged in in the first chapter, this language also recalls Richard's encounter with his father and the strange woman, the incident he came away from feeling as if he had had something "to do with something unclean" (42). Richard's choice of a sexual gesture towards Granny and Wright's adoption of sexually laden language in the description of Richard's responses to literature show Richard open to the same kinds of impulses his father is open to. But Richard will channel those impulses differently, the differentness demonstrating his discontinuity with his father. Initiated as he is in the Bluebeard scene not into the world of the flesh but into the world of story-telling, Richard's impulses serve another god.

Richard's responses to the story are not unlike the responses of an initiate, a convert, and they parallel Granny's responses to religion. Where she sees angels, he sees magical presences. His books generate in him a transcendent experience and momentarily blot out reality, making him feel "lost to reality" and so compete with her religion in which she feels dead to the world. Richard in fact adopts his grandmother's terms—devil, evil, hell—and then transforms them. From Granny's point of view, the dreamy schoolteacher is "evil," books are the "devil's stuff," Richard's desire to know, "the devil's work," and Richard himself "a little black devil" who surely is "going to burn in hell." That is all right with Richard, who appropriates the terms; he "burns to learn to read novels" (49) and "tortures his mother" as a good devil ought "to define every strange word" he comes upon, because he has learned from Granny (as surely as Frederick Douglass learned from Captain Auld) that words are the "gateway to a forbidden and enchanting land" (49).

In the course of *Black Boy* what is implicit in the Bluebeard-bathtub sequence is made explicit: if Richard is a devil, then the saint is someone who has cut him or her self off from life; if his acts are evil, then being good is akin to being dead; if he is headed for hell, then heaven is a static place where nothing much happens. Within this framework, novels *are* the devil's work, opening up possibilities for the individual in a society which depends for its existence on those possibilities being denied, a society, furthermore, which works to deny that any life other than that proscribed is possible.

Richard's reaction to this proscription is complex and germinal. At the age of twelve, having promised Granny "to pray hard," Richard goes up to his room every afternoon, "but everything I could think of saying seemed silly." Failing even at writing hymn verses, Richard claims that "the Holy Ghost was simply nowhere near me" (132). The Holy Ghost may be absent, but not so Richard's muse: "One day while killing my hour of prayer" (132), Wright writes, he is inspired to write an Indian love story. "I had made something," he writes, "no matter how bad it was; and it was mine" (133). Paradoxically, then, Richard's first work of art emerges under the pressure of Granny's religiosity. As if he had taken his directions from her, Richard creates not prayer but exactly the kind of work Granny burns, becoming exactly what she had feared he would become.

If the crucial difference between Richard and his father has been that the son succumbs not to passion but to art, then the difference between Richard and his grandmother is that while she uses religion to withdraw from a world she finds intolerable, he will seek a way through words, as Wright would put it, to alter his relationship to his environment and thereby prove himself to be a free man. From Richard's point of view, Granny and others like her fly to religion as an answer to the pain of their existence. He flees the South, however, so that he may find the words to describe the life he has known, and in describing that life create for himself (and for others) a new one. Writing stories is finally a religious activity for Richard, writing redeeming him as religion redeems Granny. While Granny's religion frees her from the world, Richard's frees him into it.

His choice of professions, then, is no accident: becoming a writer, he becomes at once an author, creator, and artist, and this may be said to specifically solve his problems. As a writer of books, he creates new worlds and thereby competes with Granny's God, the source of her authority and Richard's spiritual father; as an autobiographer, he engenders himself and so displaces his biological father. Recreating his world and himself for us, as he sees it, Wright even outwits his political fathers, white men of the South, who never imagine a black boy could become a writer. Wright does become one though, and in so doing transforms himself, permanently altering his fate and status. No longer a native son doomed to an obscure and deadened existence, he becomes Richard Wright.

<h2 style="text-align:center">REFERENCES</h2>

Brignano, Carl. *Richard Wright: An Introduction to the Man and His Work*. Pittsburgh, Pa.: University of Pittsburgh Press, 1970.

Gayle, Addison, Jr. *The Way of the World*. Garden City, N.Y.: Doubleday, 1976.

Gibson, Donald B. "Richard Wright and the Trauma of Autobiographical Rebirth." *Callaloo*, 9 (1986): 492–498.

Kinnamon, Keneth. *The Emergence of Richard Wright: A Study in Literature and Society*. Urbana: University of Illinois Press, 1972.

Shaull, Richard. Introduction, *Pedagogy of the Oppressed*, by Paulo Friere. Trans. Myra Bergman Ramos. New York: The Seabury Press, 1968.

Stone, Albert E. *Autobiographical Occasions and Original Acts*. Philadelphia: University of Pennsylvania Press, 1982.

Wright, Richard. "The Author Meets the Critics." New York radio interview, printed in *PM's Sunday Picture News*, Magazine Section, April 15, 1945, m3.

———. *Black Boy*. New York: Harper & Row, 1945.

———. "Why I Selected 'How "Bigger" Was Born.'" *This Is My Best*. Ed. Whit Burnett. Philadelphia: Blackiston & Grayson, 1942.

WILLIAM L. ANDREWS

Richard Wright and the
African-American Autobiography Tradition

T o tell the whole truth in the name of complete honesty or to conceal part of the truth out of deference to white readers' sensibilities—this dilemma and the anxiety it spawned have haunted African-American autobiography since its beginnings. The earliest black American autobiographers frequently commented on their unique dilemma: speak forthrightly and be thought a liar or censor oneself in the hope of being believed. Antebellum slave narrators introduced what Robert Stepto has called "distrust of the reader" into African-American autobiographical discourse by admitting, in the classic formulation of Harriet Jacobs, "I have not exaggerated the wrongs inflicted by Slavery; on the contrary, my descriptions fall far short of the facts" (1). By assuring her white reader that she has not told the whole truth, Jacobs paradoxically seeks to confirm the first and most important statement she makes in her autobiography: "Reader, be assured this narrative is no fiction" (1).

One way to chart the development of African-American autobiography is to track the gradual replacement of a discourse of distrust and self-restraint that relies on white-authored prefaces and appendices to authenticate and authorize black writing by a discourse that avows frank self-expression as a sign of authenticity and independent self-authorization. We know, of course, that much nineteenth-century black autobiography was structured and to

From *Style* Vol. 27, No. 2 (Summer 1993). © 1993 William L. Andrews.

some extent governed by internal rhetorical strategies and external documents designed to confirm the sincerity (i.e., the genuineness and good character) of the narrator and the sincerity (i.e., the truthfulness) of her or his story (Andrews 3–7, 19–22). What is not so well understood, perhaps, is the role that discourses of sincerity and autobiographical acts of authentication have played in the evolution of black-American autobiography into the modern era. My purpose is to situate Richard Wright's *Black Boy* (*American Hunger*) in the context of African-American autobiography's long-standing concern with sincerity and authenticity in order to show how *Black Boy* (*American Hunger*) redefined these crucial parameters and thus signaled the arrival of a new kind of discourse in the history of black autobiography in the United States.

Most antebellum slave narrators were sufficiently distrustful of, or deferential to, the sensibilities of whites that they and/or the whites who introduced their texts felt obliged to assure their readers that credibility, not self-expression, was their watchword in narrating their stories. Frederick Douglass's 1845 *Narrative* carries a preface by William Lloyd Garrison, promising the reader that while "essentially true in all its statements," Douglass's story "comes short of the reality, rather than overstate a single fact in regard to SLAVERY AS IT IS" (38). Douglass also understood how useful the discourse of sincerity could be, as is clear when he professed not to care whether some might consider him egotistical in judging his boyhood removal to Baltimore "a special interposition of divine Providence in my favor." "I prefer to be true to myself, even at the hazard of incurring the ridicule of others, rather than to be false, and incur my own abhorrence" (75), Douglass claimed. Yet in stating that he cared less about the ridicule of others than about telling the truth, Douglass indirectly promised that his reader could believe him because he had openly declared his dedication to truth, regardless of whether it placed him in a less than admirable light. By stating that he would rather be true than credible, Douglass subtly bears witness to how seriously he takes his own credibility. Only a writer who wants very much to be believed will claim to be more sincerely dedicated to truth than to credibility. A further indication of Douglass's espousal of the discourse of sincerity comes up in the appendix to his *Narrative*, where he announces that, despite all appearances to the contrary in his autobiography, he is not "an opponent of all religion." He wants his reader to understand that he means to denounce only "the hypocritical Christianity of this land" so that it will not be confused with "the pure, peaceable, and impartial Christianity of Christ," which "I love" (153). In this instance Douglass is sufficiently worried about white "misapprehensions" of his religious views that he feels obliged to declare himself a sincere Christian so that the hard truths he has told will not be dismissed by those whom he believes are still capable of moral reform.

During the crisis decade of the 1850s, occasionally a black autobiographer, most notably Harriet Jacobs, would hint at or complain of the tension between a sense of obligation to self and to the white reader's expectations.[1] This attempt to be honest about what it meant not to be fully honest in telling one's story was fairly short-lived, however. Post-Reconstruction autobiographies such as the *Life and Times of Frederick Douglass* (1881), John Mercer Langston's *From the Virginia Plantation to the National Capitol* (1894), and Booker T. Washington's *Up from Slavery* (1901) had nothing to say about the question of sincerity versus credibility in black-American autobiography. By implication, this postbellum breed of successful, progressive black autobiographer had little difficulty following Polonius's advice to Hamlet: "to thine own self be true / And it doth follow, as the night the day, / Thou canst not then be false to any man." In these lines, which represent the epitome of the traditional idea of sincerity according to Lionel Trilling (3–4), we learn that truth to self naturally and inevitably leads one to do right by everyone else, an idea that Washington espoused in *Up from Slavery* not only for himself but for all progressive-minded people, black and white.[2] Like Washington, the most famous turn-of-the-century black autobiographers represented themselves as so much in agreement with what white Americans already believed that the old anxieties about truth to self versus believability to others seemed no longer an issue.

With the rise of the so-called "New Negro" in the 1920s, the problem of self-expressiveness versus self-restraint returned to center stage in the well-known battles that black artists and intellectuals fought over what blacks should write about in general and how they should represent themselves in particular. To those, white as well as black, who prescribed any agenda, any standard of discrimination and value other than that emanating from within the artist, Langston Hughes retorted defiantly: "We younger Negro artists who create now intend to express our individual dark-skinned selves without fear or shame" (694). Despite his black critics' shame or his white critics' fears, Hughes defended himself and his frankly "racial" jazz poetry by stating: "I am sincere as I know how to be in these poems" (693). Hughes's New Negro supporters, such as Wallace Thurman and Claude McKay, championed a similar creed of artistic sincerity that granted any black writer the right, in effect, to call them as he saw them as long as he did not pander blatantly to white prejudices.

Yet while New Negro critics egged on their fellow novelists, dramatists, and poets toward greater self-expressiveness, the question of how much an autobiographer should feel free to expose about himself or herself or about the relationships of actual blacks and whites in the recent past or immediate present did not get much attention. In part this is attributable to the fact that few critics in the 1920s, black or white, are likely to have thought of autobiography at all when they considered the kinds of African-American literary "art" that needed policing or protecting. The New Negro era was a time of comparatively few noteworthy autobiographies. Those that did get a hearing were mostly by men of traditional values and outlook: successful members of the black clergy, such as Bishop William Henry Heard, author of *From Slavery to the Bishopric in the A.M.E. Church* (1924), or proteges of Washington, such as Robert Russa Moton, whose *Finding a Way Out* (1920) preached the message of the great Tuskegeean in a manner calculated to leave an image of the African-American leader as a man of "unemotional business-like self-control" (213).

During the 1920s almost all the literary New Negroes were too busy working in the more traditional belletristic genres to take the time to write personal reminiscences. One significant exception, William Pickens, who published his autobiography, *Bursting Bonds*, in the same year as Cane, evoked the familiar parameters of nineteenth-century narrative when he stated in his preface: "If I am frank, it is only to be true" (Foreword n. pag.). For Pickens, though very much the New Negro with the New Negro's determination to speak his mind, the traditional Shakespearian formulation of sincerity was still applicable: frankness about oneself was a necessary condition to telling white people the truth. Frankness was in fact the sign of truthfulness rather than, as it had often seemed to whites reading blacks, a warning flag that something unpleasantly "bitter" was about to come up. Nevertheless, even Pickens acknowledged that aspects of his experience as a New Negro in the South would defy his white reader's credibility. Thus, when recounting a year he spent in east Texas just before the outbreak of World War I, Pickens prefaced his remarks by stating that he would "not strain credulity too far by endeavoring to tell the whole truth" about the "savage treatment of colored people in this section of the civilized world," but would instead "relate only some of the believable things" (57).

Some white readers of the 1920s, particularly the more "liberal" and trendy of the white literati, seem to have been prompted by the cult of primitivism to embrace and indeed assume that black personal narratives would bare the soul of their authors. Muriel Draper's introduction to Taylor Gordon's *Born to Be* (1929) promised the white reader that this celebrated black entertainer had composed his story "with rare candor," attributable, she suggests, to his inherent "honesty, humor and complete freedom from vulgarity" as well as to his lack of both "racial self-consciousness" and "literary self-consciousness" (1). In Draper's assessment of Gordon, we find a curious resolution of the conflict between candor and truthfulness: only let the black autobiographer be "unfettered" from consciousness of himself as a black person writing, and the result will be a prodigy at liberty simply to be himself, which in fact, Draper implies, is what this Negro was "born to be." Draper's notion that an identification of selfhood with race must inhibit a black autobiographer's ability to speak fully and fairly gives us an early instance of a presumption invoked by many white critics during the first half of the twentieth century: namely, that if blacks would start writing as "people" rather than as Negroes, their (white) readers would find them more interesting and more believable. Ironically, however, in his foreword to Draper's introduction to Taylor Gordon's autobiography, Carl Van Vechten could not help raising doubts about Draper's reading of Gordon as an unself-conscious, freely expressive black autobiographer. Van Vechten applauded Gordon for his writing especially "frankly" about blacks, but of Gordon's recollections of his dealings with whites Van Vechten warned: "constantly you suspect him of concealing the most monstrous facts" (xlvi). Thus even the "new kind of personality" that Van Vechten saw in this remarkable New Negro could not be fully trusted. Van Vechten could not believe that the traditional mask of the black autobiographer had been abandoned.

The decade and a half after the New Negro Renaissance saw the publication of a number of important autobiographies by James Weldon Johnson (*Along This Way*, 1933), Claude McKay (*A Long Way from Home*, 1937), Angelo Herndon (*Let Me Live*, 1937), Mary Church Terrell (*A Colored Woman in a White World*, 1940), Langston Hughes (*The Big Sea*, 1940), W. E. B. Du Bois (*Dusk of Dawn*, 1940), Zora Neale Hurston (*Dust Tracks on a Road*, 1942), J. Saunders Redding (*No Day of Triumph*, 1942), and of course, Richard Wright (*Black Boy*, 1945). Significantly, only four of these autobiographies—Terrell's, Du Bois's, Redding's, and Wright's—have prefaces at all. Those by Johnson, McKay, Herndon, Hughes, and Hurston enter directly into the narration without so much as a hint of whether their authors have negotiated or simply ignored the old problem of self-expressiveness versus self-restraint. One might think from reading the majority of these remarkable life stories that the old problem had been rendered passe by virtue of the liberation of consciousness and expression enacted by the New Negro Renaissance. Only Terrell harked back to the hesitancy of the past when she introduced her life story with the caveat: "In relating the story of my life I shall simply tell the truth and nothing but the truth—but not the whole truth, for that would be impossible. And even if t tried to tell the whole truth few people would believe me" (n. pag.). In the "apology" that prefaces *Dusk of Dawn* Du Bois depreciated what he called "mere autobiography," but he did not attribute to black autobiography the "reticences, repressions and distortions which come because men do not dare to be absolutely frank" (1). He implied instead that selective truthfulness and lack of candor were inherent in autobiography as a form, regardless of the ethnicity of the author. For Du Bois, the solution to this problem lay in writing the sort of narrative that transcended personality altogether. His autobiography would subsume the whole vexed question of the individual's obligation to the truth under a larger, historically verifiable rubric: the Truth of a race's experience.[3] Hence the subtitle of *Dusk of Dawn* is *An Essay toward an Autobiography of a Race Concept.* By making himself a spokesman and exemplar of a supposedly desubjectivized Truth of history rather than of the self, Du Bois tried, in effect, to claim for his autobiography the ultimate sincerity of which he felt himself and his form capable: the sincerity of the historian-sociologist impartially dedicated to recovering the Truth of his era.

Du Bois's bid for ultimate sincerity did not, however, turn the tradition of African-American autobiography in a new direction with regard to the relationship of narrator, narratee, and narrative. Most of Du Bois's contemporaries in black autobiography in the 1930s and '40s showed little interest in modeling themselves on any historically verifiable idea of representativeness or typicalness. Instead of this traditional, nineteenth-century way of conceiving selfhood,[4] the likes of Hurston, Hughes, McKay, and Redding argue that they were sufficiently different—that is, temperamentally resistant to the models of their predecessors and atypical of their peers as well—that they could appeal to nothing more valid than the example of their own individuality as a standard for judging the credibility of what they said about themselves.

In *Dust Tracks on a Road*, for instance, Hurston describes herself as having felt impelled from her earliest school days "to talk back at established authority" (95). Yet even Hurston admitted that she concealed her "feeling of difference from my fellow men" out of fear that telling the truth about what she saw and felt would bring her ridicule as well as the reputation of being "a story-teller": that is, a liar (58–59). Similarly, when McKay recalled his decision not to follow the example of William Stanley Braithwaite, the most successful African-American poet of his time, the West Indian claimed with pride that his own poetic expression was "too subjective, personal and tell-tale" (28) to suit the expectations of traditionalists. Yet McKay, in the spirit of Hurston, confessed later in *A Long Way from Home* that there had been limits to his often-professed creed of full romantic self-expression. He had deliberately omitted "If We Must Die," a poem of revolutionary candor, from his first widely read volume of poetry, *Spring in New Hampshire* (1920), and it had taken a white man, Frank Harris, to sting him into full recognition of the sort of betrayal this act of self-censorship had entailed. Harris had called McKay "a traitor to [his] race" for implicitly disavowing "If We Must Die." But, wrote McKay in his autobiography, "I felt worse for being a traitor to myself. For if a man is not faithful to his own individuality, he cannot be loyal to anything" (99).

In this statement, McKay iterates once again the sentiments of Shakespeare's Polonius, affirming the long-standing Euro-American ideal of sincerity as a truth to, and of, self that ensures inevitably a communal bond of right dealing with the other. As I have tried to show, Douglass, Washington, Pickens, and Du Bois gave McKay ample precedent for believing that a black autobiographer could find a way to reconcile truth to self with a credible, socially constructive relationship to the white reader. On the other hand, as I have also tried to illustrate, from Jacobs to Hurston to Terrell, important African-American women autobiographers called attention to the gender-specific problems that arose whenever a black woman tried to speak frankly in order to expand her white reader's horizon of belief with regard to the realities of the color line. I do not want to make too much of this gendered distinction in African-American autobiography; one could easily point to black women autobiographers who do not allude in any way to the problem of sincerity as I have tried to outline it here, for instance.[5] What is more significant for the history of this tradition is the way that Richard Wright in *Black Boy (American Hunger)* tried to dispose of the whole question of whether or at what cost a black autobiographer could or should adopt the discourse of sincerity in addressing whites.

In her "Introductory Note" recommending the 1945 edition of *Black Boy* to all "morally responsible Americans," Dorothy Canfield Fisher characterizes with only three adjectives Wright's "story of a Negro childhood and youth." Fisher labels the story "honest," "dreadful," and "heartbreaking" (*Black Boy*, n. pag.). Like many white liberals before her, Fisher was proud to put her name on the line in testimony to a black autobiographer's honesty. But refusing to claim more for *Black Boy* than that it was "dreadful" and "heart-breaking" and in particular refusing to speak of how the book could enlighten the reader or help to change the social order—this failure, in other words, to attest to any desire in Wright to have an ameliorative effect on the world that his autobiography describes—constitutes a significant change in the purpose to which prefaces by whites had been traditionally put in the tradition of black American autobiography. In this sense, Fisher's preface hints at a move away from sincerity in Wright's discourse and toward a new kind of self-authentication.

We find Wright articulating this new standard of selfhood most explicitly in chapter 9 of his autobiography, wherein he discusses his last months in Jackson, Mississippi, before he left for Memphis at the age of seventeen. The aloof, defensive, and yet unyielding teenager who refused to give in to his principal over the content of his ninth-grade valedictory speech has to begin his first sustained dealings with whites in order to get a job. He plays the part of black supplicant so awkwardly that his friend Griggs takes him aside to explain the rules of the game. "Dick, look, you're black, black, black, see? ... You act around white people as if you didn't know that they were white. And they see it." Wright retorts, "I can't be a slave." But Griggs reminds him, "[Y]ou've got to eat." Therefore, he continues, "When you're in front of white people, think before you act, think before you speak. Your way of doing things is all right among our people, but not for white people" (*Black Boy (American Hunger)* 176–77). Wright's response to this advice has often been quoted by scholars as a key to the mind of the man:

> What Griggs was saying was true, but it was simply utterly impossible for me to calculate, to scheme, to act, to plot all the time. I would remember to dissemble for short periods, then I would forget and act straight and human again, not with the desire to harm anybody, but merely forgetting the artificial status of race and class. It was the same with whites as with blacks; it was my way with everybody. (177)

Wright's "way," put simply, was that of personal authenticity, not sincerity. From Douglass forward, the way of sincerity required representing oneself in such a way as to try quite deliberately not to offend whites but rather to try to show them how sincere discourse from a black autobiographer could give the white reader a truth that would set him or her free. Autobiographers like Jacobs foregrounded the calculatedness, the insincerity, of adopting a discourse of sincerity in African-American autobiography, but neither Jacobs nor Hurston nor any other black autobiographer before Wright would claim that he or she simply could not adopt that autobiographical act even though it seemed the only way to keep from alienating whites predisposed to be distrustful. What Wright suggests in his analysis of his inability to conform to Griggs's advice is that by the time he was ready to go out on his own, he was constitutionally incapable of being anyone or anything other than himself. He was, and could not help but be, authentically and inescapably himself, regardless of whom he was around, regardless of what would seem to be in his best interest or anyone else's.

The hallmark of Wright's personal authenticity in *Black Boy* is not his refusal to conform to social demands; rather, it is his constitutional inability to conform though he is told repeatedly by blacks and whites who he is to be and how he is to act in order to get along. The more people, black as well as white, judge him strange, intractable, offensive, and threatening, the more Wright encourages his reader to conclude that he was the only truly authentic person in the oppressive world in which he grew up. Every time the black boy is told to shut up or is slapped on the mouth, every time he shocks someone with his writing or is punished by someone in power for refusing to censor himself, Wright, in effect, authenticates himself as the quintessentially authentic modern writer, devoted absolutely to expression of self, indifferent to any external standard, especially that of pleasing or improving the reader. Instead of arguing that being true to himself was for the good of others and indeed made community possible, the usual justification of the discourse of sincerity, Wright's autobiography shows how truth to the self led to ruptures with every community the black writer tried to join.

Cast out by southern blacks and northern whites, hated by Dixie rednecks and Yankee reds, Wright turns his alienation from community into a badge of his intellectual and ultimately his artistic integrity. To identify himself as the supremely authentic man, he must render the entirety of society, black as well as white, profoundly inauthentic, pervasively false. This tactic, it seems to me, is why from the outset of *Black Boy* (*American Hunger*) Wright is at such pains to condemn the black southern community, to deny that black people even had a community or had the capacity for community, as is evidenced in his famous denunciation of "the cultural barrenness of black life" and his complaints about "how lacking we were in those intangible sentiments that bind man to man" (*Black Boy* (*American Hunger*) 37). Individual authenticity is not measured in the modern era by the degree to which the social order recognizes and endows one with authenticity but by the extent to which one can claim to have asserted one's self in direct opposition to that which the social order recognizes and respects. Thus from his struggles with the Seventh-Day Adventists through his disillusionment with the Communist Party, Wright fashions an image of himself as uniquely and authentically "human" by showing how every community had failed him, how "my country had shown me no examples of how to live a human life" (*Black Boy* (*American Hunger*) 365), how in the end he would have to go on alone with nothing but his inner "hunger for life" to guide him.

The discourse of authenticity pioneered in Wright's autobiography introduced a new mode of authentication for African-American autobiography in the post-World-War-II era. Not until the 1960s, however, did Wright's call provoke a response in the writings of an unprecedentedly bold group of black autobiographers who not only regarded autobiography as an important means of telling white America the truth about itself but also portrayed themselves as messengers unmuzzled by past forms of racial etiquette, as tribunes whose militant dedication to telling it like it is constituted vocal confirmation of the authority and authenticity of the selfhood they claimed. Eldridge Cleaver's opening proclamation in *Soul on Ice* (1968) about the necessity of "speaking frankly and directly" about the most volatile of personal topics—such as the attraction and repulsion of black men for white women—was designed to demonstrate the black man's commitment to "individuality" and the "salvation" of his manhood (16–17), two hallmarks of authenticity in Wright's autobiography. One of the central themes of *Coming of Age in Mississippi* (1968) is Anne Moody's accelerating alienation from family in general and her mother's expectations in particular because of an awakening of "discontent" and "rebelliousness" that cause her to behave "as if I should please myself doing whatever pleased me" (350). Others in her family may be able to stifle their sense of oppression, but as Moody comes of age, she takes pride in her inability to suppress her "discontent" with the status quo. "It had always been there. Sometimes I used to try to suppress it and it didn't show. Now it showed all the time" (351). Autobiographical writings of the 1960s by people like Cleaver and Moody testify to a process of self-discovery very much reminiscent of Wright's search for personal authenticity, except that in the 1960s the expression of such authenticity often finds its fulfillment in a sociopolitical radicalization about which Wright at the end of his autobiography seems distinctly ambivalent. While personal authenticity and radical politics dovetail in many "revolutionary" black autobiographies of the 1960s, in the Wright model the authentic man is cast out by his fellow radicals for being, in effect, too radically committed to telling everyone (even the radicals) the truth as he sees it. In considering this difference between Wright and his 1960s successors, one should remember that the second half of Wright's autobiography (*American Hunger*), which records the author's disillusionment with radical politics, did not get into print until 1977, well after the heyday of the militant black autobiographer of the 1960s.

On the verge of his death in 1963, Du Bois, the archradical among twentieth-century African-American intellectuals, would not deceive himself or his reader with the claim of having achieved full truthfulness in his final *Autobiography* (1968). The author of *Dusk of Dawn* still thought autobiography was "always incomplete, and often unreliable." His last book, therefore, would be at best "the Soliloquy of an old man on what he dreams his life has been as he sees it slowly drifting away; and what he would like others to believe" (12–13). But Du Bois's skepticism about what a black autobiographer, even with the most authentic of intentions, could say did not cause the readers of *The Autobiography of Malcolm X* (1965) to doubt Malcolm when he insisted, "I'm telling it like it is!" (273). A man who went through as many name changes and revisions of identity and political persuasions as had Malcolm had great need of the discourse of authentication, which he invoked without qualification throughout his autobiography in such statements as, "You never have to worry about me biting my tongue if something I know as truth is on my mind. Raw, naked truth exchanged between the black man and the white man is what a whole lot more of is needed in this country" (273). Even more explicitly than Wright, Malcolm predicates his authenticity as a black man on the fear he instills in whites every time he tells them the "raw, naked truth" about the racial scene in the United States. Those he labels contemptuously as "ultra-proper-talking Negroes" (284) betray their racial inauthenticity, their lack of genuine solidarity with black people, in every word of integrationist reconciliation they utter. Only by working separately toward the eradication of racism and defeatism in their separate racial groups, Malcolm concludes in the last chapter of his autobiography, can "sincere white people and sincere black people ... show a road to the salvation of America's very soul" (377). The implication of Malcolm's words is that only authentic black and white people have a chance to become sincerely socially redemptive. While the pursuit of integration would abet more role playing and pretense, racial separatism dedicated toward a common antiracist goal could foster an unprecedented "mutual sincerity" (377) between the races. In light of Polonius's classic formulation of sincerity, Malcolm might be read as applying Polonius's advice to a racial group, rather than an individual self, and promising that truth to one's race is the only way to guarantee an end to falseness to those of any other race.

The Autobiography of Malcolm X is one of the last African-American autobiographies to be introduced by a white person, in this case the journalist M. S. Handler, who, very much in the spirit of such introductions, represents Malcolm among the ranks of those "remarkable men who pulled themselves to the summit by their bootstraps" (xiv) and championed "Negroes as an integral part of the American community" (xiii). Such a testimonial, with its concluding image of Malcolm as a disillusioned separatist and a protointegrationist, calls attention to a crucial disjunction between Handler's notion of what ultimately qualified Malcolm as a sincere black writer (a perception of Malcolm's emerging acceptance of integration) and what Malcolm himself implied was the basis of a black writer's sincerity (his rejection of integration as inevitably inauthentic and self-abnegating). Like abolitionist introducers and reviewers of slave narratives, Handler betrays a lingering desire to measure a black autobiographer's sincerity according to the palatability of his or her politics and personal style; hence

Handler attempts to rehabilitate Malcolm X by promising that the private Malcolm of the autobiography had outgrown the "diabolic dialectic" (xii) of his public persona and was moving toward a more revealing and less polarizing style of self-representation.[6] Maybe Handler's well-meaning but unthinking recapitulation of the traditional role of the white introducer as "handler" in effect, as manager and manipulator of first impressions, as character reference for the sincerity of the black autobiographer—specially when contrasted with Malcolm's own powerful rhetoric of self-authentication—crystallized in an unprecedented and unmistakable way the problematic function of the white introducer and his or her discourse of sincerity. In any event, after *The Autobiography of Malcolm X*, the few whites who were asked to introduce African-American autobiographies made little attempt to adduce the sincerity of the autobiographer in question. Instead these introductions, usually written by academics, concentrate on matters of authenticity relating to the text (not the autobiographer), such as how the text came into being, how it has been edited, and what its value is to a reliable understanding of literary, cultural, or social history.[7]

In surveying the evolution of discourses of sincerity and authenticity in African-American autobiography, we need to be careful in gauging the impact of Wright's mode of self-authentication on black autobiography of the last forty years. Wright was virtually unique in predicating authenticity on the alienation of the individual from any community, black as well as white. When we celebrate Wright's contribution to African-American autobiography, we should remember that his myth of the individual could not have given us narratives of self-discovery through, rather than in spite of, community, narratives such as Maya Angelou's *I Know Why the Caged Bird Sings* (1969), Ned Cobb's *All God's Dangers* (1974), or John Wideman's *Brothers and Keepers* (1984). Wright's example of personal authenticity was sufficiently magnetic to draw the pendulum of tradition toward the polar opposition he represented, but his significance may ultimately depend more on the force that he exerted on the pendulum's swing than on the arc it has followed since his death.

If recent African-American autobiographers have felt little need to authenticate themselves in Wright's manner, the fact that they (and their publishers) have felt little need of an introducer (white or black) to testify to their sincerity or credibility may evince sufficiently their debt to Wright's conviction that an African-American autobiography could be, and had to be, self-authenticating in every sense of the term. Nowadays it is not impossible to find an African-American autobiographer invoking the old conventions of sincerity and authentication, but when such discourse turns up, as in Itabari Njeri's *Every Good-Bye Ain't Gone* (1990), we ought not be surprised to see the terms of that discourse ironically exploited. "What follows on these pages," Njeri writes in her preface to her autobiography, "began as a novel and ends up the literal truth; many might not have believed the portrayals otherwise.... But the characters in my family only seem made up. At times both comical and tragic, they have been too large for life" (6–7). In acknowledging that her African-American reality may seem "too large for life" (7) and hence for life story as well as too incredible for fiction, Njeri takes her reader back to Jacobs's dilemma in which neither telling "the literal truth" nor resorting to the subterfuge of fiction could satisfy a black woman autobiographer's need to be read as sincere and credible. Like Jacobs, Njeri wants her reader to "be assured this narrative is no fiction," but the changing status of the discourses of sincerity and authenticity enables Njeri to escape Jacobs's trap, the trap of promising to be credible by not telling the whole truth. Njeri has come to realize that fiction, for so long the bogeyman of the black autobiographer, the presumed refuge of the insincere black narrator, need not be a diversion from the truth, but may serve as the means to her ultimate autobiographical end, the telling of "literal truth."

Since this is so, Njeri need not try to prove her sincerity or demonstrate her credibility by rejecting fiction or by subscribing to the simple oppositions of fact versus fiction, authenticity versus credibility that have bedeviled African-American autobiographers for so long. Njeri can simply point out that her attempt to encompass her African-American reality in fiction brought her to the outer boundaries of probability. To break through those limits she had to make a commitment to a radical concept of autobiography. She had to reject the anxieties of African-American autobiographers who felt that their form, more than anything else, had to read credibly in order for them to he regarded as sincere. Once Njeri realized that the only way to seem sincere or credible was to write "the literal truth" of autobiography, acknowledging that such truth was almost inevitably "too large for life," she had in effect got the monkey of sincerity off her back and thrust it into her reader's lap. Is her reader prepared to accept autobiography as the closest thing to an adequate means of reconstructing a personal and family history inherently "too large" for the house of fiction or any other narrative model except autobiography itself? If so, then we as readers can join Njeri as autobiographer and put anxieties about sincerity and authenticity far enough behind us when we read texts like *Every Good-Bye Ain't Gone* so as to confront African-American life first and fully before trying to decide how to accommodate our sense of truth to it.

Notes

*Without the contributions and stimulation of the participants in the 1991 NEH Seminar for College Teachers that I directed on "The Slave Narrative Tradition in African American Literature," this essay would never have found a beginning.

1. See Samuel Ringgold Ward's acknowledgment of his bitterness toward whites, though he is aware of the danger to his credibility that such open expression of feeling entails, in *Autobiography of a Fugitive Negro*.

2. Washington contends repeatedly in *Up from Slavery* that the ambition and effort based on mere self-seeking yield neither long-term nor deeply felt success. True success comes only when one decides "to lose himself in a great cause. In proportion as one loses himself in this way, in the same degree does he get the highest happiness out of his work" (311). Thus the truest and most complete act of self-interest occurs when dedicating oneself to others.

3. "Thus very evidently to me and to others I did little to create my day or greatly change it; but I did exemplify it and thus for all time my life is significant for all lives of men" (*Dusk of Dawn* 4).

4. See, for instance, James McCune Smith's introduction to Douglass's *My Bondage and My Freedom*, in which Douglass is presented as a "representative man."

5. Most of the autobiographies reprinted in the *Schomburg Library of Nineteenth-Century Black Women Writers* (Oxford UP, 1988) and its *Supplement* (1991) do not allude to this problem.

6. Handler's attitude toward Malcolm X in his introduction to *The Autobiography* takes the approximate stance of Ephraim Peabody in his 1849 review of five slave narratives, including that of Frederick Douglass. Peabody takes Douglass to task for "extravagance," "sweeping denunciations," and "violent declarations"—just the sort of rhetoric for which Malcolm X was censured—because Peabody believes such rhetoric is likely to antagonize whites while making even Douglass's friends doubt his "real earnestness" about achieving "any great reform." By contrast the "tolerant, calm, benevolent, and wise" character of Josiah Henson's narrative demonstrates that he does not wish to alienate whites (Peabody 24–26).

7. See the introductions by Herbert Aptheker to *The Autobiography of W. E. B. Du Bois* (1968), Theodore Rosengarten to Ned Cobb's *All God's Dangers: The Life of Nate Shaw* (1974), and David J. Garrow to Jo Ann Gibson Robinson's *The Montgomery Bus Boycott and the Women Who Started It* (1987).

Works Cited

Angelou, Maya. *I Know Why the Caged Bird Signs*. New York: Random House, 1969.

Andrews, William L. *To Tell a Free Story: The First Century of Afro-American Autobiography, 1760–1865*. Urbana: U of Illinois P, 1986.

Aptheker, Herbert. Introduction. *The Autobiography of W. E. B. Du Bois*. By W. E. B. Du Bois. New York: International, 1968. 5–6.

Cleaver, Eldridge. *Soul on Ice*. New York: Dell, 1968.

Cobb, Ned. *All God's Dangers: The Life of Nate Shaw*. Ed. Theodore Rosengarten. New York: Knopf, 1974.

Douglass, Frederick. *My Bondage and My Freedom*. Ed. William L. Andrews. Introd. James McCune Smith. Urbana: U of Illinois P, 1987.

———. *Narrative of the Life of Frederick Douglass: An American Slave.* Ed. Houston A. Baker, Jr. 1845. New York: Penguin, 1982.

Draper, Muriel. Introduction. *Born to Be.* By Taylor Gordon. Seattle: U of Washington P, 1975. xlix–liv.

Du Bois, W. E. B. *The Autobiography of W. E. B. Du Bois.* Introd. Herbert Aptheker. New York: International. 1968.

———. *Dusk of Dawn: An Essay toward an Autobiography of a Race Concept.* New York: Schocken, 1968.

Fisher, Dorothy Canfield. "Introductory Note." *Black Boy.* By Richard Wright. New York: Harper, 1966. n. pag.

Garrow, David J. Introduction. *The Montgomery Bus Boycott and the Women Who Started It.* By Jo Ann Gibson Robinson. Knoxville: U of Tennessee P, 1987. ix–xv.

Gordon, Taylor. *Born to Be.* Ed. Robert Hemenway. Seattle: U of Washington P, 1975.

Handler, M. S. Introduction. *The Autobiography of Malcolm X.* By Malcolm X. New York: Grove, 1965. ix–xiv.

Heard, William Henry. *From Slavery to the Bishopric in the A. M. E. Church.* Philadelphia: A.M.E. Book Concern, 1924.

Hughes, Langston. "The Negro Artist and the Racial Mountain." *Nation* 23 June 1926: 692–94.

Hurston, Zora Neale. *Dust Tracks on a Road.* Ed. Robert E. Hemenway. 2nd ed. Urbana: U of Illinois P, 1984.

Jacobs, Harriet. *Incidents in the Life of a Slave Girl.* Ed. Jean Fagan Yellin. Cambridge: Harvard UP, 1987.

Malcolm X. *The Autobiography of Malcolm X.* Introd. M. S. Handler. New York: Grove, 1965.

McKay, Claude. *A Long Way from Home.* New York: Arno, 1969.

———. "A Negro to His Critics." *New York Tribune Books* 6 March 1932: 1, 6.

Moody, Anne. *Coming of Age in Mississippi.* New York: Dell, 1968.

Moton, Robert Russa. *Finding a Way Out.* Garden City: Doubleday, 1920.

Njeri, Itabari. *Every Good-Bye Ain't Gone.* New York: Random, 1990.

Peabody, Ephraim. "Narratives of Fugitive Slaves." *The Slave's Narrative.* Ed. Charles T. Davis and Henry Louis Gates, Jr. New York: Oxford UP, 1985. 19–28.

Pickens, William. *Bursting Bonds.* Ed. William L. Andrews. Bloomington: Indiana UP, 1991.

Robinson, Jo Ann Gibson. *The Montgomery Bus Boycott and the Women Who Started It.* Ed. David J. Gatrow. Knoxville: U of Tennessee P, 1987.

Rosengarten, Theodore. Introduction. *All God's Dangers: The Life of Nate Shaw.* By Ned Cobb. New York: Knopf, 1974. xiii–xxv.

Smith, James McCune. Introduction. *My Bondage and My Freedom.* By Frederick Douglass. Ed. William L. Andrews: Urbana: U of Illinois P, 1987. 9–23.

Stepto, Robert B. "Distrust of the Reader in Afro-American Narratives." *Reconstructing American Literary History.* Ed. Sacvan Bercovitch. Cambridge: Harvard UP, 1986. 300–22.

Terrell, Mary Church. *A Colored Woman in a White World.* Washington, D.C.: Ransdell, 1940.

Thurman, Wallace. "Negro Artists and the Negro." *New Republic,* 31 August 1927: 37–39.

Trilling, Lionel. *Sincerity and Authenticity.* Cambridge: Harvard UP, 1971.

Vechten, Carl Van. Foreword. *Born to Be.* By Taylor Gordon. Seattle: U of Washington P, 1975. xlv–xlvii

Ward, Samuel Ringgold. *Autobiography of a Fugitive Negro*. London: Snow, 1855.

Washington, Booker T. *Up From Slavery: The Booker T. Washington Papers*. Ed. Louis R. Harlan. Vol. 1. Urbana: U of Illinois P, 1972. 14 vols. 1972–1989.

Wideman, John. *Brothers and Keepers*. New York: Holt, 1984.

Wright, Richard. *Black Boy*. Introd. Dorothy Canfield Fisher. 1945. New York: Harper, 1966.

———. *Black Boy (American Hunger)*. 1977. New York: Library of America, 1991.

WARREN J. CARSON

"They Don't Look So Good, Mistah": Realities of the South in Richard Wright's Black Boy and Selected Short Fiction

I

Although Richard Wright is best known for his articulation of black urban anger and despair in his 1940 novel *Native Son*, equally important to our full assessment and understanding of Wright's social and narrative perspectives are the 1945 autobiographical installment titled *Black Boy*, its 1946 sequel *American Hunger*, and the several short stories and novellas published in *Uncle Tom's Children* (1938) and *Eight Men* (1961). In short, the frustrations that boil over in Wright's classic depiction of Chicago's South Side are grounded in the displaced hopes and expectations of the black Southern migrants. Indeed, as Wright shows time after time, the realities of blacks in the South were often virtually the same as realities of blacks in the so-called North—Up South, Down South, there was very little difference. These realities—social, economic, political, what have you—while they may have different geographical trappings, still serve to oppress, constrain, and retard the development of African Americans. These stark realities of hunger, fear of violence and reprisal, poverty, and the added treachery of fellow blacks are ubiquitous and omnipresent, so much so that Tom, the central character in Wright's "The Man Who Saw the Flood," speaks quintessentially about the black experience in the South when questioned about his own situation after a destructive flood, "They don't look so good, Mistah" (*Eight Men* 93).

From *CLA Journal* Vol. 47, No. 3 (March 2004). © 2004 by the College Language Association.

Certainly, and penetratingly so, realities in the South, especially for her black citizens, were often worse than they at first seemed, and Wright provides what Howard Ramsby calls "a not-so-generous, yet necessary, assessment of the South's treatment of people who were not white" (1) and what Wright himself called "the essential bleakness of black life in America" (*Black Boy* 45).

Black Boy, the second and more fully developed installment of Wright's full autobiographical statement, may rightfully be considered a Southern version of *Native Son*, for in *Black Boy*, readers are dragged through episode after episode of human tragedy whose sum is to render young Richard Wright a time bomb waiting to explode in much the same fashion that Bigger Thomas explodes as a product of his own sum of oppression in *Native Son*. Thus, *Black Boy* provides us an excellent backdrop against which to view and measure the extent to which Wright's fictive vision compares to and frequently meshes with his own perspective on life. Further, as John Reilly aptly notes, "It is precisely Wright's insight into the dynamics of man in society that is his strength as a writer. *Black Boy*, recording the growth and development of this insight, is thus the story of a writer's education" (288).

Let us consider, for example, the matter of hunger, something that is a constant reality for Wright and a constant theme for much of his fiction. *Black Boy* is dominated with references to hunger, but Wright is careful to differentiate among the varieties of hunger, though often in subtle ways. One such aspect of hunger is the commonplace one of physical hunger. Wright speaks frequently in *Black Boy* about the hunger that he experienced as a child. One degree is that hunger usually associated with growing children that could be abated, according to Wright, "when I ate a crust of bread" (21). Wright had experienced this variety of hunger many times while a child in Mississippi but apparently attached no real significance to it beyond that of a temporary, manageable condition. However, the frequency of hunger increases when the family moves to Memphis. Hunger becomes constant, gnawing, unabatable. Wright writes of days that he and his brother went hungry or were forced to subsist on a piece of bread and a pot of tea. Back in Mississippi, Wright again experiences severe hunger and is moved to sell his prized dog to obtain money for food. However, Wright learns a powerful lesson here. Refusing to sell the dog to a white girl for ninety-seven cents instead of the full one-dollar asking price, Wright returns home triumphant but still hungry, only to witness the dog's being run over and killed by a coal truck. His mother's singular comment is instructive: "You could have had a dollar. But you can't eat a dead dog" (81). Wright learns that pride goeth before a fall, and so, apparently, does hunger.

Black Boy contains many more references to hunger, the intensity of which continued to escalate until, Wright says, it became a "biting hunger that made my body aimlessly restless, hunger that kept me on edge, that made my temper flare, hunger that made hate leap out of my heart like the dart of a serpent's tongue, hunger that created in me odd cravings" (113–14). Wright portrays himself as quick witted, although unsophisticated at times, but he is, nevertheless, able to articulate hunger as a growing, developing, quasi-permanent condition that becomes the chief metaphor for the black experience, more specifically, the black male experience, in America. The metaphor is firmly established in the last pages of *Black Boy*, as Addison Gayle points out: "What have I got out of living in America?" Wright asks rhetorically "... [A]ll that I possessed were words and a dim knowledge that my country had shown me no examples of how to live human life. All my life I had been full of a hunger for a new way to live" (176). This "new hunger" that Wright talks about in *Black Boy* carries him, literally and figuratively speaking, to "the borders of actual starvation," where it is possible for us to see—without what David Bakish calls "the thin veneer of fiction"—just how vulnerable blacks are to the sociological oppression that forces them to grow up early" (51).

In Wright's short stories, some of which prefigure Wright's later preoccupation with hunger, others of which subsequently extend and emphasize this same preoccupation, the various characters have similar experiences with hunger. One such character is Big Boy, from "Big Boy Leaves Home." Big Boy, a large strapping youth, is constantly hungry. Early in the story he announces to his friends, Lester, Buck, and Bobo, "Ahm hungry.... Ah wished Ah hada big pota belly busters!" (*Uncle Tom's Children* 21). His various expulsions of air heighten our awareness of the emptiness of Big Boy's stomach and bowels. Later in the story, the reader comes to understand that Big Boy's hunger is one that goes deeper than physiological hunger; his yearning to go North to freedom and a better life becomes something he and his friends develop a hunger for, much like Wright's personal realization in *Black Boy*. As Big Boy hides himself in the kiln awaiting Will's truck that will sneak him away, his physical hunger and his psychological hunger meld into one. It is only after Big Boy emerges from his watery hole in the ground where he hid on his knees with the body of a dead dog and entered the safety of the trapdoor to Will's truck does his hunger begin to subside. After he has quenched his thirst, eaten the cornbread, and made sure that the truck "sped northward," his hunger eased and "[h]e turned on his side and slept" (53).

A similar situation is presented in a later story, "The Man Who Was Almost a Man," from *Eight Men*. In this story, Dave Saunders's voracious appetite for food parallels his insatiable hunger for a gun, manhood, and what he anticipates will be "a new way to live" (Gayle 176). In the same manner that Dave Saunders "scooped up peas and swallowed fat meat without chewing" and "poured his plate full of molasses and sopped it up ... with a piece of cornbread" (12), he also greedily consumed the pictures of guns in the catalog he borrowed from Joe's store. Furthermore, there is a parallel between the fact that Dave's physical hunger is not checked until he is stuffed and the fact that his hunger for manhood is not satisfied until he has obtained a gun. Ultimately, though, Dave comes to realize that it is only by leaving the presence of those who insist upon treating him like a child will he ever become a man and be able to live according to his own choices. In this regard, Dave Saunders, like Big Boy and Wright himself, also leaves home. Furthermore, Dave's hopping the train to what he perceives is manhood and freedom recalls the end of *Black Boy*, where Richard Wright himself stowed away aboard a train that sped toward the North "where [he] could live with a little less fear" (226) and perhaps enjoy a new way of life where, for Wright, a man can be a man. Thus, in rejecting the South and the compound oppression that the South exemplifies for the black man, Wright and his fictional characters, Big Boy and Dave Saunders, satisfy, if only temporarily, their hunger for freedom, life, liberty, and the pursuit of happiness.

II

Another reality that clearly did not look so good to Tom, in "The Man Who Saw the Flood," was the terror of white violence and reprisal. As Tom surveyed his loss, he found that like every other victim of the destructive powers of the flood, he would have to rebuild. Unlike the other two victims, however, Tom must begin again at a distinct disadvantage: He already owes his sharecrop boss, Mr. Burgess, eight hundred dollars. Now he needs to borrow more to make a new start; so instead of starting "from scratch" (*Eight Men* 93), Tom really must start with less than scratch. He rightly concludes, "Ahm worse off now than befo" (93). More importantly, Tom correctly assesses the power of the white man to compound the devastation of natural destruction. Burgess implicitly warns Tom, "... you got to go through with it. Two of the boys tried to run away this morning and dodge their debts, and I had to have the sheriff pick em up" (93). Tom concludes that he has no choice but to submit to the white terror.

Wright had his own experience with what he called "the white hot face of terror" (*Black Boy* 64) and observed quite early on that "Fear ... is the most dominant emotion in Negro life.... We're scared all the time ..." (qtd. in Gayle 109). In *Black Boy*, one such experience is encapsulated in the episode of the murder of Wright's Uncle Hoskins in Arkansas. Uncle Hoskins was the purveyor of a lucrative, though illegal, liquor business that had long been coveted by local whites. Because Hoskins would not relinquish his enterprise at the insistence of the whites, they murdered him in his saloon. Moreover, they issued the threat that they would kill the rest of the Hoskins family, who had to flee for their lives under cover of darkness. Wright called this his "first baptism in racist emotion" (82). As a result of this "baptism," Wright says "[a] dread of white people came to live permanently in [his] feelings and imagination" (83). Another experience was learning of the murder by whites of Bob, a young friend's brother. Of this murder, Wright says, "Bob had been caught by the white death, the threat of which hung over every black male in the South" (190). The far-reaching impact of this incident Wright recounts as follows:

> The things that influenced my conduct as a Negro did not have to happen to me directly; I needed but to hear of them to feel their full effects in the deepest layers of my consciousness. Indeed, the white brutality that I had not seen was a more effective control of my behavior than that which I knew. (190)

Wright's autobiographical account of his immersion in white terror recalls a similar account in "Big Boy Leaves Home." Because Big Boy has exposed himself, "black and naked," albeit unintentionally, to a white woman, and because a white man, Jim Harvey, has been killed, the entire black community knows that reprisal will be sure and swift. Their immediate fear is of a lynching, a fear that cuts across all ages, genders, social statuses, and code infractions. As Big Boy hides in the water-filled hole in the ground, he experiences his own "baptism in racist emotion" as he witnesses the white mob hang and burn alive his friend Bobo. Big Boy thinks to himself: "Goddamn them white folks. Thas all they wuz good fer, t run a nigger down like a rabbit. Yeah, they git yuh in a corner n they let yuh have it" (*Uncle Tom's Children* 44). If it were not enough to witness his friend's murder, Big Boy also learns through pieces of conversation that his own parents have been terrorized: When the search of their home did not yield the suspect, the whites drove Big Boy's parents from their home and set it on fire. For Big Boy, this act is a reaffirmation of the terror that the white South is capable of inflicting on black people. These acts become all too important catalysts for his leaving home.

Similarly, Silas in "Long Black Song" is further steeped in racist emotion when he returns after an extended absence from home to find that his private space and his wife have been invaded and violated by a white man—what Sharon Tucker argues is "violence and rape of weak Black women by white men" (128). Silas is unable to contain his outrage as he exclaims, "From sunup t sundown Ah works mah guts out t pay them white trash bastards what Ah owe em' n then Ah comes n finds they been in mah house. Ah can't go into their houses, n yuh know Gawddam well Ah cant. They don't have no mercy on no black folks; we's jus like dirt under their feet" (*Uncle Tom's Children* 117–18). Subsequently, Silas horsewhips and shoots the violator who foolishly returns to Silas's house to sell him a clock. Silas is fully aware that the white reaction will be imminent and violent; further, he understands the absurdity of his position. When his wife pleads with him to run or face death, Silas responds:

> It don't make no difference.... Now, its all gone. Gone ... ef Ah run erway, Ah aint got nothin. Ef Ah stay an fight, Ah aint got nothin. It don't make no difference which way Ah go.... The white folks ain never gimme a chance. They ain never give no black man a chance. There ain nothin in yo whole life kin keep you from em. They take yo land. They take yo freedom. They take yo women N then they take yo life. (125)

Wright tells us that Silas "Talked out of his life, out of a deep and final sense that now it was all over and nothing could make any difference" (125). What Silas does, however, is to make a stand: When the white mob comes, Silas "killed as many [of them] as he could and stayed on to burn" in his house (128). Clearly, to recall Tom's earlier observation, things in the South don't look so good for black people.

III

An assessment of the realities of Wright's South could not be complete without some mention of what Wright perceived as the treachery of his own people. According to one of Wright's biographers, blacks were among the early critics of *Black Boy* upon its publication for its frequent, unflattering portraits of black people. One such portrait is that of the principal of Wright's junior high school. Wright considers the principal to be a pawn of the white power structure. As such, Wright perceives that the principal's role is more to retard the development of black students by teaching them to conform to what white folks want rather than encouraging the students to think, speak, and act freely. At issue is Wright's graduation address. The principal wants Wright to deliver an address to appease the whites in the audience, an address the principal himself has written. Wright, however, insists upon delivering his own speech, much to the consternation of the principal. After a heated exchange and the principal's further efforts to manipulate the situation and subvert Wright's resolve, Wright prevails, fully aware, however, that his victory is temporary because of the principal's power to prevent him from obtaining suitable employment. Wright's position here is unmistakably clear—such individuals perform a disservice to the black youth in their charges and are due not respect, but base ingratitude for failing to empower those who might help save the race.

Other unflattering portraits include those of Wright's own family, particularly his grandmother, Mrs. Wilson, his own Uncle Tom, a retired teacher, and his Aunt Addie, a teacher just beginning her career. Wright describes his grandmother as being "as close to white as a black person could get, which was white" (24); and while the issue of color is present in the family politics, the grandmother's real shortcoming for Wright was her strict religious convictions with which he was always at odds. Two incidents related in *Black Boy* illustrate this observation. First, Wright relates Mrs. Wilson's reaction to a boarder's reading to young Wright from a novel. The grandmother considered such works immoral, trash at the very best, and forbade their presence in her house, telling young Wright that he would "burn in hell" (45). This view is directly opposite to Wright's own views and his desire to become a writer, and not only resulted in many subsequent battles between him and his grandmother, but the lack of learning created in Wright "a sense of emptiness, loss" or indeed an intellectual hunger.

Another point on which Wright and his grandmother disagreed was the strict Seventh Day Adventist religious code that Mrs. Wilson adhered to and expected her household to observe as well. Wright, as we know, resisted all such efforts to religiously instruct—constrict—him. In particular, he stood up to his grandmother on whether he could or could not work on Saturdays—the Sabbath for Seventh Day Adventists. For Wright, it was mostly a practical matter, one of whether to work and eat or observe religious dogma and go hungry. Ultimately, though, Wright rejected most religions as just another method of further restricting and controlling the black man's destiny.

Wright's fictional characters experience similar treachery from other blacks. For example, in "The Man Who Was Almost a Man," Dave Saunders perceives that the other sharecroppers, particularly the older black men, conspire with those in power, the Mr. Hawkins of the world, to keep him from becoming a man. Not only are they not supportive of Dave's own efforts to grow up and emulate what he sees as expressions of manhood, they ridicule him in the presence of whites. Such treachery is too much for Dave Saunders and, like his creator, he renounces his people and leaves town.

A more penetrating example of treachery from fellow blacks is found in

"Long Black Song." Silas holds Sarah even more responsible for his situation for failing to be vigilant and allowing herself to be seduced by a white man: "Ah gits stabbed in the back by my own blood. When my eyes is on the white folks to keep em from killing me, my own blood trips me up" (125). Much the same as Wright concludes in *Black Boy*, Silas sees the ultimate futility of life in the South for the black man: "I don't mean nothing. Yuh die if you fight. Yuh die if you don't fight. Either way yuh die and it don't mean nothing ..." (125).

IV

Taken together, these episodes from Wright's principal autobiographical statement and a sampling of his short stories underscore several main points. First, there is an obvious connection between Wright's personal experience and his fictive vision. Secondly, Wright imbues his characters with experiences similar to many things he witnessed as a child growing up in Mississippi, Tennessee, and Arkansas, endows them with similar frustrations, and provides them with similar responses. Thirdly, whatever the episode, be it autobiographical or fictional, it is designed so as to emphasize the fact that realities in the South for the black man are anything but pretty; indeed, "they don't look so good." For Wright, this perpetual unprettiness for the black man was synonymous with what America was all about as he so tragically and melodramatically shows in his work.

WORKS CITED

Bakish, David. *Richard Wright*. [1973]. New York: Ungar, 1984.

Gayle, Addison. *Richard Wright: Ordeal of a Native Son*. Garden City: Anchor, 1980.

Rambsy, Howard II. "(Re)-Introducing A Black Boy: Studying Richard Wright and His Writings in the 21st Century." *Richard Wright Newsletter* 7:2 (1999–2000): 1, 3.

Reilly, John. Afterword." *Black Boy*, by Richard Wright. New York: Harper, 1966. 286–88.

Rowley, Hazel. *Richard Wright: The Life and Times*. New York, Holt, 2001. Tucker, Sharon. "The Generation after 'Uncle Tom's'." *South Carolina Black Media Group* (April 1995): 12B.

Wright, Richard. *Black Boy* [1945]. New York: Harper, 1966.

———. *Eight Men*. New York: Pyramid, 1961.

———. *Uncle Tom's Children* [1938]. New York: Harper, 1965.

PETAR RAMADANOVIC

Black Boy's *Comedy:*
Indestructibility and Anonymity in
Autobiographical Self-Making

For my father

In his seminar on the ethics of psychoanalysis, the French psychoanalyst and philosopher Jacques Lacan says that comedy, like tragedy, is a relationship between action and desire. While tragedy "functions in the direction of a triumph of death" (*Ethics* 313) and while its action is toward death, an end game of sorts, comedy, Lacan says, has to do less with a triumph of life over death and more with what he calls the flight of life. In comedy life flies, "slips away, runs off, escapes all those barriers that oppose it, including precisely those that are the most essential, those that are constituted by the agency of the signifier" (*Ethics* 314). So, while in a tragedy the hero submits to desire and to the signifier, dying in the process, in a comedy the action continues despite the encounter with the signifier and despite the disruption this encounter creates. In a comedy, this is to say, the hero is not a character defined by her mortality (as the tragic hero is), but an agent of the endurance of life (a kind of many-in-one), where life is understood as a process of generation, a line of derivation from one individual to another and so on, following life's seemingly inexhaustible chain of transformations.

What interests me most in Lacan's understanding of comedy is the indestructibility of the comic hero, his ability to escape all obstacles and to

From *Callaloo* Vol. 27, No. 2 (Spring 2004). © 2004 Charles H. Rowell.

be renewed over and over again, since this figure resembles closely the self-restoring character we find in two different works whose main subject is autobiography—Richard Wright's *Black Boy* (*American Hunger*), the work that, arguably, defined African American autobiography for the twentieth century, and Paul de Man's seminal examination of autobiographical writing, "Autobiography as De-facement," which set the terms for subsequent treatments of this genre. My goal in this article is, first, to describe this figure and then to use it to understand autobiographical writing (in de Man's sense) and Wright's autobiography. What is pertinent for this article is, hence, not that psychoanalysis, black writing, and deconstruction, or the three authors, share some common or essential characteristics, but only that these specific works—Lacan's *Ethics*, de Man's "Autobiography as De-facement," and Wright's *Black Boy* (*American Hunger*)—make use of a similar figure, the indestructible, self-recreating hero, which will serve me to address certain aspects of autobiographical self-making.

Though the precise nature of the relation between Wright, Lacan, and de Man is not directly relevant for my essay, I should tentatively indicate that both circumstantial and substantive connections can be established between the three men and their work.[1] Circumstantial in that they draw upon some of the same phenomenological and existentialist post-Heideggerian philosophers and, of course, Freud.[2] Substantive, in that Wright's political and aesthetic project is, in its final logical consequences, a critique of the subject, as are Lacan's and de Man's.

Bearing in mind that Wright is one of the key post-Depression literary figures in the US, there is surprisingly little written on him.[3] This is partly because Wright became a canonical figure before the canon wars (and, therefore, did not need to be rediscovered or reclaimed), and partly because there is something quite disturbing about his major novel *Native Son*[4] and, perhaps less obviously, about his autobiography, which is still interpreted as if there were no substantial differences between the original version he wrote and the truncated 1945 *Black Boy* Wright published as a compromise.[5] For these reasons, we have at least in some sense yet to encounter Wright and his work. That is, at any rate, what I assume to be the case in approaching his autobiography with Lacan and de Man, and in deciding to pursue the indestructible, self-restoring figure through Wright.

PART I: LACAN AND DE MAN

In preparation for a reading of Wright's *Black Boy* (*American Hunger*), to which the second part of this article will be devoted, I will begin by reconstructing the comic hero from Lacan's text, the self-recreating, indestructible figure that I will use to put forward a basic explanation of de Man's take on autobiographical writing.

Comedy

According to Lacan, a comic hero faces and undergoes numerous life-threatening, sometimes deadly injuries but, in contrast to a tragic hero, comes out of them practically unscathed.[6] The following logic is paradigmatic for comedy: "If the comic hero trips up and lands in the soup, the little fellow nevertheless survives" (*Ethics* 314), whereas a tragic hero is definitively marked by his actions. The comic hero has an indestructible body that can receive blows without suffering them, whereas the tragic hero carries around a human, mortal body that, by definition, can suffer only one such blow. And further, while the comic self is broken into pieces, fragmented, only to be recreated, the blow of fate permanently marks the tragic self as split. These two processes—on the one hand, fragmentation and reconstitution, and on the other the splitting of the subject—make one action comic and the other one tragic, indomitable, or irreversible.

The most fitting example for a Lacanian understanding of comedy is not to be found in literature but in films, and first of all in cartoons, as Slavoj Zizek has pointed out.[7] In the *Road Runner* series, for instance, the plot is always the same: the coyote dies countless times only to be reconstituted and to begin again his chase for the bird who will inevitably outrun him. The bird is, we could say, the desire that escapes and returns as the possibility of the coyote attaining it. It is similar with action movies.[8] Rambo, for instance, comes out of an obviously life-threatening situation barely scratched, ready and fit to continue the pursuit of his goal.

In literary comedies the situation is different from movies only in degree. Since literary comedies do not perform the violation of the self and its reconstitution in the spectacular manner of films and especially cartoons, the literary comic hero may be shoved around and kicked in the ass, but more often he is humiliated, and his injury tends to be psychological rather than physical. His pain, just as in cartoons and action movies, is marvelously absent. Or, if some pain is felt, it is neither commensurate to the force of the blow nor a significant obstacle to the continuation of the comic action.

We can sum up this understanding of comedy by saying that the strike—the mortal strike of the signifier—which the hero receives in tragedy and for which tragedy prepares its audience, is, in a comedy, only a temporary obstacle that has no lasting consequences, allowing for the continuation of the pursuit of the object of desire, which is itself presented as if it were a thing (a bird, for instance) that could be, possibly, attained. Second, tragedies and comedies operate with two different but compatible notions of body: destructible and indestructible, mortal, that is, symbolic, and imaginary. Third, it should be clear from this definition of comedy and from the examples given above why I am not tying the comic to laughter, as is usually done.[9] According to the line of thinking I am developing here, the comic is essentially an action of an indestructible, enduring body that is never mortally injured. The comic body suffers or undergoes an experience without pain. This escape from pain may be, so to speak, the body of laughter, precisely that which makes us laugh, as well as a description of what happens when we laugh (namely, a dissolution of ego boundaries), but one should not posit a causal relation between laughter and the comic described here, or equate them. The comic rather enacts one of the two fundamental fantasmatic structures, and laughter identifies a response, an epiphenomenon that the comic action may or may not provoke.

If both tragedy and comedy are, in Lacan's understanding, defined in the relation of action and desire, in a tragedy the hero finds his or her limitation in desire. The tragic hero encounters his desire as his limit, and further, he encounters the limit (his finitude) that he cannot survive *as* his desire. Comedy, however, is not, for Lacan, the simple inversion of tragedy. It is not a genre in which the hero triumphs because he overcomes this limit and is placed in the position of being able to obtain the object of desire. Instead, the comic hero shows the medium in which he exists for what it is, namely, fiction. It is precisely because he is a fictional creation, an image, that the comic character can escape the obstacles he faces.

In a Lacanian understanding, both comedy and tragedy confirm that the phallus (the signifier) is indeed a signifier. The phallus is, simply, "phallus"—a fantasmatic or aesthetic creation—which, nevertheless, has some real, tangible effects. On the one hand, the phallus can be replicated, substituted with other signifers, infinitely deferred, denied, erased, etc.; but on the other hand, the phallus cannot be avoided or transcended. If there is a decisive show-down with the signifier—the uncovering of the limit of the field of signification, as in Lacan's reading of *Antigone*—the structure of the encounter is tragic. If there is a celebration of the signifier as phallus, for instance, if there is an acknowledgment of the relation between phallus and the male sexual organ, the event is comic.[10]

Before we get to Wright, I want to use this understanding of the comic figure to read Paul de Man's "Autobiography as De-facement." The purpose of this analysis is to make apparent the link between this figure and autobiography, which is the subject of this article, and to show that in de Man's text, autobiographical self-making operates on the same comic supposition of the subject's indestructibility and ability to recreate him- or herself.

Autobiography

The import of de Man's 1979 "Autobiography as De-facement" is not that it redefines autobiography but that it offers a new way to understand that an autobiography is an attempt at restoring an author's identity (an attempt that includes a deformation of the represented identity). His overall argument relies on the following two assumptions. First, autobiography is neither the most factual of literary genres, nor an undecidable mix of truth and fiction, as some of his contemporaries suggested; rather, it is a particular "figure of reading or of understanding that occurs, to some degree, in all texts" (de Man 921).[11] (As we shall see in some detail below, interpretations of Wright's autobiography have been dominated by notions of literature's referent philosophically close to those against which de Man lays out his theory of autobiographical writing. Wright's readers have been deciding, either directly or tacitly, what the relation is between the truth of the work's critique of racism and the fact that it does not accurately portray its author's life.) The second assumption of "Autobiography as De-facement" is that reading and understanding are themselves processes through which a subject is formed. De Man assumes that the process of reading (of writing, as well) is analogous to autobiographical self-making in the sense that they both involve, and unfold through, a series of imaginary self-identifications. That all texts contain an autobiographical moment means hence that one of the fundamental textual acts is a reciprocal identification between the author (or the reader) and the self in the narrative, the goal of identification being the restoration of the author's (reader's) identity. It is not surprising then—since autobiography is a figure of reading, since all texts have an autobiographical moment—that de Man's test-case in this article is not a common example of autobiography but Wordsworth's *Essays upon Epitaphs*. In what is for our purposes a crucial passage of "Autobiography as De-facement," de Man concludes:

> Wordsworth's claim for restoration in the face of death, in the *Essays upon Epitaphs*, is grounded in a consistent system of thought, of metaphors and of diction that is announced at the beginning of the first essay and developed throughout. It is a system of mediations that converts the radical distance of an either/or opposition in a process allowing movement from one extreme to the other by a series of transformations that leave the

negativity of the initial relationship (or lack of relationship) intact. One moves, without compromise, from death *or* life to life *and* death. (925, de Man's emphasis)

Leaving aside the subtleties of de Man's theory, and using the terms we developed in the reading of Lacan, we can say that Wordsworth, in order to restore himself, resorts to a comic strategy (in the terms identified above) when the poet replaces the disjunctive logic of life *or* death with a conjunctive opportunity, life *and* death.[12] The restorative transformation leaves intact what de Man calls the initial relationship, which is the relation—or, more accurately, the non-relation—of the subject to his mortality. If the negativity of this non-relation is not changed, this means that, in practical terms, the poet, the autobiography's author, recognizes the inevitability of a physical death, the disruption that it causes, and continues despite it, creating in his writing the impression of his endurance and unity over time. Autobiographical writing in de Man's (and Wordsworth's) understanding thus—despite the fact that it leaves this negativity intact—transforms what we can call the tragic choice, life *or* death, into a comic restorative possibility, life *and* death.

The same comic, that is, restorative, feature of autobiographical writing can be deduced from the definition of prosopopoeia, which is for de Man the main trope of this genre. Prosopopoeia is, in de Man's words, "the fiction of an apostrophe to an absent, deceased or voiceless entity, which posits the possibility of the latter's reply and confers upon it the power of speech" (de Man 926). Prosopopoeia links together entities that belong to two different realms, the present and the absent, the living and the dead, the immediate and the distant, being and thing, and, we can add, that which we believe to be actual and that which we should know is imagined. In an autobiography, prosopopoeia relates the present self of the author to a series of younger, past selves. The effect of this connection is that all past versions of "me" are, first, given voice, then transformed into selves, and then these selves are identified with the author. Prosopopoeia thus gathers together various past, absent voices under one, enduring name, and the character in autobiography is restored as one self-identical subject who survives the blows of time, forgetting the discontinuity of experience, etc., as his self is given the comic qualities we described above.

We should emphasize, however, that autobiography understood in de Man's sense is not reducible to comedy.[13] As opposed to comedy, autobiography acknowledges that its protagonist is finite and can suffer an indelible blow. It is, then, a condition of autobiographical writing (as opposed to comedy) that it recognizes the finitude of its subject. But autobiography posits the final end of the subject at some undetermined future point that, in most works of this kind, is assumed to be beyond the narrative's range (Wordsworth's is a very unusual case in this respect). Autobiography, as opposed to comedy, must therefore distinguish between the final end of the author's life (future) and the temporary disruptions that have taken place in the past.

Based on this discussion of de Man, we can offer a provisional understanding of autobiography. It is a writing defined by the author's now moment, from which the author projects a fantasmatic, subjective unity onto the past and creates a continuity between past and present, the absent selves and a given self that is present to itself. The restoration of this character—the link between various selves that gives the impression of an individual's unity and continuity over time—reveal the same structure, that of the self-regenerating hero we found in Lacan's understanding of comedy. The "I" in the autobiographical narrative represents the ego's belief in its indestructibility, which is the fundamental phantasm that comedy supports.

In what follows, I will analyze Richard Wright's *Black Boy* (*American Hunger*), trying to extend the provisional understanding of autobiography given above. Let it be said here that when Lacan addresses issues relevant for autobiography, he maintains, as he does in "Aggressivity in Psychoanalysis," that "man's ego can never be reduced to his experienced identity" (*Écrits* 20). This is to say that a part of the ego remains obscure in the recounting of one's life. The subject of autobiography is thus, for Lacan, divided between the ego he or she cannot know and the subject of "experienced identity." Or, if the autobiographer gets to know the opaque part of the ego, this very experience is no longer of the ego but of the strange parts that constitute it, the fragments with which the author cannot identify precisely because of their alien character. The author, we can say, discovers more than he bargained for and more than he can accept as his or her self. This fragmentation, or defacement in de Man's terms, happens in at least some form in every autobiographical text. It is provoked by the restorative—that is, in the terms I have developed in this article, comic—movement that defines this kind of writing.

PART II: *BLACK BOY* (*AMERICAN HUNGER*)

Though diverse in their particulars, interpretations of Wright share the common underlying notion that socio-historical factors are crucial for understanding African American literature.[14] This seems only appropriate, since most influential explanations of why African American literature emphasizes socio-historical factors rely on Wright. For instance, in *Black*

Literature in America, Houston A. Baker, Jr. cites Wright's lecture "The Literature of the Negro in the United States": "Truly, you must now know that the word Negro in America means something not racial or biological but something purely social, something made in the United States" (Baker 2). What Wright says in the lecture, however, is only that "Negro-ness" in America is a socio-historical construct, and not that socio-historical factors have a determinative influence on Negro literature. Believing that "Negro-ness" is not an essential or a biological category, in this lecture Wright begins to interrogate how it is that literature interacts with and changes the notion of "black" or "Negro," which is the process and the phenomenon also described in his autobiography. Leaving aside the complex issue of socio-historical factors, it is to this Wright that I will turn in my reading of *Black Boy* (*American Hunger*).

The Truth of Fiction

As mentioned above, the issue that both tacitly and directly has marked the reception of Richard Wright's autobiography is the relation between its truth and its fiction. The assumption is that in order to read Wright's narrative, we need to decide how it relates to the reality of growing up poor and black in the Jim Crow South, and this is what I will do before I introduce my reading of the specific form of self-restoration (as well as self-defacement) we find in *Black Boy* (*American Hunger*). The usual interpretation takes the narrator's comment on a particular tale about the murder of a black woman by a white mob—"I did not know if the story was factually true or not, but it was emotionally true" (Wright 73)—and applies it to the entire work, which is then read as an account of a collective African American experience.

The implication is that though *Black Boy* (*American Hunger*) is not true to the life of any particular individual, it does render truly, in an emotional sense, the life of black people in the segregated South. If Wright's work is not an autobiography in the strict sense of this term—because it does not correspond to the author's life and does not adequately render its facts, which can be (and have been) otherwise corroborated either by Wright himself or by others—the logic goes, it does live up to its subtitle "a record of childhood and youth" because, to borrow the phrase Timothy Dow Adams uses, it does "ring true" (Adams 302, 306). The text of Wright's work, however, presents a more complex choice than that between two notions of truth, truth as adequation (correct autobiography) or truth as semblance (emotionally true autobiography).

The full sentence from *Black Boy* (*American Hunger*) in which "emotional truth" appears goes as follows: "I did not know if the story [of the black woman's murder] was factually true or not, but it was emotionally true because I had already grown to feel that there existed men against whom I was powerless, men who could violate my life at will" (Wright 73). The sentence says, first, that *regardless whether the story was factual*, irrespective of the tale's authenticity, the story *corresponded to a particular feeling* Richard Wright had as a boy. The sentence then names the reason for the black boy's reaction to the tale: because he had *already* realized "that there existed men against whom I was powerless, men who could violate my life at will." What this sentence is out to explain, therefore, is not the difference between two kinds of truth but, rather, the impact this story had on Wright as a boy. After the story reminds the black boy that there are men who can violate him at will, he is "resolved that I would emulate"—that is, imitate, behave like, the black woman—"if I were ever faced with a white mob" (Wright 73). He imagines that he would "conceal a weapon, pretend that I had been crushed by the wrong done to one of my loved ones; then, just when they thought I had accepted their cruelty as the law of my life, I would let go with my gun and kill as many of them as possible before they killed me" (Wright 73–4).

Upon hearing the story, the boy places himself in the position of the black woman, assumes her role, and enacts the tale with himself as the main character. The role playing, this mise-en-scène, we are lead to understand, helps the boy identify and articulate his feelings. As Wright says, it gave "form and meaning to confused defensive feelings that had long been sleeping in me" (Wright 74). The boy achieves this sublimation not by externalizing the violence—say, killing the kitten or fighting back against the gang of street boys, as he has done in earlier episodes—but, first, by internalizing the violence (when he identifies with the injury suffered by the woman in the murderous tale) and, then, by acting out the violence in his daydream. The daydreamed story itself contains both of these moments: the boy first internalizes the pain, suffers because of "the wrong done to one of my loved ones" and then, "just when they thought I had accepted their cruelty as the law of my life," he projects the violence outward. He lets go with his gun and kills as many of the white people as he can before they kill him. The tale, his identification with it, and the ensuing daydream are the boy's way to ward off the *possibility* of violation, to prepare himself for the violence that may threaten him in the future, but also for the violence that has *already* happened to him.[15]

In his "imaginings" (Wright 74), the black boy does precisely what he sees people around him incapable of doing: he stands up for himself and his people against an oppressive, life-threatening environment. He has to do this in his fantasies because, as Wright explains three short paragraphs before he introduces the tale, the young man he was "had no power to make things happen outside of me in the objective world" (Wright 72). But the boy's fantasies are not simply the expression of his powerlessness; they endow the otherwise "bare and bleak" world of the boy's youth "with unlimited potentials." The boy's fantasies redeem this world "for the sake of my hungry and cloudy yearning" (Wright 73) and, of course, help him survive in the segregated Southern society. The young man's fantasies have this effect not because they endow the black boy with movie-hero-like powers, but because his daydreams help him establish the imaginary unity of his ego by emphasizing his limitations, as in the scene of his death, with which the described fantasy ends.

If, then, we are to find in our interpretation of the oft-quoted sentence the logic that the whole of *Black Boy* (*American Hunger*) follows, we can suggest that Wright's autobiography is an attempt to redeem the violent world of his childhood and youth through his writing and, in the process, to give himself a definite, unified identity, keeping whole what Wright calls his "emotional integrity" (Wright 74). Wright is thus not warning the reader about the kind of truth *Black Boy* (*American Hunger*) presents; instead, he is explaining that the story he tells is, with respect to the "objective world" of his boyhood and youth, a redeeming flight, which is itself a way to introduce possibilities into a world that otherwise held none for him and his race except, of course, physical flight in the form of migration north. We then also see that Wright creates this record of his life from two perspectives simultaneously: from the perspective of the young man needing to flee the threatening reality of the world around him *and* from the perspective of the one who understands the origin, purpose, fictive nature, but also futility and impotence of the boy's imaginings. The writer who has managed to emancipate himself from Southern culture, and has turned to writing about it and himself, understands that "what had been taken for our emotional strength"—the boy's imaginative scenarios, but also some forms of Southern African American cultural production—"was our negative confusions, our flights, our fears, our frenzy under pressure" (Wright 37).

The truth of the universe Wright describes, its poetic truth given in retrospect, is that writing is *the* way of survival. Like nothing else—more than religion, more than some traditional African American art forms, and more than the black boy's imaginative flights—it gives, to use Wright's words, "form and meaning to" the black boy's "confused defensive feelings" (Wright 74). Writing, that is to say, holds *the* possibility for a future that, once the boy becomes an emancipated writer, will offer a vantage point from which to see the Southern way of life for what it is.[16]

There are, however, at least two problems with the reading of Wright

I have just offered (in addition to the assumption that writing is more emancipatory than other art forms). First, the Northern enlightenment of his character can be posited only belatedly, after the fact, and thus the enlightenment cannot in and of itself explain the fundamental puzzle of this work: the way that the Southern ignorance relates to the critical consciousness it helped to build. The suggested interpretation fits the first published, 1945 version of Wright's autobiography better than it does *Black Boy* (*American Hunger*) because the former celebrates the enlightened writer who has managed to emancipate himself from the darkness of the Jim Crow South, and the latter very much complicates this story.[17] The 1945 *Black Boy* has, ultimately, a teleological if not outright religious meaning in that it sees the survival of the Southern past in terms of the later, Northern redemption and enlightenment. Its story is incoherent in the sense that the character, the black boy, and the subject telling the story of his life, the intellectual who is the product of the North, are not sufficiently related to each other.[18]

The second problem is that the enlightened narrator is not aware—until the very end of *Black Boy* (*American Hunger*), as we shall see below—that his autobiographical narrative responds to and stems from the same source as the boy's imaginings and, for that matter, has the same cause as the dogmatic flight into religion of, for instance, the black boy's grandmother, a flight rejected by both the black boy and the narrator. What we see here is the specific logic, the specific pattern of autobiographical restoration that Wright seems to follow and that we need to describe more precisely in order to be able to understand his autobiography. The pattern will become more obvious if we look at a paragraph that relates the enlightened, older narrator to the black boy.

Illusion

In the forgiveness scene at the end of the first chapter, Wright has not seen his father for a quarter of a century. When they meet again, Wright, approximately thirty years of age, comments:

> I forgave him and pitied him as my eyes looked past him to the unpainted wooden shack [in which the father lived]. From far beyond the horizons that bound this bleak plantation there had come to me through my living the knowledge that my father was a black peasant who had gone to the city seeking life, but who had failed in the city; a black peasant whose life had been hopelessly snarled in the city, and who had at last fled the city— that same city which had lifted me in its burning arms and borne

me toward alien and undreamed-of shores of knowing. (Wright
34–5)

Wright meets with his father as an educated man capable of seeing his father
for who he is (a black peasant who has failed in life) beyond the idealized
image that the son maintained in his youth when he looked at this father with
awe, fear, and hatred (Wright 10–11). The father had failed in the city,
moreover in *the same* city that is the origin of the son's knowledge. After this
is established, the passage and the whole first chapter close with a striking,
complex metaphor of the Northern city endowed with proper parental
characteristics. We could say that the passage described a moment of
disillusionment if it were not for the fact that one Southern illusion—the
idealized image of the hated and envied father—is substituted for another,
Northern illusion—the idealized image of the paternal city bearing Wright
to new horizons of knowledge. The old illusion is not simply replaced by the
new one but repeated in it since the basic form of idealized (paternal)
identification is extended as the older Wright turns toward the new object.

     What is most important for us in this example is the repetitive pattern,
the logic that one attitude is repeated in another one, for a similar restorative
repetition is evident in the way the autobiography's main character reacts to
the world around him.

     From the very first trial when, as a bored four-year-old, he almost
burns down his home, to the very last one, his exclusion from the Federal
Writers' Project, the main character reacts to the circumstances allotted to
him with utter surprise and with a readiness to learn in order to benefit from
the predicaments in which he finds himself. This cycle of punishment and
survival, surprise and willingness to learn, repeats over and over again.[19] The
last repetition happens at the very close of the autobiography when, after an
unsuccessful attempt to meet with the head of the local Communist party,
Wright, a writer in his late twenties, tossing and turning in his bed,
formulates his perennially surprised attitude toward the world around him.
He says: "Nothing that I could think of could explain the reality I saw. My
mind was like an ulcer whenever it touched upon what had happened to my
relations with the party. I asked myself why a million times, and there were
no answers" (Wright 379).

     The reason why the Communist party does not want him in its ranks
is, however, obvious: it is precisely because this black man *asks why*. Here, as
elsewhere in the book, Wright's character does not know the reality, the
order that he sees, and reacts with disbelief to the situation in which he finds
himself. Instead of learning from his trials, he repeats the cycle that begins
with his failure to understand the world around him, continues through the

punishment he receives for his behavior, and seemingly ends with his enlightenment, his having learned the lesson, only to begin the cycle again. We see that, contrary to the accepted interpretation, the question Wright asks over and over again does not demand a clarification of the Communist Party's attitude any more than his "why," repeated throughout the work, calls for an understanding of any particular problem at hand. "Why" is rather a device, a poetic device, which allows Wright to repeat the cycle of self-restoration again and again. For, finally, to understand racism means, at least in some sense, also to accept it. This is precisely what Wright's character cannot bring himself to do and what distinguishes him from all other black characters in *Black Boy* (*American Hunger*).

On this understanding, the one who did not learn when he was four that he should accept the way things are, as his younger brother had already done, will have never learned but, in his extraordinary, enduring, stubborn naivete, will have disturbed if not undone the order of the world. Wright, to borrow his image, "gnawed" (Wright 384) at the racist reality he could not accept until—in his writing—there appeared something different. We then begin to see that all forms of repetition in this work, its fictions, and its illusions, are not just flights from a given Jim Crow reality, or a redemptive compensation for past sufferings, but attempts, literally, to rewrite what was.[20]

Self-restoration

On the penultimate page of his autobiography, Wright decides that what he calls "his problem" is not out there in the world with other people, but "here with me." With the narrator's turn toward himself, his main question changes. It is no longer a "why," as it has been throughout the work, but:

> Well, what had I got out of living in the city? What had I got out of living in the South? What had I got out of living in America? I paced the floor, knowing that all I possessed were words and dim knowledge that my country had shown me no examples of how to live a human life. All my life I had been full of a hunger for a new way to live ... (Wright 383)

We are thus told that this autobiography is, in fact and finally, a search for a way to live a life, and that the repetitions (the cycles of self-restoration enacting past violations and leading to their restitution, as well as the black boy's imaginative flights and the illusion-disillusionment-illusion cycle) were

not an end in themselves but Wright's means of emancipation from the
society that defined him. Lacking examples that he could follow, in his
autobiographical writing Wright invents his own role-model. He does so
using an indestructible, self-recreating hero endowed with the ability to
renew himself and thus survive the tremendous obstacles he faces. Wright
does this by fictionalizing his life as a means toward an end whose meaning
is revealed only in the closing pages of the autobiography when the narrator
changes the question from the surprised "Why is this happening to me?" to
the decisive "What had I got out of living in America?" and addresses himself
as the narrator of this story of a black man's childhood and youth. What
Wright creates beyond the self-regenerating comic hero and beyond the
social models available to a young Southern Negro is the self of a writer, the
self *in* this narrative of emancipation whose last words, as we shall see,
suggest that his self-definition is beyond words.

Monologic

On the last two pages of *Black Boy* (*American Hunger*), in the process of
turning toward himself, the narrator realizes that he cannot be reconciled
with the world. He cannot fulfill his redemptive dream—which has been the
goal of his writing—of "achieving a vast unity" between him and the world
he has known, nor can he join together his present and his past (Wright 384).
But then, following the rule of Wright's autobiographical writing that an
illusion, once identified as an illusion, is repeated in another one, the final
sentence of the autobiography returns to unity. This time it is the essential
unity of "us all," the inexpressible thing which makes us human. The means
to create and keep alive this dream are identified as words. But at the end of
his book Wright's use of words is not as dialogic or dialectic as his story-
telling has seemed throughout the autobiography, where unifying restoration
has been the task of narratives describing borrowed and actual events that
happened in Richard Wright's life. Explaining how he has written this
autobiography, the writer says:

> I would hurl words into this darkness [that stands between inside
> and outside, present and past] and wait for an echo, and if an echo
> sounded, no matter how faintly, I would send other words to tell,
> to march, to fight, to create a sense of hunger for life that gnaws
> in us all, to keep alive in our hearts a sense of the inexpressibly
> human. (Wright 384)

Before we reach a conclusion to this reading of *Black Boy* (*American*

Hunger), here is a brief summary of the interpretative turns we have traced thus far. First, in its 1945 version, it is a narrative whose purpose is to redeem the past in the implied future of the enlightened author. Second, the restored version of Wright's autobiography, the 1991 *Black Boy* (*American Hunger*), connects, on the one hand, the South, ignorance, and the past, with, on the other hand, the North, enlightenment, and the present. Once the two are brought into a relation, they are supposed to culminate in a triumphant image of an African American writer—his "emotional integrity whole" (Wright 74)—identical to the hero of his autobiography who has managed to overcome adversity and who has returned to cast a critical look at the racist society in which he was born, grew up, and became a writer. But, third, as we saw above, this is precisely what does not happen in *Black Boy* (*American Hunger*). What Wright was supposed to express, his past in words, which is the very premise of an autobiography, and what was to have been the response of the enlightened author to Jim Crow America, gives way to and is replaced by the assertion that the human essence is beyond words or, which is the same thing, beyond fictional representation.

The kind of reflexivity that appears at the end of *Black Boy* (*American Hunger*), the imaginative echoing of the past in the present, reveals that this autobiography cannot be grounded as a dialectical, unifying process between the self and the other, present and past. While *Black Boy* (*American Hunger*) aims to establish and maintain the "emotional integrity" of its enlightened hero and, by implication, of its author, the realization Wright reaches at the end is that no such restoration is possible. The immediate context of this failure is the racism of Jim Crow society, which makes the psychological integration of a black individual difficult and political inclusion as an equal citizen in American democracy impossible. But racism is not the cause of the breakdown of the dialectic whose task was to create the unified identity of an enlightened author. Nor can the breakdown be understood in terms of that racism. The cause of the dissolution is rather the dialectic of emancipatory, restorative autobiographical writing, Wright's intention to render his life in writing and create an autonomous, whole, and wholly critical individual. At the end of his work, Wright realizes that an autobiographical writing is, in the final instance, a failed dialectical writing and, in this specific sense, a mono-logical writing. Mono-logical because it miscarries in what it must do, bring an "I" into a relation with itself; with itself as a function of the "I"'s iterability in an autobiographical narrative, in others, in the past, and in what we suppose are things that define us essentially or fundamentally (Jim Crow racism in Wright's case). As we shall see below, the autobiography that fails to bear out a dialectical unity achieves something else.

Paternity

After this conclusion concerning the final moment of Wright's *Black Boy* (*American Hunger*), we are prepared to return to de Man to make explicit a characteristic of autobiographical writing that he only alludes to. Though de Man's "Autobiography as De-facement" abounds with uses of the term "name" and, in effect, describes the processes of naming and of assuming a name, the essay offers no direct recognition that autobiography is the only writing genre that explicitly makes the writing subject's origin *and* destiny its primary concerns, not just destiny as it is presented in "Autobiography as De-facement." Consider, for instance, de Man's commentary on the metaphor of the sun in Wordsworth's *Essays upon Epitaphs*, which immediately precedes his introduction of prosopopoeia:

> Knowledge and mind imply language and account for the relationship set up between the sun and the text of the epitaph: the epitaph, says Wordsworth, "is open to the day; the sun looks down upon the stone, and the rains of heaven beat against it." The sun becomes the eye that *reads* the text of the epitaph. And the essay tells us what this text consists of, by way of a quotation from Milton that deals with Shakespeare: "What need'st thou such weak witness of thy *name*?" In the case of poets such as Shakespeare, Milton or Wordsworth himself, the epitaph can consist only of what he calls "the naked name" (p. 113), as it is read by the eye of the sun.

De Man then interprets this description:

> At this point, it can be said of "the language of the senseless stone" that it acquires a "voice," the *speaking* stone counterbalancing the *seeing* sun. The system passes from sun to eye to language as name and as voice. We can identify the figure that completes the central metaphor of the sun and thus completes the tropological spectrum that the sun engenders: it is the figure of prosopopoeia. (925–6, emphases de Man's)

Yes, the main figure of this discourse is prosopopoeia, but the analysis of the tropological spectrum cannot end with that conclusion. The stock mythical trope of the sun symbolizing the Father; the homonyms "sun" and "son," "eye" and "I"; the line of generation from Shakespeare to Milton to Wordsworth to de Man himself; the transformation of a voiceless into a speaking entity, one entity replacing another, etc., all lead us to read the basic plot of autobiography (in de Man's sense) as a story of self-restoration, where the subject's origin and destiny are brought together as the "son" assumes the position previously held by the "father." Not a biological father, to be sure, but a father figure whom the son has chosen for himself as Wordsworth does when he invokes Milton and as Milton does in the poem that testifies to Shakespeare's greatness. In all of these instances the younger man asks Milton's ambiguous question: "What need'st thou such weak witness of thy *name*?"Ambiguous not simply because it is an assertion that Shakespeare— "Dear son of memory, great heir of Fame"—is a timeless author, but because, appropriating the tradition that culminates with the bard, Milton asserts himself in the bard's place. An heir, this symbolic son, does not only choose a father for himself, he also configures the way in which this name of the father signifies, the way it becomes a name and a part of a new tradition—the son's name and the son's tradition.

   We saw above that Wright, who was looking for role-models and, in his writing, rejected those that were available to him,[21] did so to transform the world and also (perhaps firstly) in order to make himself. The self-making is thematized under the trope of hunger, which begins as an associative link with Wright's father: "As the days slid past the image of my father became associated with my pangs of hunger, and whenever I felt hunger I thought of him with a deep biological bitterness" (Wright 16). Gradually, this hunger becomes the hunger for the knowledge and the emancipation from Southern ignorance the author will achieve in the Northern city. Now we can explicitly state that Wright's hunger has the same significance as the metaphor of the sun in motion in Wordsworth's text and prosopopoeia in de Man's. It invokes the paternal figure under which the author restores and recreates himself.

   This paternal figure is, as we see in Wright, a function in speech, not a concrete father or even a father figure such as God. It stands for the anonymity, the namelessness, of the father and designates that the paternal figure is unidentifiable in any other way but as a function. Given our source, Wright's *Black Boy* (*American Hunger*), it is, then, more precise to call it the no-name of the father since, in Wright's case, autobiography is meant to secure the paternal function as a function, without fixing its content or naming its bearer.

Conclusion

   If, as de Man suggests, autobiography restores and, at the same time, disfigures, this is not a consequence of the fact that the human world is mediated by language, that everything that is restored in language is also negated, dis-figured or de-faced by this very restoration.[22] Autobiography restores *and* disfigures, rather, because it makes obvious that the human being is, essentially, a linguistic being, the result (that is, the subject) of the linguistic predicament whose essence is inexpressible (Wright) and whose knowledge is privative (de Man), but also, whose universe is pre-configured in a certain way. As Lacan shows and as we have discovered in both Wright and de Man, human beings are subject to a given configuration of their symbolic universe, which is structured around the signifier or around the no-name of the father. That our universe is pre-configured means that the subject, in the very process of assuming its subject position, has to rearticulate or rewrite the entire system in order to be, in order to become what and who he is.

As we saw in our reading of Wright, this rearticulation, this rewriting does not lead to an establishment of a specific, positive identity but to the recognition that the act of self-making is, ultimately, an anonymous act; i.e., it is an act leading to the understanding that there is nothing that can define or that can guarantee our humanity, whose cause and meaning remain beyond words.

We can arrive at the same conclusion with a glance at the history of autobiography as a genre. History of autobiography as a genre is, in fact, a history of the doubt that, on the one hand, autobiography is to be counted among the literary genres and, on the other, that it can present a historical or any other truth. The persistent doubt also concerns, not surprisingly, the proper way to name the subject in the autobiographical narrative; whether he should be identified by the first or the third person pronoun,[23] by the author's proper name or his other appellations such as "black boy." Whatever the decision of the author, whether his main character is finally an "I," a "he," a "Richard Wright," or a "black boy," *the narrative has, in an ontological sense, the same significance* since in a writing that pretends to be a record (Wright's work is subtitled "A record of Childhood and Youth"), nearness invokes and implies a distance, identity implies its erasure, singularity implies iterability, the assertion of truth implies the presence of fictional representation, etc. All this should confirm that though autobiography is a self-making, it is neither about (of) the self nor about (of) the other—same or different, truth or fiction, present or absent. Rather, it is about the inexpressible or anonymous something which allows us—in this modern historical epoch, which starts approximately with the proclamation that *all men are created equal*—to identify these specular pairs: self/other, same/different, truth/fiction, author/character, etc.

As we have seen, autobiographical writing presents its subject as an indestructible, self-restorative, and, by implication, self-generative, self-creating entity. But, as we also have seen, the subject of autobiography has to recognize this imaginary, comic nature of autobiographical self-restoration for what it is, a defacing autofiction[24] or, in Sandra Adell's terms, a defacing auto-text. What is, strictly speaking, funny—because also laudable—about the attempt to self-construct, to engender oneself, is the fantasy (the bourgeois fantasy par excellence), present in Wright and supported by de Man and Lacan, that a man can be self-made.[25] The comic transformations and the author's recognition of their nature *allow the emergence of the ontologically*, not historically, *prior*, negativity, which could, then, fundamentally undermine the assumed, given, pre-ordered, historically determined system—Jim Crow and family, in Wright's case, metaphysics in Lacan's and de Man's—but only if this negativity is maintained as a *radical* negativity. Only if, to use de Man's words, "the negativity of the initial relationship (or lack of relationship) is left intact" (de Man 925).[26] That is, only if the negativity is left beyond the dialectic of naming. This is certainly not the case either in the black boy's daydreams or in the flight into religion described by Wright. It is, however, precisely what his *Black Boy (American Hunger)*, taken in its entirety, attempts to do.

It follows from this analysis of the comic figure that autobiography (and the autobiographical moment that all works of fiction share, according to both Wright and de Man) is *about (or of) that which the dialectic between the self and the other, the same and the different, truth and fiction, author and character, even black and white cannot sublate (bring into relation) but which, paradoxically, makes the relation between these and all other specular pairs possible. The challenge of interpretation, as we see in de Man and Wright—be it an interpretation of one's life or a reading of an autobiography—is to find a way to address that nameless, inexpressible, or anonymous something ("a sense of the hunger [...] that gnaws in us all" in Wright's terms; negativity in de Man's) that escapes the dialectic of specular pairs and can be identified only indirectly, through the displacing effects it has on an autobiographical narrative and, hence, on the creation and disfiguration of identity.*

Regarding Richard Wright, the problem that remains to be comprehended is why he agreed not to publish the version of his autobiography that we know today. The accepted and incomplete answer is that Wright knew that the symbolic revolution he had performed with *Black Boy (American Hunger)* would not have been sufficient for the Negro author to gain the independence he sought. Wright, the self-supporting writer, the logic goes, published the 1945 version of *Black Boy* because being selected for the Book-of-the-Month Club virtually insured that his work would be a best-seller and that its author would continue to enjoy the financial privileges of stardom such as they were in the immediate aftermath of the Second World War. A thorough reexamination of Wright's oeuvre, which is still to come, should add a clarification, explaining the implications of Wright's compromise in terms of what he meant by writing and what writing meant to him.

NOTES

1. Sandra Adell has already shown this in her excellent chapter "The Auto-Text." The main difference between Adell's undertaking and mine is that hers is a more strictly Lacanian reading of Wright. We also read two different versions of Wright's autobiography; Adell the *Black Boy* and I the original version.

2. Though neither of Wright's biographies, nor Lacan's by Rudinesco, mentions that the two men met, it is likely, since they moved in similar Parisian intellectual circles, that they at least knew of each other.

3. The MLA Bibliography lists three hundred seventy-three titles on, for instance, Toni Morrison's *Beloved* (1987) and only sixty-one titles on Wright's *Black Boy*. The 1991 publication of the original *Black Boy* (*American Hunger*) has not spurred a general reevaluation of scholarship on Wright's autobiography as it should have.

4. I have elaborated on this in my article "Native Son's Tragedy."

5. The 1945 edition of *Black Boy* is roughly one fourth shorter than the original version, which was titled *American Hunger*, and was published for the first time (in the restored, integral version) only in 1991, more than thirty years after Wright's death in 1960. The 1945 *Black Boy* is not simply the Southern part of the experience described in the original manuscript. It is a narrative with a different meaning, shaped by the sensibilities of the Book-of-the-Month Club luminaries, who, as Jeff Karem has shown, cared more for their idea of what an authentic, local story should be than for the complex story of American racism Wright had to tell. I should add here that all parts of Wright's autobiography not published in *Black Boy* were published prior to 1991 as separate articles.

6. As throughout his lectures on *Antigone*, Lacan is here following Aristotle's *Poetics*, which famously asserts that no aspect of comedy should be painful or destructive. Lacan offers an explanation for this phenomenon that goes beyond the scope of Aristotle's analysis.

7. In *The Sublime Object of Ideology*, Zizek briefly analyzes the *Tom and Jerry* series (134).

8. The influence of movies on Wright is obvious and has been elaborated on in Ross Pudaloff's "Celebrity as Identity: *Native Son* and Mass Culture."

9. The most recent example is Simon Critchley's critique of Lacan.

10. In Lacan's understanding, there are no essential or ontological differences between comic and tragic heroes—both are articulated along the same axis relating desire and action. It is these articulations, however, that differ in the ways outlined in my extension of Lacan's basic proposition that in comedy the triumph of death is deferred.

11. In an unpublished essay titled simply "On Literature," Wright make a similar point. "[A]ll writing is," Wright says, "a secret form of autobiography" (Rowley 410). I should mention here that the conclusion that there are autobiographical elements in all writing is not itself new. See for instance Lacoue-Labarthe's "The Echo of the Subject" (142), originally published the same year as de Man's "Autobiography as De-facement." In this essay Lacoue-Labarthe follows a post-Heideggerian theoretical path similar to the one engaged in de Man. The main difference between the two essays is that the latter addresses the field of literary studies directly and is thus closer to my present purposes.

12. In one of his rare discussions of comedy in "Rhetoric of Temporality," de Man follows Baudelaire's text "De l'essence du rire," focusing on the notion of *dédoublement*, which de Man translates as "self-duplication" and "self-multiplication." Understood in this way, *dédoublement* resembles closely some of the characteristics of the Lacanian comic hero—namely, the comic hero does not feel pain because of a doubling. De Man pursues *dédoublement* as a relationship between two types of consciousness and two types of self-reflexivity, the philosophical and the ordinary, the ironic and the merely comic, privileging the philosophical and ironic consciousness.

13. This is also to say that the intention of my article is not to read Wright's autobiography as a comedy but as a narrative whose protagonist fits the indestructible, self-recreating figure we find in Lacan's reading of *Antigone*. Wright's autobiography has been read as a comedy by Marc Guidry, who assumes it to be a comedy because the main character triumphs over the adverse environment when he escapes the confines of Southern Jim Crow. Guidry stops short of explaining why there is a similarity between the two genres (comedy and autobiography) or what it is that this similarity consists of.

14. One is tempted to call Craig Werner's "Bigger's Blues: *Native Son* and the Articulation of Afro-American Modernism," published in Kinnamon's collection, an exception to this rule (that there is no decisive critique of the notion of socio-historical factors in works on Wright). But Werner examines Wright in order to assert the primacy of certain existential and experiential characteristics—"fragmentation, alienation, sense-making" (121)—and, thus, the primacy of a version of socio-historical factors over and against a modernist aesthetics that can itself be defined by the same terms, fragmentation, alienation, construction. Similarly, Michel Fabre, throughout his work on Wright, discusses the writer's poetics in terms of his life experiences, even as Fabre wants to contest the claim that Wright follows naturalist and realist paradigms. See, for instance, Michel Fabre, "Beyond Naturalism?" published in Bloom's collection.

15. Prior to the telling of the story of the black woman, on page 7, the black boy is "lashed so hard and long" by his mother that he loses consciousness. On pages 13 and 14, his mother forces him to bury the kitten he has killed and orders him to pray to God to spare his life. On page 16, a gang of boys beats him up on the street. On page 17, they do it again. On page 18, he is threatened with a whipping by his mother if he does not fight back against the boys. He is forced to drink alcohol in a bar and, after he gets drunk, he is punished for it by his mother (20). His mother punishes him for writing four-letter words (25). Etc.

16. See Jan Mohamed for a reading of Wright's autobiography in terms of possibilities the author creates for himself.

17. To the best of my knowledge, there are no works on *Black Boy* that convincingly contest this emancipation.

18. Consider, for instance, the difference between the ending of the 1945 *Black Boy*— "With ever watchful eyes and bearing scars, visible and invisible, I headed North, full of a hazy notion that [...] if men were lucky in their living on earth they might win some redeeming meaning for their having struggled and suffered here beneath the stars" (*Native Son/Black Boy* 285)—and the original version: "This was the culture from which I sprang. This was the terror from which I fled" (Wright 257).

19. While the pattern we see here dramatizing an overcoming of obstacles can be found in much of African American folklore and literature, Wright's version is distinct in that his repetitions rearticulate the relationship between an individual-writer and a collective whose ideology the character cannot accept or completely reject. The pattern in Wright, as we shall promptly see, leads to radical renewal, the complete self-

invention of a black person as a writer. On Wright and folklore see Baker (1972) and Ellison.

20. It is because Wright attempts to rewrite the past that his autobiography is a work of fiction. What the goals and implications of this rewriting are we shall see below.

21. The most significant of Wright's rejections is of his mother, who was a school teacher and who appears in *Black Boy* (*American Hunger*) as a sickly, poor, cruel, uneducated if not stupid woman whom the main character will have to support, sharing with her his meager earnings. To be more precise, the narrator accepts his mother only after she has been transformed into a symbol of poverty, ignorance, and helplessness. In Wright words: "My mother's suffering grew into a symbol in my mind, gathering to itself all the poverty, the ignorance, the helplessness; the painful, baffling, hunger-ridden days and hours; the restless moving, the futile seeking, the uncertainty, the fear, the dread; the meaningless pain and the endless suffering" (Wright 100). In a striking contrast, Wright's dedication of his *Native Son* reads: "To my mother who, when I was a child at her knee, taught me to revere the fanciful and the imaginative."

22. I assume that the negation, dis-figuration, and de-facement are connoted in de Man's use of the adjective "privative" at the end of his article where he says: "As soon as we understand the rhetorical function of prosopopoeia as positing voice or face by means of language, we also understand that what we are deprived of is not life but the shape and the sense of a world accessible only in the *privative* way of understanding" (de Man 930, emphasis added).

23. Or even by the second person singular pronoun, as in, for instance, the prologue of Mary Karr's recent memoir titled *Cherry*.

24. The term "autofiction" was coined by Serge Doubrovsky to describe his work *Fils*.

25. The fantasy, needless to say, is not limited to the three works examined here but is a common, masculine modernist motif present in some form already in Milton and Wordsworth and, perhaps most famously, in James Joyce's *A Portrait of the Artist as a Young Man*. In the film entitled *Psychoanalysis*, Lacan himself declares faking an American accent: "En quoi je suis un *self-made man*" (*Télévision* 8).

26. De Man's identification of the initial relationship as the subject's being-towards-death, in Heidegger's terms, should be understood as emphasizing the non-relational nature of human finitude and not as an attempt to posit human mortality as some quasi-absolute or ultimate referent against which all other relations are measured. Therefore, we understand de Man to be saying that the initial relationship, such as, for instance, human finitude, is precisely that kind of relationship which exceeds relationality. It is initial not because it takes place prior to other relations, but because it is not reified in them and remains a non-relation.

WORKS CITED

Adams, Timothy Dow. "'I Do Believe Him Though I Know He Lies': Lying as Genre and Metaphor in *Black Boy*." *Richard Wright: Critical Perspectives Past and Present*. Eds. Henry Louis Gates, Jr. and K. A. Appiah. New York: Amistad, 1993: 302–315.

Adell, Sandra. "The Auto-Text: On Inscripting Otherness; or Alas, Poor Richard, Poor Maya." *Double-Consciousness/Double Bind: Theoretical Issues in Twentieth-Century Black Literature*. Urbana: University of Illinois Press, 1994: 56–89.

Baker, Houston A. Jr. *Black Literature in America*. New York: McGraw-Hill, 1971.

———. *Long Black Song: Essays in Black American Literature and Culture*. Charlottesville:

University of Virginia Press, 1972.

———, ed. *Twentieth Century Interpretations of Native Son*. Englewood Cliffs, N.J.: Prentice-Hall, 1972.

Baudelaire, Charles. *Curiosités esthétiques: L'Art romantique et autres Ouvres critiques*. Ed. H. Lemaître. Paris: Garnier, 1962.

Bloom, Harold, ed. *Richard Wright*. New York: Chelsea House Publishers, 1987.

Critchley, Simon. *Ethics-Politics-Subjectivity: Essays on Derrida, Levinas and Contemporary French Thought*. New York: Verso, 1999.

de Man, Paul. "Autobiography as De-facement." *MLN* 94 1979: 919–930.

———. "Rhetoric of Temporality." *Blindness and Insight*. Minneapolis: University of Minnesota Press, 1988: 187–228.

Doubrovsky, Serge. *Fils*. Paris: Éditions Galilée, 1977.

Ellison, Ralph. *Shadow and Act*. New York: Random House, 1964.

Fabre, Michel. "Beyond Naturalism?" *Richard Wright*. Ed. Harold Bloom. New York: Chelsea House Publishers, 1987: 37–56.

Gates, Henry Louis Jr. and K. A. Appiah, eds. *Richard Wright: Critical Perspectives Past and Present*. New York: Amistad, 1993.

Guidry, Marc. "Richard Wright's Wrighting: The Autobiographical Comedy of *Black Boy*." *Publications of the Mississippi Philological Association* 1990: 104–108.

Jan Mohamed, Abdul R. "Negating the Negation: The Construction of Richard Wright." *Richard Wright: Critical Perspectives Past and Present*. Eds. Henry Louis Gates, Jr. and K. A. Appiah. New York: Amistad, 1993: 285–301.

Joyce, James. *A Portrait of the Artist as a Young Man*. New York: Penguin, 1993.

Karem, Jeff. "'I Could Never Really Leave the South': Regionalism and the Transformation of Richard Wright's American Hunger." *American Literary History* 13.4, 2001: 694–715.

Karr, Mary. *Cherry*. New York: Penguin, 2000.

Kinnamon, Keneth. *New Essays on Native Son*. New York: Cambridge University Press, 1990.

Lacan, Jacques. *Télévision*. Paris: Seuil, 1973.

———. "Aggressivity in Psychoanalysis." *Écrits: A Selection*. Trans. Alan Sheridan. New York: Norton, 1977: 8–29.

———. *The Ethics of Psychoanalysis*. Trans. Dennis Porter. New York: Norton, 1992.

Lacoue-Labarthe, Philippe. "The Echo of the Subject." Trans. Barbara Harlow. *Typography: Mimesis, Philosophy, Politics*. Ed. Christopher Fynsk. Cambridge, Mass.: Harvard University Press, 1989: 139–207.

Pudaloff, Ross. "Celebrity as Identity: *Native Son* and Mass Culture." *Richard Wright: Critical Perspectives Past and Present*. Eds. Henry Louis Gates, Jr. and K. A. Appiah. New York: Amistad, 1993: 156–170.

Ramadanovic, Petar. "Native Son's Tragedy: Traversing the Death Drive with Bigger Thomas." *Arizona Quarterly* (Summer 2003) 59:2, 81–106.

Rampersad, Arnold. *Richard Wright: A Collection of Critical Essays*. Englewood Cliffs, NJ: Prentice Hall, 1995.

Rowley, Hazel. *Richard Wright: The Life and Times*. New York: Henry Holt, 2001.

Werner, Craig. "Bigger's Blues: *Native Son* and the Articulation of Afro-American Modernism." *New Essays on Native Son*. Ed. Keneth Kinnamon. New York: Cambridge University Press, 1990: 117–152.

Wright, Richard. "The Literature of the Negro in the United States." *White Man Listen!* Doubleday: New York, 1964.

———. *Native Son/Black Boy*. New York: Harper and Row, 1987.

———. *Black Boy (American Hunger)*. New York: Harper Collins, 1993.

Zizek, Slavoj. *The Sublime Object of Ideology*. New York: Verso, 1997.

Chronology

1908	Richard Nathaniel Wright is born September 4 on Rucker's Plantation, some twenty miles east of Natchez, Mississippi, the first child of Nathaniel Wright, a sharecropper, and Ella Wilson Wright, a schoolteacher.
1910	Brother Leon Alan Wright is born September 24.
1911–1912	Ella Wright leaves the farm with her children and goes to Natchez to live with her family. Richard accidentally sets fire to his grandparents' house.
1913–1914	The Wright family moves to Memphis. Richard's father leaves his family to live with another woman.
1915–1916	Richard enters school for the first time. He drops out to take care of his ill mother; then he and his brother are placed in an orphanage for a short time. Eventually they move in with their maternal grandparents in Jackson, Mississippi, and then with Wright's aunt Maggie and uncle Silas Hopkins.
1917	Uncle Silas is murdered by whites.
1918–1919	The Wrights settle again with Ella's mother in Jackson. Wright is forced to leave school to find work. Ella's deteriorating health culminates in a stroke, leaving her paralyzed.

1920	Wright attends the Seventh-Day Adventist school taught by his aunt Addie, but rebels against its strict rules.
1921	Wright transfers to the public Jim Hill School, where he excels academically and gains friends.
1922	Wright works various jobs after school and during summer, including work as a newsboy and as a secretary/accountant to an insurance agent—enabling him to afford books, food, and clothing for the first time.
1923–1924	Wright attends Smith-Robertson Junior High. His first short story, "The Voodoo of Hell's Half-Acre," is published in the black newspaper *Jackson Southern Register*.
1925	Graduates as valedictorian of his ninth-grade class. Leaves public schooling, and leaves Jackson for Memphis.
1927–1928	Wright moves to Chicago, where he works part time for the post office and begins to write in earnest.
1930	Loses his job due to the stock market crash.
1931	Publishes short story "Superstition" in *Abbott's Monthly Magazine*, an African-American journal.
1933	Wright joins the Chicago John Reed Club and writes revolutionary poetry for *Left Front*. He joins the Communist Party and is hired to supervise a youth club organized to counter juvenile delinquency among African-Americans on the South Side.
1935	Continues publishing poetry, and tries unsuccessfully to sell his first novel (*Lawd Today!*). Wright expands his acquaintances among left-wing writers and is hired by the Federal Writer's Project.
1936	Organizes the Communist Party–sponsored National Negro Congress. His short story "Big Boy Leaves Home" appears in *The New Caravan*.
1937	Moves to New York, where he becomes the Harlem editor of the *Daily Worker* and helps launch the magazine *New Challenge*. His story "Fire and Cloud" wins first prize of $500 in a contest sponsored by *Story* magazine.
1938	*Uncle Tom's Children: Four Novellas* is published to wide acclaim.
1939	Receives a Guggenheim fellowship. Marries Dhimah Rose Meadman, a white ballet dancer.
1940	*Native Son* is published and becomes a best-seller. The book

	receives national attention as a Book of the Month Club selection. Wright's marriage to Meadman fails.
1941	Wright marries Ellen Poplar, a Communist organizer from Brooklyn. The play *Native Son* is produced on Broadway by Orson Welles and John Houseman. Wright collaborates with Edwin Rosskam on *Twelve Million Black Voices: A Folk History of the Negro in the United States.*
1942	Daughter Julia is born.
1944	Wright's break with the Communist Party becomes public with the publication of "I Tried to Be a Communist" in *The Atlantic Monthly.*
1945	*Black Boy*, published in March, receives excellent reviews, and is accepted by the Book of the Month Club.
1946	Wright travels to France in May as a guest of the French government, where he is well received by French intellectuals.
1947	Decides to move his family to France permanently.
1949	A second daughter, Rachel, is born in January. Wright writes the film version of *Native Son.*
1951	The film *Native Son* opens in Buenos Aires. Thirty minutes of film are cut by censors for the U.S. premier; the film fails in the U.S.
1952	Wright refuses to return to the United States, citing risk of subpoena by an anti-Communist Congressional investigating committee.
1953	*The Outsider* is published in March to mixed reviews. Wright travels throughout Africa's Gold Coast.
1954	Wright travels in Spain. Publishes *Black Power* and *Savage Holiday.*
1955	Attends the Bandung Conference in Indonesia.
1956	*The Color Curtain: A Report on the Bandung Conference* is published.
1957	*White Man, Listen!*, a collection of lectures, is published.
1958	*The Long Dream* is published in October, but reviews are mostly unfavorable. When Wright attempts to renew his passport, he is harassed by the American embassy for his former Communist associations.
1959	Wright's mother dies.

1960   *The Long Dream*, adapted from the novel, has only a one-
            week run on Broadway. Wright prepares more than eight
            hundred of his haiku for publication. *Eight Men*, a
            collection of short stories, is ready for publication. Wright
            dies of an apparent heart attack on November 28.

Contributors

HAROLD BLOOM is Sterling Professor of the Humanities at Yale University. He is the author of 30 books, including *Shelley's Mythmaking* (1959), *The Visionary Company* (1961), *Blake's Apocalypse* (1963), *Yeats* (1970), *A Map of Misreading* (1975), *Kabbalah and Criticism* (1975), *Agon: Toward a Theory of Revisionism* (1982), *The American Religion* (1992), *The Western Canon* (1994), and *Omens of Millennium: The Gnosis of Angels, Dreams, and Resurrection* (1996). *The Anxiety of Influence* (1973) sets forth Professor Bloom's provocative theory of the literary relationships between the great writers and their predecessors. His most recent books include *Shakespeare: The Invention of the Human* (1998), a 1998 National Book Award finalist, *How to Read and Why* (2000), *Genius: A Mosaic of One Hundred Exemplary Creative Minds* (2002), *Hamlet: Poem Unlimited* (2003), *Where Shall Wisdom Be Found?* (2004), and *Jesus and Yahweh: The Names Divine* (2005). In 1999, Professor Bloom received the prestigious American Academy of Arts and Letters Gold Medal for Criticism. He has also received the International Prize of Catalonia, the Alfonso Reyes Prize of Mexico, and the Hans Christian Andersen Bicentennial Prize of Denmark.

RALPH ELLISON achieved international fame with his first novel, *Invisible Man*, winner of the National Book Award in 1952. He also wrote *Juneteenth*, published after his death, and two collections of essays, *Shadow and Act* (1964) and *Going to the Territory* (1986).

DAN McCALL is Professor of American Studies at Cornell University. He is the author of *The Example of Richard Wright* and the novels *Messenger Bird* and *Jack the Bear*, and the editor of *Melville's Short Novels* (Norton Critical Editions).

CLAUDIA C. TATE was a professor of English and African-American studies at Princeton University known for her contributions to African-American literary criticism. Her books included *Black Women Writers at Work*; *Domestic Allegories of Political Desire: The Black Heroine's Text at the Turn of the Century*; *Psychoanalysis and Black Novels: Desire and the Protocols of Race*; and *The Works of Katherine Tillman*.

CHARLES T. DAVIS co-edited *The Slave's Narrative* with Henry Louis Gates, Jr. He was also the author of *Black is the Color of the Cosmos: Essays on Afro-American Literature and Culture, 1942–1981*.

HORACE A. PORTER is the author of *Jazz Country: Ralph Ellison in America*; *Stealing the Fire: The Art and Protest of James Baldwin*; *The Making of a Black Scholar: From Georgia to the Ivy League*; and one of the editors of *Call and Response: The Riverside Anthology of the African American Literary Tradition*. He is a professor in the English Department at the University of Iowa.

YOSHINOBU HAKUTANI is a professor in the English Department at Kent State University. He is the editor of *Critical Essays on Richard Wright*; *The Critical Response in Japan to African American Writers* (with Toru Kiuchi and Robert J. Butler); *Theodore Dreiser and American Culture: New Readings*; *Modernity in East-West Literary Criticism: New Readings*; and *Postmodernity and Cross-Culturalism*.

KENETH KINNAMON's books include *The Emergence of Richard Wright: A Study in Literature and Society*; *New Essays on* Native Son; *Critical Essays on Richard Wright's* Native Son; and *Conversations with Richard Wright* (with Michel Fabre).

DONALD B. GIBSON is the editor of *Five Black Writers: Essays on Wright, Ellison, Baldwin, Hughes, and LeRoi Jones*; *Modern Black Poets: A Collection of Critical Essays*; and *Black and White: Stories of American Life* (co-edited with Carol Anselment). He is also the author of *The Politics of Literary Expression: A Study of Major Black Writers*.

ELIZABETH J. CINER is Senior Lecturer in English at Carleton College. She has written on the subject of freedom in Wright's fiction, and she has worked to encourage multiculturalism in American schools.

WILLIAM L. ANDREWS teaches at UNC-Chapel Hill. He is the author of *To Tell a Free Story: The First Century of Afro-American Autobiography, 1760–1865*. He also co-edited *The Norton Anthology of African American Literature*; *The Oxford Companion to African American Literature*; and *The Literature of the American South: A Norton Anthology*.

WARREN J. CARSON is an associate professor of English and chair of the Department of English and Foreign Languages at the University of South Carolina, Spartanburg. He has published essays and reviews in a number of scholarly journals, including the *African American Review*, the *Southern Literary Review*, and *Appalachian Heritage*.

PETAR RAMADANOVIC is Assistant Professor of English at the University of New Hampshire.

Bibliography

Abcarian, Richard, ed. *Richard Wright's Native Son: A Critical Handbook.* Belmont, Calif.: Wadsworth Pub. Co, 1970.

Andrews, William L. "Richard Wright and the African American Autobiography Tradition." *Style* 27, no 2 (Summer 1993): 271–285.

Bakish, David. *Richard Wright.* New York: Ungar, 1973.

Baldwin, James. "Everybody's Protest Novel." *Notes of a Native Son.* Boston: Beacon, 1955. 85–114.

———. "Richard Wright." *Encounter* 16 (April 1961): 58–60.

Bloom, Harold, ed. *Richard Wright: Modern Critical Views.* New York: Chelsea House Publishers, 1987.

Bone, Robert. *Richard Wright.* Minneapolis: University of Minnesota Press, 1969.

Brignano, Russell C. *Richard Wright: An Introduction to the Man and His Works.* Pittsburgh: University of Pittsburgh Press, 1970.

Carson, Warren J. "'They Don't Look So Good, Mistah': Realities of the South in Richard Wright's *Black Boy* and Selected Short Fiction." *CLA Journal* 47, no. 3 (March 2004): 299–309.

Davis, Charles T. "From Experience to Eloquence: Richard Wright's *Black Boy* as Art." *Chant of Saints: A Gathering of Afro-American Literature, Art, and Scholarship.* Michael S. Harper and Robert B. Stepto, ed. Urbana: University of Illinois Press, 1979. 425–439.

Denissova, Tamara. "Richard Wright: The Problem of Self-Identification" *Mississippi Quarterly* 50, no. 2 (Spring 1997): 239–253.

Ellison, Ralph. "Richard Wright's Blues." *Shadow and Act*. New York: Random House, 1964. 77–94.

Fabre, Michel. *The Unfinished Quest of Richard Wright*. New York: Morrow, 1973, second edition, 1993.

Felgar, Robert. *Richard Wright*. Boston: Twayne, 1980.

Hayley, Mitchell, ed. *Readings on Richard Wright's* Black Boy. San Diego: Greenhaven, 2000.

Gates, Henry Louis, Jr., and K.A. Appiah, eds. *Richard Wright: Critical Perspectives Past and Present*. New York: Amistad, 1993.

Gayle, Addison. *Richard Wright: Ordeal of a Native Son*. Garden City, N.Y.: Anchor Press/Doubleday, 1980.

Gibson, Donald B. "Richard Wright's *Black Boy* and the Trauma of Autobiographical Rebirth." *Callaloo*, No. 28, Richard Wright: A Special Issue (Summer 1986): 492–498.

Hakutani, Yoshinobu, ed. *Critical Essays on Richard Wright*. Boston: G.K. Hall, 1982.

Howe, Irving. "Black Boys and Native Sons." *A World More Attractive*. New York: Horizon, 1963. 98–110.

Joyce, Joyce A. *Richard Wright's Art of Tragedy*. Iowa City: University of Iowa Press, 1986.

Kinnamon, Keneth. *The Emergence of Richard Wright: A Study in Literature and Society*. Urbana: University of Illinois Press, 1972.

———, ed. *Critical Essays on Richard Wright's* Native Son. New York: Twayne Publishers, 1997.

———, and Michel Fabre, eds. *Conversations with Richard Wright*. Jackson: University Press of Mississippi, 1993.

Macksey, Richard, and Frank E. Moorer, eds. *Richard Wright: A Collection of Critical Essays*. Englewood Cliffs, N.J.: Prentice-Hall, 1984.

Margolies, Edward. *The Art of Richard Wright*. Preface by Harry T. Moore. Carbondale: Southern Illinois University Press, 1969.

Maxwell, William J. *New Negro, Old Left: African-American Writing and Communism Between the Wars*. New York: Columbia University Press, 1999.

McCall, Dan. *The Example of Richard Wright*. New York: Harcourt, Brace & World, 1973.

Miller, Eugene E. *Voice of a Native Son: The Poetics of Richard Wright*. Jackson: University Press of Mississippi, 1990.

Ramadanovic, Petar. "*Black Boy*'s Comedy: Indestructibility and Anonymity in Autobiographical Self-Making." *Callaloo* 27, no. 2 (Spring 2004): 502–521.

Reilly, John M. *Richard Wright: The Critical Reception.* New York: Franklin, 1978.

Rowley, Hazel. *Richard Wright: The Life and Times.* New York: Henry Holt, 2001.

Scherr, Athur. "Richard Wright's *Black Boy* and 'The Ethics of Living Jim Crow': A Sidelight on Motives." *Southern Studies* 11, no. 1-2. (Spring–Summer 2004): 39–46.

Tate, Claudia C. "*Black Boy*: Richard Wright's 'Tragic Sense of Life.'" *Black American Literature Forum* 10, no. 4 (Winter 1976): 117–119.

Trotman, C. James, ed. *Richard Wright: Myths and Realities.* New York: Garland Publishing, Inc., 1988.

Walker, Margaret. *Richard Wright, Daemonic Genius: A Portrait of the Man, a Critical Look at His Work.* New York: Warner Books, 1988.

Webb, Constance. *Richard Wright: A Biography.* New York: Putnam, 1968.

Williams, John A., and Dorothy Sterling. *The Most Native of Sons: A Biography of Richard Wright.* Garden City, N.Y.: Doubleday, 1970.

Acknowledgments

"Richard Wright's Blues" by Ralph Ellison. © 1945 by the Antioch Review, Inc. (renewed 1972). First appeared in the *Antioch Review* Vol. 5, No. 2. Reprinted by permission of the Editors.

"An American Life" by Dan McCall. From *The Example of Richard Wright*. pp. 103–135. © 1969 Dan McCall. Reprinted by permission.

"*Black Boy*: Richard Wright's 'Tragic Sense of Life'" by Claudia C. Tate. From *Black American Literature Forum* 10, no. 4, pp. 117–119. © 1976 *African American Review*. Reprinted by permission.

"From Experience to Eloquence: Richard Wright's *Black Boy* as Art" by Charles T. Davis. From *Chant of Saints: A Gathering of Afro-American Literature, Art, and Scholarship*. Michael S. Harper and Robert B. Stepto, ed. pp. 425–439. © 1979 by University of Illinois Press. Reprinted by permission.

"The Horror and the Glory: Richard Wright's Portrait of the Artist in *Black Boy* and *American Hunger*" by Horace A. Porter. From *Richard Wright: A Collection of Critical Essays*. Richard Macksey and Frank E. Moorer, ed. pp. 55–67. © 1984 Horace A. Porter. Printed by permission of the author.

"Creation of the Self in Richard Wright's *Black Boy*" by Yoshinobu Hakutani. From *Black American Literature Forum* 19, no. 2 (Summer 1985), pp. 70–75. © 1985 *African American Review*. Reprinted by permission.

"Call and Response: Intertexuality in Two Autobiographical Works by Richard Wright and Maya Angelou" by Keneth Kinnamon. From *Studies in Black American Literature*, Vol. 2. *Belief vs. Theory in Black American Literary Criticism*. Joe Weixlmann and Chester Fontenot, ed. pp. 121–134. © 1986 Keneth Kinnamon. Reprinted by permission.

"Richard Wright's *Black Boy* and the Trauma of Autobiographical Rebirth" by Donald B. Gibson. From *Callaloo*, No. 28 (1986): 492–498. © Charles H. Rowell. Reprinted with permission of The Johns Hopkins University Press.

"Richard Wright's Struggle with Fathers" by Elizabeth J. Ciner. From *Richard Wright: Myths and Realities*. C. James Trotman, ed. pp. 125–136. © 1988 C. James Trotman. Reprinted by permission.

"Richard Wright and the African-American Autobiography Tradition" by William L. Andrews. From *Style* 27, No. 2 (Summer 1993), pp. 271–285. © 1993 William L. Andrews. Reprinted by permission.

"'They Don't Look So Good, Mistah': Realities of the South in Richard Wright's *Black Boy* and Selected Short Fiction" by Warren J. Carson. From *CLA Journal* 47, No. 3 (March 2004), pp. 299–309. © 2004 by the College Language Association. Reprinted by permission.

"*Black Boy*'s Comedy: Indestructibility and Anonymity in Autobiographical Self-Making" by Petar Ramadanovic. From *Callaloo* 27, No. 2 (Spring 2004), pp. 502–521. © 2004 Charles H. Rowell. Reprinted with permission of The Johns Hopkin's University Press.

Index

Characters in literary works are indexed by first name (if any), followed by the name of the work in parentheses